2003 Supplement

Constitutional Law

2003 Supplement

Constitutional Law

Fourth Edition

Geoffrey R. Stone
Harry Kalven, Jr., Distinguished Service Professor of Law
University of Chicago Law School

Louis M. Seidman
Professor of Law
Georgetown University Law Center

Cass R. Sunstein
Karl N. Llewellyn Professor of Jurisprudence
University of Chicago Law School and
Department of Political Science

Mark V. Tushnet
Carmack Waterhouse Professor of Constitutional Law
Georgetown University Law Center

Pamela S. Karlan
Kenneth & Harle Montgomery Professor of Public Interest Law
Stanford Law School

ASPEN
PUBLISHERS

1185 Avenue of the Americas, New York, NY 10036
www.aspenpublishers.com

Permissions
Aspen Publishers
1185 Avenue of the Americas
New York, NY 10036

Printed in the United States of America

Library of Congress Cataloging-in-Publication Data

Constitutional law / Geoffrey R. Stone . . . [et al.]. — 4th ed.
    p.   cm.
    Includes bibliographical references and index.
    ISBN 0-7355-2016-X (casebound)
    0-7355-3477-2 (supplement)
    1. Constitutional law — United States. I. Stone, Geoffrey R.

KF4549.C647   2001
342.73 — dc21   00-065069

ISBN 0-7355-3477-2

1 2 3 4 5 6 7 8 9 0

About Aspen Publishers

Aspen Publishers, headquartered in New York City, is a leading information provider for attorneys, business professionals, and law students. Written by pre-eminent authorities, our products consist of analytical and practical information covering both U.S. and international topics. We publish in the full range of formats, including updated manuals, books, periodicals, CDs, and online products.

Our proprietary content is complemented by 2,500 legal databases, containing over 11 million documents, available through our Loislaw division. Aspen Publishers also offers a wide range of topical legal and business databases linked to Loislaw's primary material. Our mission is to provide accurate, timely, and authoritative content in easily accessible formats, supported by unmatched customer care.

To order any Aspen Publishers title, go to *www.aspenpublishers.com* or call 1-800-638-8437.

To reinstate your manual update service, call 1-800-638-8437.

For more information on Loislaw products, go to *www.loislaw.com* or call 1-800-364-2512.

For Customer Care issues, email *CustomerCare@aspenpublishers.com*; call 1-800-234-1660; or fax 1-800-901-9075.

Aspen Publishers
A Wolters Kluwer Company

Contents

Contents

CHAPTER 8.   THE CONSTITUTION AND RELIGION 227

CHAPTER 9.   THE CONSTITUTION, BASELINES, AND THE PROBLEM OF PRIVATE POWER 237

Table of Cases

Italics indicate principal and intermediate cases.
All references are to page numbers in the main text.

Table of Authorities

Acknowledgments

Bollinger, Lee C. & Geoffrey R. Stone, eds. Eternally Vigilant: Free Speech in the Modern Era. Copyright © 2002 by the University of Chicago. All rights reserved.

Post, The Constitutional Status of Commercial Speech, 48 UCLA L. Rev. 1, 2-4, 14, 49, 53-54 (2000). Copyright © 2000, The Regents of the University of California. All rights reserved.

Rubenfeld, Jed. The First Amendment's Purpose, 53 Stan. L. Rev. 767, 768-769 (2001). Copyright © 2001 by Stanford Law Review. Reproduced with permission of Stanford Law Review in the format textbook via Copyright Clearance Center.

Sunstein, Cass. R. republic.com. Copyright © 2001 by Princeton University Press. Reprinted by permission of Princeton University Press.

2003 Supplement
Constitutional Law

1

THE ROLE OF THE SUPREME COURT IN THE CONSTITUTIONAL ORDER

A. Introduction: Some Notes on the History and Theory of the Constitution

Page 22. At the end of section 7 of the Note, add the following:

See also M. Tushnet, The New Constitutional Order (2003), for an argument that the constitutional arrangements that prevailed in the United States from the 1930s to the 1990s have ended. Tushnet suggests that the nation's new constitutional order is characterized by divided government, ideologically organized parties, and subdued constitutional ambition.

B. The Basic Framework

Page 35. Before *Note: Constitutions, Democracy, and Judicial Review,* add the following:

For a detailed treatment of the historical issues, see Larry D. Kramer, Foreword: We the Court, 115 Harv. L. Rev. 4 (2001). Kramer urges that for the framers, the "Constitution was *not* ordinary law, *not* peculiarly the stuff of courts and judges." Instead it was "a special form of popular law, law made by the people to bind their governors." Id. at 10. For many members of the revolutionary generation, constitutional principles were subject to "popular enforcement," id. at 40, that is, public insistence on compliance with the Constitution, rather than judicial activity. "It was the legislature's delegated responsibility to decide whether a proposed law was constitutionally authorized, subject to oversight by the people. Courts simply had nothing to do with it, and they were acting as interlopers if they tried to second-guess the legislature's decision." Id. at 49. Kramer traces the controversial early growth of the practice of judicial review, with many seeing it as an "act of resistance." Id. at 54. At the founding, a "handful of participants saw a role for judicial review, though few of these imagined it as a powerful or important device, and none seemed anxious to emphasize it. Others were opposed . . . . The vast majority of participants were still thinking in terms of popular constitutionalism and so focused on traditional political means of enforcing the new charter; the notion of judicial review simply never crossed their minds." Id. at 66.

In Kramer's account, constitutional limits would be enforced not through courts, but as a result of republican institutions and the citizenry's own commitment to its founding document. Kramer raises serious doubts about the account in *Marbury v. Madison* and in particular about judicial supremacy in the interpretation of the Constitution. He suggests that for some of the framers, judicial review was "a substitute for popular resistance" and to be used "only when the unconstitutionality of a law was clear beyond dispute."

Page 45.   In the second paragraph, before the last sentence, add the following:

For an illuminating comparative discussion, based on the experience in Israel, see Barak, Foreword: A Judge on Judging: The Role of a Supreme Court in a Democracy, 116 Harv. L. Rev. 16 (2002). Barak emphasizes the important role of the Supreme Court of Israel (of which he is the President) in protecting civil liberties and in maintaining a balance between security and liberty; his treatment of terrorism is worth special attention. Barak stresses the general importance of a judicial check on the elected branches. For a quite different view, see Sunstein and Vermeule, Interpretation and Institutions, 101 Mich. L. Rev. 885 (2003), arguing that it is important to consider the institutional capacities (or lack thereof) of various actors, including courts, and that much is missed by approaches that emphasize what ideal courts should do. For a provocative treatment of the role of the judiciary under emergency conditions, see Gross, Chaos and Rules: Should Responses to Violent Crises Always Be Constitutional?, 112 Yale L.J. 1011 (2003).

Page 108.   After the third paragraph, add the following:

A divided Court built on Northeastern Fla. Chapter in Gratz v. Bollinger, 539 U.S. ___ (2003). Patrick Hamacher, a plaintiff in the case, objected to an affirmative action program used by the University of Michigan in undergraduate admissions. The problem was that while Hamacher said that he intended to apply for admission as a transfer student, he had not actually made any such application. Dissenting, Justice Stevens urged that because Hamacher had not yet applied, his claim of injury was conjectural and hypothetical. The Court disagreed. It said that for standing, it was enough that Hamacher claimed that "he was 'able and ready' to apply as a transfer student" if the university stopped using race in undergraduate admissions. This claim of intent supported standing "to seek prospective relief with respect to the University's continued use of race in undergraduate admissions."

E. "Case or Controversy" Requirements and the Passive Virtues

Page 135.   Before Section F, add the following:

BUSH v. GORE
531 U.S. 98 (2000)

PER CURIAM: . . .

[Following an agonizingly close presidential election in Florida, the Florida Supreme Court ordered a manual recount of undervotes — ballots on which no vote had been registered during the machine count — in all counties that had not yet completed a recount. In addition, it ordered that additional votes recovered during prior but untimely manual recounts in several other counties be included in the vote total.]

II

B

The individual citizen has no federal constitutional right to vote for electors for the President of the United States unless and until the state legislature chooses a statewide election as the means to implement its power to appoint members of the Electoral College. U.S. Const., Art. II, §1. This is the source for the statement in McPherson v. Blacker, 146 U.S. 1, 35 (1892), that the State legislature's power to select the manner for appointing electors is plenary; it may, if it so chooses, select the electors itself, which indeed was the manner used by State legislatures in several States for many years after the Framing of our Constitution. Id., at 28-33. History has now favored the voter, and in each of the several States the citizens themselves vote for Presidential electors. When the state legislature vests the right to vote for President in its people, the right to vote as the legislature has prescribed is fundamen-

3

tal; and one source of its fundamental nature lies in the equal weight accorded to each vote and the equal dignity owed to each voter. The State, of course, after granting the franchise in the special context of Article II, can take back the power to appoint electors. See id., at 35 ("[T]here is no doubt of the right of the legislature to resume the power at any time, for it can neither be taken away nor abdicated") (quoting S. Rep. No. 395, 43d Cong., 1st Sess.).

The right to vote is protected in more than the initial allocation of the franchise. Equal protection applies as well to the manner of its exercise. Having once granted the right to vote on equal terms, the State may not, by later arbitrary and disparate treatment, value one person's vote over that of another. See, e.g., Harper v. Virginia Bd. of Elections, 383 U.S. 663, 665 (1966) ("[O]nce the franchise is granted to the electorate, lines may not be drawn which are inconsistent with the Equal Protection Clause of the Fourteenth Amendment"). It must be remembered that "the right of suffrage can be denied by a debasement or dilution of the weight of a citizen's vote just as effectively as by wholly prohibiting the free exercise of the franchise." Reynolds v. Sims, 377 U.S. 533, 555 (1964). . . .

Much of the controversy seems to revolve around ballot cards designed to be perforated by a stylus but which, either through error or deliberate omission, have not been perforated with sufficient precision for a machine to count them. In some cases a piece of the card—a chad—is hanging, say by two corners. In other cases there is no separation at all, just an indentation.

The Florida Supreme Court has ordered that the intent of the voter be discerned from such ballots. For purposes of resolving the equal protection challenge, it is not necessary to decide whether the Florida Supreme Court had the authority under the legislative scheme for resolving election disputes to define what a legal vote is and to mandate a manual recount implementing that definition. The recount mechanisms implemented in response to the decisions of the Florida Supreme Court do not satisfy the minimum requirement for non-arbitrary treatment of voters necessary to secure the fundamental right. Florida's basic command for the count of legally cast votes is to consider the "intent of the voter." This is unobjectionable as an abstract proposition and a starting principle. The problem inheres in the absence of specific standards to ensure its equal application. The formulation of uniform rules to determine intent based on these recurring circumstances is practicable and, we conclude, necessary. . . .

An early case in our one person, one vote jurisprudence arose when a State accorded arbitrary and disparate treatment to voters in its different counties. Gray v. Sanders, 372 U.S. 368 (1963). The Court found a constitutional violation. We relied on these principles in the context of the Presidential selection process in Moore v. Ogilvie, 394 U.S. 814 (1969), where we invalidated a county-based procedure that diluted the influence of citizens in larger counties in the nominating process. There we observed that "[t]he idea that one group can be granted greater voting strength than another is hostile to the one man, one vote basis of our representative government." Id., at 819.

The State Supreme Court ratified this uneven treatment. It mandated that the recount totals from [several] counties [be] included in the certified total [even though] each of the counties used varying standards to determine what was a legal vote. Broward County used a more forgiving standard than Palm Beach County, and uncovered almost three times as many new votes, a result markedly disproportionate to the difference in population between the counties. . . .

In addition to these difficulties the actual process by which the votes were to be counted under the Florida Supreme Court's decision raises further concerns. That order did not specify who would recount the ballots. The county canvassing boards were forced to pull together ad hoc teams comprised of judges from various Circuits who had no previous training in handling and interpreting ballots. Furthermore, while others were permitted to observe, they were prohibited from objecting during the recount.

The recount process, in its features here described, is inconsistent with the minimum procedures necessary to protect the fundamental right of each voter in the special instance of a statewide recount under the authority of a single state judicial officer. Our consideration is limited to the present circumstances, for the problem of equal protection in election processes generally presents many complexities.

The question before the Court is not whether local entities, in the exercise of their expertise, may develop different systems for implementing elections. Instead, we are presented with a situation where a state court with the power to assure uniformity has ordered a statewide recount with minimal procedural safeguards. When a court orders a statewide remedy, there must be at least some assurance that the rudimentary requirements of equal treatment and fundamental fairness are satisfied. . . .

Upon due consideration of the difficulties identified to this point, it is obvious that the recount cannot be conducted in compliance with the requirements of equal protection and due process without substantial additional work. It would require not only the adoption (after opportunity for argument) of adequate statewide standards for determining what is a legal vote, and practicable procedures to implement them, but also orderly judicial review of any disputed matters that might arise. In addition, the Secretary of State has advised that the recount of only a portion of the ballots requires that the vote tabulation equipment be used to screen out undervotes, a function for which the machines were not designed. If a recount of overvotes were also required, perhaps even a second screening would be necessary. . . .

The Supreme Court of Florida has said that the legislature intended the State's electors to "participat[e] fully in the federal electoral process," as provided in 3 U.S.C. §5. [This provision is part of a complex scheme dealing with Congressional procedures for the counting of electoral votes, enacted in the wake of the disputed presidential election of 1876. The statute provides that

[if] any State shall have provided, by laws enacted prior to the day fixed for the appointment of the electors, for its final determination of any controversy or contest concerning the appointment of [electors] by judicial or other [methods], and such determination shall have been made at least six days before the time fixed for the meeting of the electors, such determination made pursuant to such law so existing on said day, and made at least six days prior to said time of meeting of the electors, shall be [conclusive]].

That statute, in turn, requires that any controversy or contest that is designed to lead to a conclusive selection of electors be completed by December 12. That date is upon us, and there is no recount procedure in place under the State Supreme Court's order that comports with minimal constitutional standards. Because it is evident that any recount seeking to meet the December 12 date will be unconstitutional for the reasons we have discussed, we reverse the judgment of the Supreme Court of Florida ordering a recount to proceed. . . .

None are more conscious of the vital limits on judicial authority than are the members of this Court, and none stand more in admiration of the Constitution's design to leave the selection of the President to the people, through their legislatures, and to the political sphere. When contending parties invoke the process of the courts, however, it becomes our unsought responsibility to resolve the federal and constitutional issues the judicial system has been forced to confront.

The judgment of the Supreme Court of Florida is reversed, and the case is remanded for further proceedings not inconsistent with this opinion.

CHIEF JUSTICE REHNQUIST, with whom JUSTICE SCALIA and JUSTICE THOMAS join, concurring.

We join the per curiam opinion. We write separately because we believe there are additional grounds that require us to reverse the Florida Supreme Court's decision.

I

We deal here not with an ordinary election, but with an election for the President of the United States. . . .

[In] Anderson v. Celebrezze, 460 U.S. 780, 794-795 (1983), we said: "In the context of a Presidential election, state-imposed restrictions implicate a uniquely important national interest. For the President and the Vice President of the United States are the only elected officials who represent all the voters in the Nation."

In most cases, comity and respect for federalism compel us to defer to the decisions of state courts on issues of state law. That practice reflects our understanding that the decisions of state courts are definitive pronouncements of the will of the States as sovereigns. Cf. Erie R. Co. v. Tompkins, 304 U.S. 64 (1938). Of course, in ordinary cases, the distribution of powers among the branches of a State's government raises no questions of federal constitutional law, subject to the requirement that the government be republican in character. See U.S. Const., Art. IV, §4. But there are a few exceptional cases in which the Constitution imposes a duty or confers a power on a particular branch of a State's government. This is one of them. Article II, §1, cl. 2, provides that "each State shall appoint, in such Manner as the *Legislature* thereof may direct," electors for President and Vice President. (Emphasis added.) Thus, the text of the election law itself, and not just its interpretation by the courts of the States, takes on independent significance.

In McPherson v. Blacker, 146 U.S. 1 (1892), we explained that Art. II, §1, cl. 2, "conveys the broadest power of determination" and "leaves it to the legislature exclusively to define the method" of appointment. Id., at 27. A significant departure from the legislative scheme for appointing Presidential electors presents a federal constitutional question.

3 U.S.C. §5 informs our application of Art. II, §1, cl. 2, to the Florida statutory scheme, which, as the Florida Supreme Court acknowledged, took that statute into account. [If] we are to respect the legislature's Article II powers, therefore, we must ensure that postelection state-court actions do not frustrate the legislative desire to attain the "safe harbor" provided by §5.

In Florida, the legislature has chosen to hold statewide elections to appoint the State's 25 electors. Importantly, the legislature has delegated the authority to run the elections and to oversee election disputes to the Secretary of State (Secretary), Fla. Stat. §97.012(1) (2000), and to state circuit courts, §§102.168(1), 102.168(8). Isolated sections of the code may well admit of more than one interpretation, but the general coherence of the legislative scheme may not be altered by judicial interpretation so as to wholly change the statutorily provided apportionment of responsibility among these various bodies. In any election but a Presidential election, the Florida Supreme Court can give as little or as much deference to Florida's executives as it chooses, so far as Article II is concerned, and this Court will have no cause to question the court's actions. But, with respect to a Presidential election, the court must be both mindful of the legislature's role under Article II in choosing the manner of appointing electors and deferential to those bodies expressly empowered by the legislature to carry out its constitutional mandate.

In order to determine whether a state court has infringed upon the legislature's authority, we necessarily must examine the law of the State as it existed prior to the action of the court. Though we generally defer to state courts on the interpretation of state law [there] are of course areas in which the Constitution requires this Court to undertake an independent, if still deferential, analysis of state law.

For example, in NAACP v. Alabama ex rel. Patterson, 357 U.S. 449 (1958), it was argued that we were without jurisdiction because the petitioner had not pursued the correct appellate remedy in Alabama's state courts. Petitioners had sought a state-law writ of certiorari in the Alabama Supreme Court when a writ of mandamus, according to that court, was proper. We found this state-law ground inadequate to defeat our jurisdiction because we were "unable to reconcile the procedural holding of the Alabama Supreme Court" with prior Alabama precedent. 357 U.S. at 456. The purported state-law ground was so novel, in our independent estimation, that "petitioner could not fairly be deemed to have been apprised of its existence." 357 U.S. at 457.

Six years later we decided Bouie v. City of Columbia, 378 U.S. 347 (1964), in which the state court had held, contrary to precedent, that the state trespass law applied to black sit-in demonstrators who had consent to enter private property but were then asked to leave. Relying upon *NAACP*, we concluded that the South Carolina Supreme Court's interpretation of a state penal statute had impermissibly broadened the scope of that statute beyond what a fair reading provided, in violation of due process. See 378 U.S. at 361-362. What we would do in the present case is precisely parallel: Hold that the Florida Supreme Court's interpretation of the Florida election laws impermissibly distorted them beyond what a fair reading required, in violation of Article II. . . .

II

Acting pursuant to its constitutional grant of authority, the Florida Legislature has created a detailed, if not perfectly crafted, statutory scheme that provides for appointment of Presidential electors by direct election. [The] legislature has designated the Secretary of State as the "chief election officer," with the responsibility to "obtain and maintain uniformity in the application, operation, and interpretation of the election laws." §97.012. The state legislature has delegated to county canvassing boards the duties of administering elections. §102.141. Those boards are responsible for providing results to the state Elections Canvassing [Commission]. Cf. Boardman v. Esteva, 323 So. 2d 259, 268, n. 5 (1975) ("The election process . . . is committed to the executive branch of government through duly designated officials all charged with specific duties. . . . [The] judgments [of these officials] are entitled to be regarded by the courts as presumptively correct. . . .").

After the election has taken place, [the] county canvassing boards must file certified election returns with the Department of State by 5 p.m. on the seventh day following the election. §102.112(1). . . .

The state legislature has also provided mechanisms both for protesting election returns and for contesting certified election results. Section 102.166 governs protests. Any protest must be filed prior to the certification of election results by the county canvassing board. §102.166(4)(b). Once a protest has been filed, "the county canvassing board may authorize a manual recount." §102.166(4)(c). If a sample recount conducted pursuant to §102.166(5) "indicates an error in the vote tabulation which could affect the outcome of the election," the county canvassing board is instructed to: "(a) Correct the error and recount the remaining precincts with the vote tabulation system; (b) Request the Department of State to verify the tabulation software; or (c) Manually recount all ballots," §102.166(5). In the event a canvassing board chooses to conduct a manual recount of all ballots, §102.166(7) prescribes procedures for such a recount.

Contests to the certification of an election, on the other hand, are controlled by §102.168. The grounds for contesting an election include "receipt of a number of illegal votes or rejection of a number of legal votes sufficient to change or place in doubt the result of the election." §102.168(3)(c). [Section] 102.168(8) provides that "the circuit judge to whom the contest is presented may fashion such orders as he or she deems necessary to ensure that each allegation in the complaint is investigated, examined, or checked, to prevent or correct any alleged wrong, and to provide any relief appropriate under such circumstances." In Presidential elections, the contest period necessarily terminates on the date set by 3 U.S.C. §5 for concluding the State's "final determination" of election controversies.

In its first decision, Palm Beach Canvassing Bd. v. Harris, 772 So. 2d 1220 (2000) (*Harris I*), the Florida Supreme Court extended the 7-day statutory certification deadline established by the legislature. This modification of the code, by lengthening the protest period, necessarily shortened the contest period for Presidential elections. Underlying the extension of the certification deadline and the shortchanging of the contest period was, presumably, the clear implication that certification was a matter of significance: The certified winner would enjoy presumptive validity, making a contest proceeding by the losing candidate an uphill battle. In its latest opinion, however, the court empties certification of virtually all legal consequence during the contest, and in doing so departs from the provisions enacted by the Florida Legislature.

The court determined that canvassing boards' decisions regarding whether to recount ballots past the certification deadline (even the certification deadline established by *Harris I*) are to be reviewed de novo, although the election code clearly vests discretion whether to recount in the boards, and sets strict deadlines subject to the Secretary's rejection of late tallies and monetary fines for tardiness. Moreover, the Florida court held that all late vote tallies arriving during the contest period should be automatically included in the certification regardless of the certification deadline (even the certification deadline established by *Harris I*), thus virtually eliminating both the deadline and the Secretary's discretion to disregard recounts that violate it.

Moreover, the court's interpretation of "legal vote," and hence its decision to order a contest-period recount, plainly departed from the legislative scheme. Florida statutory law cannot reasonably be thought to require the counting of improperly marked ballots. Each Florida precinct before election day provides instructions on how properly to cast a vote, §101.46; each polling place on election day contains a working model of the voting machine it uses, §101.5611; and each voting booth contains a sample ballot, §101.46. In precincts using punch-card ballots, voters are instructed to punch out the ballot cleanly:

> AFTER VOTING, CHECK YOUR BALLOT CARD TO BE SURE YOUR VOTING SELECTIONS ARE CLEARLY AND CLEANLY PUNCHED AND THERE ARE NO CHIPS LEFT HANGING ON THE BACK OF THE CARD.

Instructions to Voters, quoted in Touchston v. McDermott, 2000 WL 1781942, *6 & n. 19 (CA11) (Tjoflat, J., dissenting). No reasonable person would call it "an error in the vote tabulation," Fla. Stat. §102.166(5), or a "rejection of legal votes," Fla. Stat. §102.168(3)(c), when electronic or electromechanical equipment performs precisely in the manner designed, and fails to count those ballots that are not marked in the manner that these voting instructions explicitly and prominently specify. The scheme that the Florida Supreme Court's opinion attributes to the legislature is one in which machines are required to be "capable of correctly counting votes," §101.5606(4), but which nonetheless regularly produces elections in which legal votes are predictably not tabulated, so that in close elections manual recounts are regularly required. This is of course absurd. The Secretary of State, who is authorized by law to issue binding interpretations of the election code, §§97.012, 106.23, rejected this peculiar reading of the statutes. See DE 00-13 (opinion of the Division of Elections). The Florida Supreme Court, although it must defer to the Secretary's interpretations, see Krivanek v. Take Back Tampa Political Committee, 625 So. 2d 840, 844 (Fla. 1993), rejected her reasonable interpretation and embraced the peculiar one. See Palm Beach County Canvassing Board v. Harris, No. SC00-2346 (Dec. 11, 2000) (*Harris III*).

But [in] a Presidential election the clearly expressed intent of the legislature must prevail. And there is no basis for reading the Florida statutes as requiring the counting of improperly marked ballots. . . .

III

The scope and nature of the remedy ordered by the Florida Supreme Court jeopardizes the "legislative wish" to take advantage of the safe harbor provided by 3 U.S.C. §5. December 12, 2000, is the last date for a final determination of the Florida electors that will satisfy §5. Yet in the late afternoon of December 8th—four days before this deadline—the Supreme Court of Florida ordered recounts of tens of thousands of so-called "undervotes" spread through 64 of the State's 67 counties. This was done in a search for elusive—perhaps delusive—certainty as to the exact count of 6 million votes. But no one claims that these ballots have not previously been tabulated; they were initially read by voting machines at the time of the election, and thereafter reread by virtue of Florida's automatic recount provision. No one claims there was any fraud in the election. The Supreme Court of Florida ordered this additional recount under the provision of the election code giving the circuit judge the authority to provide relief that is "appropriate under such circumstances." Fla. Stat. §102.168(8) (2000).

Surely when the Florida Legislature empowered the courts of the State to grant "appropriate" relief, it must have meant relief that would have become final by the cut-off date of 3 U.S.C. §5. In light of the inevitable legal challenges and ensuing appeals to the Supreme Court of Florida and petitions for certiorari to this Court, the entire recounting process could not possibly be completed by that date. . . .

Given all these factors, and in light of the legislative intent identified by the Florida Supreme Court to bring Florida within the "safe harbor" provision of 3 U.S.C. §5, the remedy prescribed by the Supreme Court of Florida cannot be deemed an "appropriate" one as of December 8. It significantly departed from the statutory framework in place on November 7, and authorized open-ended further proceedings which could not be completed by December 12, thereby preventing a final determination by that date.

For these reasons, in addition to those given in the per curiam, we would reverse.

JUSTICE STEVENS, with whom JUSTICE GINSBURG and JUSTICE BREYER join, dissenting.

The Constitution assigns to the States the primary responsibility for determining the manner of selecting the Presidential electors. See Art. II, §1, cl. 2. When questions arise about the meaning of state laws, including election laws, it is our settled practice to accept the opinions of the highest courts of the States as providing the final answers. On rare occasions, however, either federal statutes or the Federal Constitution may require federal judicial intervention in state elections. This is not such an occasion.

The federal questions that ultimately emerged in this case are not substantial. Article II provides that "[e]ach State shall appoint, in such Manner as the Legislature thereof may direct, a Number of Electors." It does not create state legislatures out of whole cloth, but rather takes them as they come—as creatures born of, and constrained by, their state constitutions. [The] legislative power in Florida is subject to judicial review pursuant to Article V of the Florida Constitution, and nothing in Article II of the Federal Constitution frees the state legislature from the constraints in the state constitution that created it. [The] Florida Supreme Court's exercise of appellate jurisdiction therefore was wholly consistent with, and indeed contemplated by, the grant of authority in Article II. . . .

Nor are petitioners correct in asserting that the failure of the Florida Supreme Court to specify in detail the precise manner in which the "intent of the voter," Fla. Stat. §101.5614(5) (Supp. 2001), is to be determined rises to the level of a constitutional violation. We found such a violation when individual votes within the same State were weighted unequally, see, e.g., Reynolds v. Sims, but we have never before called into question the substantive standard by which a State determines that a vote has been legally cast. And there is no reason to think that the guidance provided to the factfinders, specifically the various canvassing boards, by the "intent of the voter" standard is any less sufficient—or will lead to results any less uniform—than, for example, the "beyond a reasonable doubt" standard employed everyday by ordinary citizens in courtrooms across this country.

Admittedly, the use of differing substandards for determining voter intent in different counties employing similar voting systems may raise serious concerns. Those concerns are alleviated—if not eliminated—by the fact that a single impartial magistrate will ultimately adjudicate all objections arising from the recount process. . . .

What must underlie petitioners' entire federal assault on the Florida election procedures is an unstated lack of confidence in the impartiality and capacity of the state judges who would make the critical decisions if the vote count were to proceed. Otherwise, their position is wholly without merit. The endorsement of that position by the majority of this Court can only lend credence to the most cynical appraisal of the work of judges throughout the land. It is confidence in the men and women who administer the judicial system that is the true backbone of the rule of law. Time will one day heal the wound to that confidence that will be inflicted by today's decision. One thing, however, is certain. Although we may never know with complete certainty the identity of the winner of this year's Presidential election, the identity of the loser is perfectly clear. It is the Nation's confidence in the judge as an impartial guardian of the rule of law.

I respectfully dissent.

JUSTICE SOUTER, with whom JUSTICE BREYER joins, [dissenting]. . . .

Petitioners have raised an equal protection claim (or, alternatively, a due process claim), in the charge that unjustifiably disparate standards are applied in different electoral jurisdictions to otherwise identical facts. It is true that the Equal Protection Clause does not forbid the use of a variety of voting mechanisms within a jurisdiction, even though different mechanisms will have different levels of effectiveness in recording voters' intentions; local variety can be justified by concerns about cost, the potential value of innovation, and so on. But evidence in the record here suggests that a different order of disparity obtains under rules for determining a voter's intent that have been applied (and could continue to be applied) to identical types of ballots used in identical brands of machines and exhibiting identical physical characteristics (such as "hanging" or "dimpled" chads). I can conceive of no legitimate state interest served by these differing treatments of the expressions of voters' fundamental rights. The differences appear wholly arbitrary.

In deciding what to do about this, we should take account of the fact that electoral votes are due to be cast in six days. I would therefore remand the case to the courts of Florida with instructions to establish uniform standards for evaluating the several types of ballots that have prompted differing treatments, to be applied within and

12

among counties when passing on such identical ballots in any further recounting (or successive recounting) that the courts might order.

Unlike the majority, I see no warrant for this Court to assume that Florida could not possibly comply with this requirement before the date set for the meeting of electors, December 18. . . .

I respectfully dissent.

JUSTICE GINSBURG, with whom JUSTICE STEVENS joins, and with whom JUSTICE SOUTER and JUSTICE BREYER join as to Part I, dissenting.

I . . .

Rarely has this Court rejected outright an interpretation of state law by a state high court. Fairfax's Devisee v. Hunter's Lessee, 7 Cranch 603 (1813), NAACP v. Alabama ex rel. Patterson, 357 U.S. 449 (1958), and Bouie v. City of Columbia, 378 U.S. 347 (1964), cited by The Chief Justice, are three such rare instances. But those cases are embedded in historical contexts hardly comparable to the situation here. Fairfax's Devisee, which held that the Virginia Court of Appeals had misconstrued its own forfeiture laws to deprive a British subject of lands secured to him by federal treaties, occurred amidst vociferous States' rights attacks on the Marshall Court. The Virginia court refused to obey this Court's *Fairfax's Devisee* mandate to enter judgment for the British subject's successor in interest. That refusal led to the Court's pathmarking decision in Martin v. Hunter's Lessee, 1 Wheat. 304 (1816). *Patterson,* a case decided three months after Cooper v. Aaron, 358 U.S. 1 (1958), in the face of Southern resistance to the civil rights movement, held that the Alabama Supreme Court had irregularly applied its own procedural rules to deny review of a contempt order against the NAACP arising from its refusal to disclose membership lists. [*Bouie*], stemming from a lunch counter "sit-in" at the height of the civil rights movement, held that the South Carolina Supreme Court's construction of its trespass laws — criminalizing conduct not covered by the text of an otherwise clear statute — was "unforeseeable" and thus violated due process when applied retroactively to the petitioners.

The Chief Justice's casual citation of these cases might lead one to believe they are part of a larger collection of cases in which we said that the Constitution impelled us to train a skeptical eye on a state court's portrayal of state law. But one would be hard pressed, I think, to find additional cases that fit the mold. As Justice Breyer convincingly explains, this case involves nothing close to the kind of recalcitrance by a state high court that warrants extraordinary action by this Court. The Florida Supreme Court concluded that counting every legal vote was the overriding concern of the Florida Legislature when it enacted the State's Election Code. The court surely should not be bracketed with state high courts of the Jim Crow South.

13

The Chief Justice says that Article II, by providing that state legislatures shall direct the manner of appointing electors, authorizes federal superintendence over the relationship between state courts and state legislatures, and licenses a departure from the usual deference we give to state court interpretations of state law. The Framers of our Constitution, however, understood that in a republican government, the judiciary would construe the legislature's enactments. See U.S. Const., Art. III; The Federalist No. 78 (A. Hamilton). In light of the constitutional guarantee to States of a "Republican Form of Government," U.S. Const., Art. IV, §4, Article II can hardly be read to invite this Court to disrupt a State's republican regime. Yet The Chief Justice today would reach out to do just that. By holding that Article II requires our revision of a state court's construction of state laws in order to protect one organ of the State from another, The Chief Justice contradicts the basic principle that a State may organize itself as it sees fit. See, e.g., Gregory v. Ashcroft, 501 U.S. 452, 460 (1991) ("Through the structure of its government, and the character of those who exercise government authority, a State defines itself as a sovereign."); Highland Farms Dairy v. Agnew, 300 U.S. 608, 612 (1937) ("How power shall be distributed by a state among its governmental organs is commonly, if not always, a question for the state itself."). Article II does not call for the scrutiny undertaken by this Court. . . .

II . . .

I cannot agree that the recount adopted by the Florida court, flawed as it may be, would yield a result any less fair or precise than the certification that preceded that recount. . . .

I dissent.

JUSTICE BREYER . . . dissenting. . . .

II

[This portion of Justice Breyer's opinion was joined by Justices Stevens, Ginsburg, and Souter.]

Despite the reminder that this case involves "an election for the President of the United States," (Rehnquist, C.J., concurring), no preeminent legal concern, or practical concern related to legal questions, required this Court to hear this case, let alone to issue a stay that stopped Florida's recount process in its tracks. With one exception, petitioners' claims do not ask us to vindicate a constitutional provision designed to protect a basic human right. See, e.g., Brown v. Board of Education, 347 U.S. 483 (1954). Petitioners invoke fundamental fairness, namely, the need for procedural fairness, including finality. But with the one "equal protection" exception, they rely upon law that focuses, not upon that basic need, but upon the constitutional allocation of power. . . .

Of course, the selection of the President is of fundamental national importance. But that importance is political, not legal. And this Court should resist the temptation unnecessarily to resolve tangential legal disputes, where doing so threatens to determine the outcome of the election.

The Constitution and federal statutes themselves make clear that restraint is appropriate. They set forth a road map of how to resolve disputes about electors, even after an election as close as this one. That road map foresees resolution of electoral disputes by state courts. See 3 U.S.C. §5. [But] it nowhere provides for involvement by the United States Supreme Court.

To the contrary, the Twelfth Amendment commits to Congress the authority and responsibility to count electoral votes. A federal statute, the Electoral Count Act, enacted after the close 1876 Hayes-Tilden Presidential election, specifies that, after States have tried to resolve disputes (through "judicial" or other means), Congress is the body primarily authorized to resolve remaining disputes. See Electoral Count Act of 1887, 24 Stat. 373, 3 U.S.C. §§5, 6, and 15.

The legislative history of the Act makes clear its intent to commit the power to resolve such disputes to Congress, rather than the courts:

> "The two Houses are, by the Constitution, authorized to make the count of electoral votes. They can only count legal votes, and in doing so must determine, from the best evidence to be had, what are legal votes. . . . The power to determine rests with the two Houses, and there is no other constitutional tribunal." H. Rep. No. 1638, 49th Cong., 1st Sess., 2 (1886) (report submitted by Rep. Caldwell, Select Committee on the Election of President and Vice- President). . . .

Given this detailed, comprehensive scheme for counting electoral votes, there is no reason to believe that federal law either foresees or requires resolution of such a political issue by this Court. Nor, for that matter, is there any reason to that think the Constitution's Framers would have reached a different conclusion. Madison, at least, believed that allowing the judiciary to choose the presidential electors "was out of the question." Madison, July 25, 1787 (reprinted in 5 Elliot's Debates on the Federal Constitution 363 (2d ed. 1876)).

The decision by both the Constitution's Framers and the 1886 Congress to minimize this Court's role in resolving close federal presidential elections is as wise as it is clear. However awkward or difficult it may be for Congress to resolve difficult electoral disputes, Congress, being a political body, expresses the people's will far more accurately than does an unelected Court. And the people's will is what elections are about. . . .

[The history of the disputed election of 1876, including] the participation in the work of the electoral commission by five Justices, including Justice Bradley, did not lend that process legitimacy. Nor did it assure the public that the process had worked fairly, guided by the law. Rather, it simply embroiled Members of the Court in parti-

15

san conflict, thereby undermining respect for the judicial process. And the Congress that later enacted the Electoral Count Act knew it.

This history may help to explain why I think it not only legally wrong, but also most unfortunate, for the Court simply to have terminated the Florida recount. Those who caution judicial restraint in resolving political disputes have described the quintessential case for that restraint as a case marked, among other things, by the "strangeness of the issue," its "intractability to principled resolution," its "sheer momentousness, . . . which tends to unbalance judicial judgment," and "the inner vulnerability, the self-doubt of an institution which is electorally irresponsible and has no earth to draw strength from [citing A. Bickel, The Least Dangerous Branch 184 (1962)]." Those characteristics mark this case. . . .

I fear that in order to bring this agonizingly long election process to a definitive conclusion, we have not adequately attended to that necessary "check upon our own exercise of power," "our own sense of self-restraint." United States v. Butler, 297 U.S. 1, 79 (1936) (Stone, J., dissenting). Justice Brandeis once said of the Court, "The most important thing we do is not doing." Bickel, supra, at 71. What it does today, the Court should have left undone. I would repair the damage done as best we now can, by permitting the Florida recount to continue under uniform standards.

I respectfully dissent.

Note: *Bush v. Gore*

1. *Standing and the political question doctrine.* The Court's opinion in Bush v. Gore implicates many of the considerations raised in the prior sections' discussions of standing and political questions. On the issue of standing, consider the following: If the injury identified in the per curiam is the exclusion of valid undervotes in some counties because those counties are using a more stringent standard for assessing voter intent and the exclusion of valid overvotes by an incomplete recount process, who has standing to raise these claims?

Does George W. Bush have standing? Why? Bush was not himself a registered voter in Florida who could claim a violation of his equal protection rights.

In this respect, consider Tribe, eroG v. HsuB and Its Disguises: Freeing *Bush v. Gore* from Its Hall of Mirrors, 115 Harv. L. Rev. 170, 229-31 (2001):

> [I]t is hardly credible—indeed, it borders on the fantastic—to argue that Bush himself lacked standing to press an equal protection claim in the Florida lawsuit. . . . [H]e surely had third-party standing. His injury was obvious: the Florida Supreme Court was in essence [replacing the certification he had received with] . . . a recount to be conducted by a process he regarded as an unconstitutional roulette game rigged in favor of his opponent. . . . Bush potentially had standing on this theory to represent at least those who had voted for him and whose votes stood to be devalued during a recount. More generally, he shared

with all the voters a sufficiently common interest in protecting the integrity of the vote count to ensure his standing as third-party plaintiff. . . . Because of the significant obstacles any individual voter would face in seeking to ensure a fair count, Bush not only had standing but was particularly well placed to assert voters' equal protection rights—even though his ultimate goal was to have some of their votes excluded.

Is "insuring the integrity of the vote count" the kind of "shared individuated right" as to which the Court has traditionally denied standing? Consider in this regard Karlan, Nothing Personal: The Evolution of the Newest Equal Protection from *Shaw v. Reno* to *Bush v. Gore*, 79 N.C.L. Rev. 1345, 1357-60, 1363-64 (2001):

> One striking thing about the Supreme Court's opinion in Bush v. Gore is that it doesn't distinguish [among the different potential claims of injury in fact.] But its general tone seems to focus largely on the claims of individual excluded voters, rather than on voters whose preferred candidate was potentially disadvantaged by the recount the Florida Supreme Court ordered. Perhaps this was a tactical decision by the majority, which sought to avoid having its decision appear partisan: to say that the injury was suffered only by Republican voters whose overall voting strength was diluted by the recount standard would have made explicit that this was a case about partisan outcomes rather than abstract principles. . . .
>
> [George W. Bush] is an especially unlikely candidate for third party standing. It is hard to see George W. Bush as the champion of a claim by undervoters in overwhelmingly Democratic Palm Beach County that they are being denied equal protection because their votes would have been included under the more liberal Broward County standard. Indeed, Bush's third-party complaint . . . alleged, among other things, that the standard used in Broward County was partisan, inconsistent, and unfair. The relief he sought was a declaration that "the illegal votes counted in Broward County under the new rules established after the election should be excluded under the Due Process Clause . . . ." Nothing in that proposed remedy vindicates the rights of excluded voters in Palm Beach County or elsewhere . . . .
>
> The equal protection right of individual voters to participate can really be vindicated only by expanding the scope of the prescribed recount. The only equal protection right that can be vindicated by abolishing recounts altogether is a group-based aggregation interest that depends on the partisan composition of the unrecovered pool, precisely the issue the Supreme Court seemed to want to avoid by couching its discussion in individualistic, atomistic terms. . . .
>
> Whatever interest the Supreme Court's decision vindicated, it was not the interest of an identifiable individual voter. Rather it was a perceived systemic interest in having recounts conducted according to a uniform standard or not at all. . . .

17

Is Bush an appropriate plaintiff to raise this more systemic claim? Would he be an appropriate plaintiff to raise the Article II claim? For additional discussions of the question of standing, consider Chemerinsky, *Bush v. Gore* Was Not Justiciable, 76 Notre Dame L. Rev. 1093, 1097 (2001) (arguing that Bush lacked first-party standing to raise the equal protection claim because he did not personally suffer an equal protection injury and that he lacked third-party standing because the injured voters could themselves have brought a lawsuit and he lacked the sort of relationship to them that is required to permit him raise their claims); Hoffman, Book Review, 95 Nw. U.L. Rev. 1533, 1548-50 (2001) (suggesting that the deluge of lawsuits filed by individual voters immediately after the election rebut the idea that "Florida voters were unable to raise the equal protection claims on their own" and that Bush should therefore be accorded third-party standing and suggesting that the Court's neglect of the question of standing reflects the doctrine's essential indeterminacy); Levinson and Young, Who's Afraid of the Twelfth Amendment?, 29 Fla. St. U.L. Rev. 925 (2001) (discussing who, if anyone, has standing to raise claims under the Twelfth Amendment); Shane, Disappearing Democracy: How *Bush v. Gore* Undermined the Federal Right to Vote for Presidential Electors, 29 Fla. St. U. L. Rev. 535, 562, n.125 (2001) (suggesting, despite "the prudential rule against so-called third-party standing, which ordinarily bars even injured parties from seeking federal judicial intervention where the cause of their alleged injury is a violation not of their own rights but of another person's," that in Bush v. Gore, "at least three factors argue persuasively for permitting the candidates to litigate their supporters' rights: the close interrelationship of the candidate's and voters' interests, the certainty that the candidates would be vigorous proponents of the voters' rights, and the possibility that direct voter suits might be deterred by uncertainty among the voters as to which of them were specifically affected by the state tabulation practices in dispute"); Tushnet, Renormalizing *Bush v. Gore*: An Anticipatory Intellectual History, 90 Geo. L.J. 113, 120 (2001) (suggesting that the question of standing in Bush v. Gore is complicated by the fact that several of the Justices in the majority had "mounted a major challenge to the entire idea of vote dilution" on the ground that discerning such an injury would require "'federal courts to make decisions based on highly political judgments —judgments that courts are inherently ill-equipped to make'").

On the subject of the political question doctrine, consider whether Article II and the twelfth amendment represent a textual commitment of the question of who is entitled to a state's electoral votes to Congress. Is this an implication of Justice Breyer's dissent? Does this explain the per curiam's decision to rely on the equal protection clause in light of *Baker*'s assurance that the equal protection clause provides judicially enforceable standards for overseeing the political process? See Karlan, Equal Protection: *Bush v. Gore* and The Making of a Precedent, in The Unfinished Election of 2000 (J.N. Rakove ed. 2001). For an extensive discussion of the evolution of the political question doctrine and its relevance to Bush v. Gore, see Issacharoff, Political Judgments, in The Vote, supra. Issacharoff argues that the overall structure of the Electoral Count Act of 1887—the source for 3 U.S.C. §5—commits the questions raised in the Florida process to political actors. He quotes Senator John Sherman—coincidentially both one of the sponsors of the act and one of the prime movers behind the equal protection clause—arguing on the floor of the Senate against Supreme Court involvement in presidential election controversies:

> Another plan which has been proposed in the debates at different times and I think also in the constitutional convention, was to allow questions of this kind to be certified at once to the Supreme Court for its decisions in case of a division between the two Houses. If the House should be one way and the Senate the other, then it was proposed to let the case be referred directly to the prompt and summary decision of the Supreme Court. But there is a feeling in this country that we ought not to mingle our great judicial tribunal with political questions, and therefore this proposition has not met with much favor. It would be a very grave fault indeed and a very serious objection to refer a political question in which the people of the country were aroused, about which their feelings were excited, to this great tribunal, which after all has to sit upon the life and property of all the people of the United States. It would tend to bring that court into public odium of one or the other of the two great parties. Therefore that plan may probably be rejected as an unwise provision. I believe, however, that it is the provision made in other countries.

17 Cong. Rec. 817-818 (1886) (Sen. Sherman). Issacharoff argues that had the Electoral Count Act been followed more faithfully, the relevant players in the dispute would have been Florida's governor and its legislature and the newly elected members of Congress. He observes:

> No doubt, this scenario would look to many modern observers like a pure power grab, a partisan circumvention of orderly legal processes. But why is it either surprising or alarming that an electoral deadlock should be resolved by political officials and bodies elected by the same voters? [In] the heated rhetorical battle of Election 2000, no charge was bandied about with greater derision than the claim that one or another group of partisans was engaged in partisanship. But it was, after all, a partisan election that was at stake. It hardly seems an affront to democratic self-governance to channel the ultimate resolution of a true electoral deadlock into other democratically-elected branches of government.

2. *The merits of the Court's decision.* The Court's decision has been subjected to voluminous scholarly and popular discussion. In general, the scholarship has been scathing in its treatment of the per curiam's equal protection analysis. For representative examples, see, e.g., Klarman, *Bush v. Gore* Through the Lens of Constitutional History, 89 Cal. L. Rev. 1721 (2001); Sunstein, Order without Law, in The Vote, *supra*. See also infra pages 20-28, 68. Much of the criticism focuses not on the ab-

stract equal protection question of whether a vote should have the same likelihood of being included regardless of where the vote was cast—a sort of "equal protection for ballots"—but on the question of remedy: Did stopping the manual recount actually protect any voter's equal protection interest? For a defense of the equal protection holding, see Lund, The Unbearable Rightness of *Bush v. Gore*, 23 Cardozo L. Rev. 1219 (2002).

Most defenders of the outcome of Bush v. Gore have defended the case either on the grounds advanced in the Chief Justice's concurrence or on more pragmatic grounds—in Judge Richard Posner's phrase, that it averted a "constitutional train-wreck." For representative samples of this scholarship, see, e.g., Epstein, "In Such Manner as the Legislature Thereof May Direct": The Outcome in *Bush v. Gore* Defended, in The Vote, supra; R.A. Posner, Breaking the Deadlock: The 2000 Election, the Constitution, and the Courts (2001).

Ultimately, despite the per curiam's embrace of an equal protection rationale for finding the ongoing recount unconstitutional, doesn't the per curiam's justification for stopping the recount depend on a weak version of the Article II argument, that is, that the Florida legislature's desire to invoke the safe-harbor provision of 3 U.S.C. §5 outweighs the state's interest in continuing to recount ballots under a more uniform process?

And with respect to the Article II rationale, what is the Court's basis—and particularly the concurrence's basis—for reading Article II as a grant of special power to a state's legislature? Isn't the legislature a creature of the state constitution?

Consider the exchange between the concurrence and Justice Ginsburg's dissent on the nature of Supreme Court review of state courts' determinations of state law. Does the concurrence's citation of *NAACP* and *Bouie* suggest that the Supreme Court here was overturning Florida law because it thought the Florida Supreme Court was not just mistaken in its interpretation of Florida law but deliberately dishonest? Is the invocation of those cases a sign that the concurrence rested on pragmatic rather than doctrinal grounds?

More generally, the Article II issue raises a question about when a state judicial decision construing state law raises federal questions. Always? How convinced, and with what evidence, must a federal court be that a state judicial decision departs from the legislature's intent and preexisting law? At one end of the spectrum, a state law might be entirely clear, particularly if the situation involved in the current case has arisen before and there are long-standing judicial and administrative interpretations. At the other end, consider a state election statute that has never before been construed by the state courts or interpreted by executive agencies: When the state courts interpret such a statute in the midst of an election, what possible baseline can the federal courts use to assess whether that interpretation is faithful? In such cases, is a federal court doing anything other than simply second-guessing the state court? With respect to the related questions whether the Florida Supreme Court properly interpreted the state's election code, whether its interpretations constituted a change sufficient to violate due process, and the implications of Article II for these questions, consider R. Posner, Breaking the Deadlock: The 2000 Election, the Constitution, and the Courts 152 (2001) (describing the Article II argument and the concurrence's charge that the Florida Supreme Court had changed Florida law as a "respectable" argument); Epstein, "In such Manner as the Legislature Thereof May Direct": The Outcome in *Bush v. Gore* Defended, in The Vote: Bush, Gore and the Supreme Court 13, 19-35 (C.R. Sunstein & R.A. Epstein eds., 2001) (arguing that the Florida Supreme Court adopted a process for conducting election challenges that deviated in substantial respects from the process set out in the state election code and that this shift violated Article II); Klarman, *Bush v. Gore* Through the Lens of Constitutional History, 89 Calif. L. Rev. 1721, 1733-46 (2001) (arguing that nothing in Article II suggests that federal courts should be less deferential to state-court rulings in the context of a presidential election and that nothing in the Florida courts' rulings violated Article II in any event); Krent, Judging Judging: The Problem of Second-Guessing State Judges' Interpretation of State Law in *Bush v. Gore*, 29 Fla. St. U.L. Rev. 493 (2001) (arguing that the Florida Supreme Court's constructions of Florida law were plausible and that the concurrence's "conclusion that the Florida Court's decision was so unforeseeable that it changed law is nothing short of startling"); Kramer, The Supreme Court in Politics in The Unfinished Election of 2000, at 105, 146-47 (J.N. Rakove ed., 2001) (claiming that "with [one] possible exception . . . , the Florida court arguably had better interpretations [of state law] on every issue" than the Supreme Court did); Schapiro, Conceptions and Misconceptions of State Constitutional Law in *Bush v. Gore*, 29 Fla. St. U.L. Rev. 661 (2001) (arguing that the concurrence was plagued by a flawed conception of state constitutionalism and the role of state courts in the state constitutional order).

3. *Questions of institutional respect and institutional competence.* On the more general question of what Bush v. Gore shows about the Supreme Court's role in the constitutional order, consider the following views:

a. Garrett, Institutional Lessons from the 2000 Presidential Election, 29 Fla. St. U.L. Rev. 975, 975-76, 979-80, 982-83 (2001):

[T]he Bush-Gore election concretely illustrates that institutional design is a crucial consideration in determining which part of the government is best suited to render particular decisions. When institutions must become involved in majoritarian political decisions such as the selection of a President, it may be better to rely largely on the political branches than on the judiciary for several reasons. This allocation of decisionmaking authority is preferable because of the greater democratic credentials of Congress. . . . In addition, there is a less-often recognized advantage of institutional design enjoyed by the legislature. . . . [T]he legislature can adopt procedural frameworks to shape decisionmaking and restrain partisan opportunism before a particular controversy arises. In the case of the

21

2000 election, the United States Congress actually had a framework in place . . . [The Electoral Count Act long antedated the Bush-Gore election and] would have ensured that decisions were made transparently so voters could have held politicians accountable both for their ultimate decision and for the manner in which they reached it.

In contrast, . . . the Supreme Court's early intervention into the 2000 election reveals the greater possibility for strategic behavior when an institution acts ex post with relatively full information about how its decisions will affect particular and concrete interests. The presidential election thus provides on the federal level both an example of ex ante rules—the Electoral Count Act—and an example of ex post decisionmaking—the judicial interventions into the political process. While the former contained gaps because its drafters did not foresee all the problems that could arise in a presidential election, the latter provided substantial leeway for opportunistic behavior designed to advance the Justices' preferences. . . .

Although the Constitution's equal protection guarantee was adopted long before the presidential dispute in 2000, it is so open-textured and vague that virtually all the specification occurs when it is applied to particular cases. As an ex ante framework, it is essentially all gap to be filled in the future. Not only did the Court articulate its specification of equal protection for the first time in this case, but it also explicitly limited the doctrine's applicability to the case before it, evading the protection against self-interested decisionmaking that generality in rules can provide. . . .

Others have defended the Supreme Court's repeated intervention into the election contest as a courageous move to save the country from crisis—courageous because the Justices adopted an aggressive role at some risk to the reputations of their institution and themselves. Such fears of a political disaster are overstated, and they reflect an elitist distrust of the relatively messy arena of politics. Congress would not have discharged its responsibility to determine any election contest without some amount of heated rhetoric, opportunistic behavior, and partisan wrangling. However, Congress had the ability to apply [the Electoral Count Act] in a transparent and accountable way.

While others . . . have worried that the Court's decision[s] . . . will damage its long-term reputation, my concern focuses on the damage to the legislative branch. When judges work so hard to keep a case away from our elected representatives, using a novel legal rationale that is not supported with the kind of argument and analysis of precedent that similar holdings have been, their distrust of the political branches is palpable. Furthermore, when those who harshly criticize the Court's opinion as lawless and unprincipled nonetheless defend it as a necessary protection against the chaos that they predict would have consumed the country, this analysis feeds the distrust of Congress already prevalent. . . .

b. Priest, Reanalyzing *Bush v. Gore*: Democratic Accountability and Judicial Overreaching, 72 U. Colo. L. Rev. 953, 963-64 (2001):

[T]he set of events leading up to Bush v. Gore can best be understood as a battle between two courts over the mechanisms of control of the election process in Florida. The Florida Supreme Court . . . claimed through its decisions that it, not the elected Secretary of State, should make the determinative political judgment as to how the Florida election process was to be managed. . . . In Bush v. Gore, the United States Supreme Court reinstated control over the Florida election process to the democratically elected official politically accountable for those decisions, control that had been wrested from that official by the Florida Supreme Court. As a consequence, the United States Supreme Court in Bush v. Gore restored to the citizens of Florida the power to hold politically accountable the official responsible for determining how the election was to proceed.

c. Sunstein, Order Without Law, 68 U. Chi. L. Rev. 757, 758-59 (2001):

The Court's decision in Bush v. Gore did have two fundamental virtues. First, it produced a prompt and decisive conclusion to the chaotic post-election period of 2000. Indeed, it probably did so in a way that carried more simplicity and authority than anything that might have been expected from the United States Congress. The Court might even have avoided a genuine constitutional crisis. Second, the Court's equal protection holding carries considerable appeal. On its face, that holding has the potential to create the most expansive, and perhaps sensible, protection for voting rights since the Court's one-person, one-vote decisions of mid-century. . . .

The Court's decision also had two large vices. First, the Court effectively resolved the presidential election not unanimously, but by a 5-4 vote, with the majority consisting entirely of the Court's most conservative justices. Second, the Court's rationale was not only exceedingly ambitious but also embarrassingly weak. However appealing, its equal protection holding had no basis in precedent or in history. It also raises a host of puzzles for the future, which the Court appeared to try to resolve with its minimalist cry of "here, but nowhere else." . . .

From the standpoint of constitutional order, the Court might well have done the nation a service. From the standpoint of legal reasoning, the Court's decision was very bad. In short, the Court's decision produced order without law. . . .

d. Karlan, Unduly Partial: The Supreme Court and the Fourteenth Amendment in *Bush v. Gore*, 29 Fla. St. U.L. Rev. 587, 600-01 (2001):

[Bush v. Gore] was political, in the broad sense of the word. The Court was trying to wrap its decision in the mantle of its most popularly and jurisprudentially successful intervention into the political process: the one-person, one-vote cases. This is a familiar strategy. Consider Planned Parenthood v. Casey, the case in which the Court reaffirmed the central right to reproductive autonomy recognized in Roe

v. Wade. The joint opinion written by Justices O'Connor, Kennedy, and Souter invoked another iconic Equal Protection Clause case, Brown v. Board of Education. It too treated the responsibility of articulating binding principles of constitutional law as an unsought responsibility. And it saw a special dimension "present whenever the Court's interpretation of the Constitution calls the contending sides of a national controversy to end their national division by accepting a common mandate rooted in the Constitution." It identified only two such occasions "in our lifetime, . . . the decisions of Brown and Roe."

Perhaps the Supreme Court saw Bush v. Gore as a third such occasion. Once again, the Court was asking the nation to end its close division by accepting a common mandate rooted in the Constitution and accepting a judicial resolution. And as between the Equal Protection Clause—source of some of the Supreme Court's finest moments—and the other contenders, it was no contest. If the Supreme Court was going to stop the recount, it had to use a constitutional provision with a pedigree. The Equal Protection Clause provided exactly that. Moreover, it allowed the Court to invoke the specter of unfair treatment of voters, whereas the other available constitutional contenders protected either the prerogative of state legislatures (Article II, Section 1) or, even worse, the interests of candidate George W. Bush (the Due Process Clause . . . .)

e. Pildes, Democracy and Disorder, 68 U. Chi. L. Rev. 695, 696-700, 714-15 (2001):

Bush v. Gore is the most dramatic moment in a constitutionalization of the democratic process that has been afoot for nearly forty years, ever since Baker v. Carr dramatically lowered the "political question" barrier to judicial oversight of politics. . . .

[In cases regulating politics,] the formal sources of legal judgment are sufficiently open-textured as not to compel directly a uniquely determinate conclusion. At that point, the implicit understandings of democracy with which all judges necessarily work—whether American democracy is fragile or secure, whether it functioned better or worse at some (partially hypothesized) moment in the past, whether democracy means order and structure or chaos and tumult—have the greatest latitude to operate. . . .

[At the time the Court decided Bush v. Gore, it faced the possibility] of the ultimate resolution emerging from a political struggle within Congress over a possibly competing slate of Florida electors . . . much as Congress was the ultimate dispute resolver in the 1876 Hayes-Tilden election or in the internal civil war in Rhode Island that lay behind Luther v. Borden. . . .

When a justice stares at this kind of political resolution of a disputed presidential election, does that justice see the specter of a "constitutional trainwreck?" A dangerous mechanism to be avoided at nearly all costs, a mechanism that conjures up images of disorder, turbulence, political instability, indeed, "crisis?" Does the very novelty of the Electoral Count Act process, one not invoked for over a hundred years, increase the judicial sense of a system racing to the brink, a race from which judicial rescue is desperately needed? Or does a justice see other disputed presidential elections of 1800 and 1876—elections freighted with profound substantive conflicts genuinely tearing the country apart, unlike in 2000—and yet elections in which political institutions adequately resolved the dispute. . . ? A deep historical sensibility about the elections of 1800 or 1876 is not needed to ask such questions. For we can also ask whether the recent presidential impeachment process was a "constitutional trainwreck" or, again more to the point, whether the constitutional order would have been improved had the Supreme Court determined for the country what constituted "high Crimes and Misdemeanors" within the meaning of the Constitution?

Whether democracy requires order, stability, and channeled, constrained forms of engagement, or whether it requires and even celebrates relatively wide-open competition that may appear tumultuous, partisan, or worse, has long been a struggle in democratic thought and practice (indeed, historically it was one of the defining set of oppositions in arguments about the desirability of democracy itself). . . . [Justices] regularly seem to group themselves into characteristic and recurring patterns of response . . . . These patterned responses suggest that it is something beyond law, or facts, or narrow partisan politics in particular cases, that determine outcomes; it is, perhaps, cultural assumptions and historical interpretations, conscious or not, that inform or even determine these judgments.

　　f. Yoo, In Defense of the Court's Legitimacy, 68 U. Chi. L. Rev. 775, 776, 779-81 (2001):

[C]oncerns about the Court's legitimacy are overblown. While it is certainly too early to be sure, the Court's actions, and their impact on the political system, come nowhere close to approaching the circumstances that surrounded earlier, real threats to the Court's standing. The Court did not decide any substantive issues— on a par with abortion or privacy rights, for example—that call upon the Court to remain continually at the center of political controversy for years. Instead, the Court issued a fairly narrow decision in a one-of-a-kind case—the procedures to govern presidential election counts—that is not likely to reappear in our lifetimes. Rather than acting hypocritically and lawlessly, the Court's decision to bring the Florida election dispute to a timely, and final, end not only restored stability to the political system but was also consistent with the institutional role the Court has shaped for itself over the last decade. . . .

The Court's authority has come under serious question four times in our history: the Marshall Court, the Taney Court's decision in Dred Scott, the Court's early resistance to the New Deal, and the Warren Court's fight against segregation and its expansion of individual liberties. Close inspection of these periods show that they bear little resemblance to Bush v. Gore. . . .

The defining characteristic of several of these periods was the persistent, central role of the Court in the political disputes of the day. Contrast these periods with Bush v. Gore. In Bush v. Gore, the Court sought to resolve a narrow legal issue involving the selection of presidential electors. The question bears no constitutional implications for the resolution of any significant and ongoing social issues of today—abortion, race relations, education, social security, defense. The decision poses no bar to a society that seeks to use the democratic process to resolve any pressing social problems. While the Democratic party has reason to be dissatisfied with the outcome of Bush v. Gore, it has no interest in challenging the legal reasoning of the decision in the future. It is highly unlikely that the Court will remain a central player in future presidential election contests. . . .

g. Klarman, Bush v. Gore Through the Lens of Constitutional History, 89 Cal. L. Rev. 1721, 1722, 1747-48, 1761-64 (2001):

[H]istory's verdict on a Supreme Court ruling depends more on whether public opinion ultimately supports the outcome than on the quality of the legal reasoning or the craftsmanship of the Court's opinion. . . .

The principal variable influencing the Court's reputation is how popular or unpopular its decisions are. Second, . . . the intensity of that sentiment—how strongly supporters and opponents feel about the underlying issue—influences the Court's standing. Third, [is how convinced opponents are] . . . that the Court decision resolving that issue will be implemented, rather than evaded or even nullified. . . . Fourth, the relative power of the constituencies that support and oppose the Court's rulings may be relevant. . . . Fifth, some constitutional issues linger, while others fade away. Controversial decisions on topics that quickly become obsolete are unlikely to do the Court much long-term harm. Sixth, public opinion changes, often quite dramatically, on some constitutional issues but not others. . . . Seventh, Justices sometimes, but not always, enjoy subsequent opportunities to adjust their original decision, thus modulating results that initially proved controversial. Eighth, contentious constitutional decisions sometimes come in packages. A ruling that might not have significantly impaired the Court's standing had it been an isolated event, may weaken an institution already under siege because of contemporaneous decisions. . . .

Half the country, the half that voted for Al Gore, thinks the result in Bush v. Gore was wrong; many think it was egregiously so. . . . Yet, while nearly all Democrats criticize *Bush*, it is not clear how intense their opposition is. Surely most Americans are more energized by presidential elections than by flag burning. On the other hand, relatively few Gore supporters seem to have manifested an intensity of commitment for their candidate approaching that displayed by right-tolifers in opposition to Roe v. Wade. Indeed, a principal reason that Gore found himself in the Florida predicament that he did (recall that all the political scientists' models predicted a relatively comfortable victory for him) was the relative lack of enthusiasm evinced by many Democrats for their party's candidate. Thus one might surmise that many Democrats' opposition to Bush v. Gore will be lukewarm at best. My hunch, however, is that this supposition is mistaken. . . . This efficacious a ruling, on this divisive an issue, is certain to generate tremendous resentment toward the Court.

As to the relative power of the constituencies impacted by the Court's decision, both Democrats and Republicans have plenty of political and economic clout in American society. Thus, Bush v. Gore is not a case where the Court's critics are relatively disadvantaged in the public relations battle that follows the ruling. On the other hand, it is hard to think of a constitutional issue that is more destined to become obsolete. George W. Bush will be president, possibly as a result of the Supreme Court's ruling, for four years. If he serves eight years, an intervening independent cause, a second electoral victory, will greatly reduce the Court's responsibility for the second term. . . . Moreover, the Supreme Court's ruling in *Bush*, by design, will have implications for no other constitutional issue. . . . Memories of what most Democrats will regard as the (at least attempted) judicial theft of a presidential election will survive, but they will be just that—memories. . . .

On the other hand, unlike with racial segregation, where public opinion transformed over time, popular attitudes toward Bush v. Gore probably never will change very much. Democrats are likely always to believe that the Supreme Court intervened in the 2000 presidential election because the conservative Justices preferred George W. Bush for president. Perhaps some attitudes will change if Bush proves to be a particularly good or bad President, but probably not too many. Moreover, unlike with the death penalty, the Supreme Court almost certainly will enjoy no future opportunities to revisit the issue in Bush . . . and thus to fix its "mistake." Once elected president, Bush cannot be "unelected."

Finally, from the "basket of issues" perspective, the Rehnquist Court might survive Bush v. Gore reasonably unscathed, because the remainder of the Court's constitutional jurisprudence has been such a political grab bag of results. . . . While the Rehnquist Court arguably has been the most activist in history, its activism does not manifest a consistent political valence. In recent years, liberals generally have won on issues involving abortion, school prayer, gender discrimination, and freedom of speech. Conservatives, on the other hand, have triumphed on issues such as affirmative action, minority voting districts, public aid to parochial schools, federalism, the death penalty, and (usually) criminal procedure. . . . Perhaps Democratic ire over Bush v. Gore is somewhat ameliorated by the Rehnquist Court's continuing propensity to distribute a substantial share of constitutional victories to liberals.

h. Seidman, What's So Bad About Bush v. Gore? An Essay on Our Unsettled Election, 47 Wayne L. Rev. 953, 958-62, 1024, 1026 (2001):

According to the Official Story, constitutional law settles otherwise destabilizing political disputes through reference to a meta-agreement. . . . This agreement, whether embodied in the constitutional text, or in doctrine and tradition that has glossed it, prevents the community from coming unraveled. Sometimes the agreement is substantive, as for example, when the Constitution directly prohibits certain outcomes like laws depriving people of property without just compensation. More often it is procedural, as when the Constitution allocates decision making authority to a branch of the federal government, the states, or the private sphere. . . .

For this story to make sense, four preconditions must be satisfied. First, there must be agreement on the metalevel. Second, there must be a discourse capable of mediating between the contested political level and the uncontroversial metalevel. Third, there must be an institution capable of engaging in the discourse. And finally, the institution and the discourse it utilizes must be "neutral" in the sense that they must not themselves be caught up in the very political controversy that they are supposed to settle. Conventionally, it is thought that the Constitution provides the area of agreement, that an arcane and specialized form of reasoning—legal reasoning—provides the mediating discourse, that the Supreme Court is uniquely capable of engaging in this discourse, and that both the Court and the discourse are free from political entanglements. . . .

[None of these was true in Bush v. Gore.] The Court's decision does not pass the "straight face" test when judged according to the aspirations for legal analysis required to make the Official Story plausible. There is no reason to take the decision seriously, and it portends precisely nothing with regard to future doctrinal developments. But it is also wrong to condemn the decision because it is political. There simply was no neutral, apolitical way in which the case could have been decided . . . .

All of which suggests that what's gone bad is not the Supreme Court, but instead the Official Story. How is it that the Supreme Court was able to play this role once stripped of the protective covering of legality . . . ?

Three possibilities suggest themselves. First, the Court may have prevailed through deception. Perhaps the decision is parasitic on the reputation for legality or integrity that the Court has built up over the years or on the pseudo-religious imagery that it uses to obscure its exercise of power. . . . The Court's decision had the external trappings of legality, even though it lacked the requisite substance. . . .

A second possibility is that the Supreme Court provided a useful focal point even though its decision was correctly perceived to be partisan rather than legal. Although the country was sharply divided about the election's outcome, there was near unanimity in the desire to get the matter over with. Even if the Supreme Court was acting nonlegally, it was at least able to settle the issue in a peaceful and orderly fashion.

The trouble with this account is that it fails to explain why people were prepared to endorse settlement by the Supreme Court, rather than another institution. After all, the federal judiciary was not the only possible focal point. The 2000 election might have been settled by the Florida Supreme Court, by the Florida Legislature, or, most plausibly, by the United States Congress. . . .

[There is also] a third possibility—one that turns the Official Story inside out. There is a chance that Bush v. Gore may begin a process of laying a more attractive and realistic foundation for constitutionalism than the Official Story provides. The very fact that the Court is not politically independent and that it could not settle the matter in a disinterested, apolitical fashion might set us down a path toward a more mature version of constitutional law. The politically tendentious character of the Court's reasoning demonstrates that our core constitutional commitments are subject to political manipulation. Ironically, public understanding of this malleability makes our politics more, rather than less, inclusive. It does so by suggesting that constitutional law, properly understood, does not settle disputes by ruling certain substantive positions out-of-bounds. . . .

Constitutional law best serves the ends of community when it opens up, rather than closes down, political argument. Nor should the Supreme Court's prestige depend upon its political neutrality. Instead, it earns that prestige when it utilizes concepts and a vocabulary that are sufficiently open-textured to allow the losers, using the same concepts and vocabulary, to claim that the Court's decision is wrong.

With respect to the deluge of academic commentary about Bush v. Gore, consider the analysis offered in Tushnet, Renormalizing Bush v. Gore: An Anticipatory Intellectual History, 90 Geo. L.J. 113, 113-16, 124-25 (2001):

The critical legal studies claim that law, properly understood, was indistinguishable from politics, properly understood, was quite threatening to the self-understanding of legal elites. . . . Legal elites are heavily invested in insisting that there is a real difference between law and politics. They are also invested, though slightly less so, in insisting that judges typically do law rather than politics. These investments . . . meant that something had to be done to take the sting out of the criticisms that [Bush v, Gore] was infected by blatant partisanship. . . . so that we can return to our belief that law is sensibly distinguishable from politics. . . .

I will identify several major techniques of renormalization. The first is simple enough: Ignore the case. Treat it as a unique event in the legal universe, unlikely ever to be repeated. . . . The difficulty that ignoring the case poses for legal elites is precisely that the decision presents itself as law, and for legal elites, judicial

29

decisions are distinguished from executive ones, for example, precisely because executive decisions need have no implications for the future—can be sui generis —in ways that judicial decisions must.

The second renormalization technique . . . acknowledges that the decision in Bush v. Gore cannot really be regarded as an example of courts operating at anywhere near their best and may even be a (hopefully) isolated case in which law was in fact reduced to politics. . . . [T]he Court, and the nation, confronted a chaotic situation implicating both the selection of the nation's most important public official and an impending constitutional crisis. The Court, in this view, was in a position to resolve the crisis in a statesmanlike way. Perhaps the Court's legal theory was thin, but a barely adequate legal theory may be sufficient when invoked to avert a serious constitutional crisis. . . .

[A third] technique of renormalization . . . [tries] to work out the doctrinal implications of the Court's innovations . . . .

A final technique of renormalization is in some ways the most interesting. It involves the generalized invocation of rule-of-law norms, typically in the form of assertions that the Supreme Court's decision, while perhaps incorrect, nonetheless deserves respect because the Court is our nation's voice of the law. . . . Not surprisingly, this creates something of a psychological difficulty, related to, but not quite the same as, the phenomenon of cognitive dissonance. People find it hard to think that decisions with which they disagree are nevertheless justified. People also find it hard to give up on the ideal of the rule of law. The outcome is predictable. As time passes, people come to think that the decisions with which they initially disagreed were actually not wrong. I think we can expect to see, and I think reasonably soon, progressives asserting that, as a matter of fact, Bush v. Gore was correctly decided.

As indeed it was. After all, the equal protection doctrine the case articulated can certainly be turned to progressive uses. . . . And that, to conclude, would be another vindication of a different critical legal studies claim, this one about the indeterminacy of legal doctrine.

2
THE POWERS
OF CONGRESS

A. Introduction

Page 142. After Note 5, add the following:

5a. *Enhancing social capital.* Consider the argument of Mazzone, The Social Capital Argument for Federalism, 11 S. Cal. Interdis. L. J. 27, 42, 59 (2001):

> [Dividing] authority [increases] the points of political power over which citizens can exert influence in order to achieve their goals. [A] political environment in which there are multiple sites for influence promotes social capital because such an environment is conducive to a large number of interest groups in which citizens actively participate. [Federalism] provides opportunities for smaller groups of active citizens to organize and pursue their goals in a variety of settings rather than relegating vast numbers of citizens to passive roles in a large national advocacy group which pursues its members' interests in Washington. [Decentralization also] increases the sites of political decisionmaking. [In] a decentralized system, however, power ultimately rests in the central authority, providing incentives for citizen groups to seek influence by strengthening their resources at the national level.

5b. *Doctrinal implications?* Assuming that a political system should advance the values of federalism, do the ones listed above provide guidance on what the content of a judicially enforced doctrine of federalism should be?

B. The Basic Issues: Federalism and Judicial Review

Page 157. After Note 4, add the following:

4a. *Political Safeguards and "Horizontal Aggrandizement."* Baker & Young, Federalism and the Double Standard of Review, 51 Duke L.J. 75 (2001), distinguish

between "vertical aggrandizement"—the accretion of power to the national government—and "horizontal aggrandizement," which they define as a mechanism "by
which a majority of states [imposes] their own policy preferences on a minority of
states with different preferences." While skeptical of the effectiveness of political
safeguards to protect against vertical aggrandizement, Baker and Young argue that
the political safeguards, whether in the form of structural limits built into the Constitution or in the form of the factors Kramer emphasizes, will not guard against horizontal aggrandizement. They identify three circumstances in which horizontal
aggrandizement might occur: when "people in some states simply do not approve of
certain activities permitted in other states, even though the activity in the other states
does not affect them directly," when some states try "to capture a disproportionate
share of federal monetary or regulatory largesse" by imposing as a national standard
requirements that these states would follow even in the absence of a national rule,
and "when states seek federal regulation to avoid externalities [associated] with regulating a particular subject at the state level," as when a local regulation might cause
investors to locate in other states. Id. at 118-20.

Do the political safeguards of federalism operate effectively in connection with
horizontal aggrandizement? Consider these responses: (1) In the situations described,
"[prior] to the adoption of the coercive federal statute there was already a federal law
regime in place that constrained state autonomy," and "Congress [was] called upon
to [decide] what kind of state autonomy it should promote." Barron, A Localist Critique of the New Federalism, 51 Duke L.J. 377, 418 (2001). What is at stake is the
distribution of power among the states to impose their policies on other states, and
the Constitution provides no reason to prefer the distribution of power that exists
before a particular statute is enacted over the distribution of power that exist after-
wards. (2) The Civil War and its outcome demonstrate, or establish, that the Constitution is not concerned about avoiding horizontal aggrandizement.

C. The Evolution of Commerce Clause Doctrine: The Lessons (?) of History

Page 164. After the first paragraph of section 5 of the Note, add the following:

Cushman, Formalism and Realism in Commerce Clause Jurisprudence, 67 U. Chi.
L. Rev. 1089 (2000), argues that the Court during this period applied the tests available to it in a principled way, related to its contemporaneous doctrine regarding state
power to regulate interstate commerce and dealing with due process limits on state
regulatory power. According to Cushman, the Supreme Court confined state regulatory power to businesses affected with a public interest. With respect to the "stream

of commerce" test, only those "local" enterprises "affected with a public interest" could be located in a stream of interstate commerce, and with respect to *Shreveport*, that case "recognized federal power to regulate the intrastate rates charged by an interstate business affected with a public interest. So long as the power of Congress to regulate interstate rates remained confined to businesses affected with a public interest, its derivative power to regulate intrastate rates would remain similarly confined." Id. at 1129, 1131.

Page 200.   At the end of section 1 of the Note, add the following:

Consider Shane, Federalism's "Old Deal": What's Right and Wrong with Conservative Judicial Activism, 45 Villanova L. Rev. 201, 221 (2000):

Compare [a] national anti-prostitution statute with a hypothetical federal law purporting to mandate compulsory education in some East Asian language as a prerequisite to high school graduation. The first regulates economic activity and the second not. Yet, the second law is obviously grounded in economic motivations that probably do not animate the first. There is no reason consistent with the Commerce Clause why Congress' commerce-driven compulsion of Asian language education should be more suspect than its morally driven regulation of prostitution.

Page 201.   After section 2 of the Note, add the following:

2a. *Defining "commercial activities."* Consider Ides, Economic Activity as a Proxy for Federalism: Intuition and Reason in *United States v. Morrison*, 18 Const. Comment. 563, 568, 569 (2002): Relying on law-and-economics analysis, Ides argues that "the rapist [forcibly] takes that to which he has no right. The consequence [is] a forced transfer of wealth [to] the rapist. [In] short, rape is an economic crime, and the act of rape constitutes economic activity." Under this approach, is there anything that is not economic activity? See Choper, Taming Congress's Power Under the Commerce Clause: What Does the Near Future Portend?, 55 Ark. L. Rev. 731, 738, 740 (2003), suggesting that Congress "could enact a nationwide law prohibiting all robbery," and "could make it unlawful to injure any individual or business that carries insurance to cover the economic effects of the criminal act." Nelson and Pushaw, Rethinking the Commerce Clause: Applying First Principles to Uphold Federal Commercial Regulations but Preserve State Control Over Social Issues, 85 Iowa L. Rev. 1, 108 (1999), suggest that Congress can regulate commerce defined to include three areas: first, "buying and selling goods; the production of such merchandise; [and] incidents of that production, such as environmental and safety effects"; second, "the compensated provision of services"; and, third, "the means by which commerce is transacted," including negotiable instruments and security interests in property. Note that the latter category would make it permissible for Congress to enact a federal law of mortgages. Choper asks: "Is barring possession or use of marijuana an attempt by Congress to impose a political, moral, cultural, or social view? Or does it seek to regulate an international business?" *Supra* at 742.

After section 3 of the Note, add the following:

3a. *Perverse effects?* Consider Vermeule, Does Commerce Clause Review Have Perverse Effects?, 46 Villanova L. Rev. 1325, 1330, 1334-35 (2001): "The proponent of Commerce Clause review assumes that if Congress enacts policy P and the courts strike it down, the decision has increased decentralization. [But] if the courts' rules allow [Congress] to enact P so long as P is broadened to include some admittedly constitutional policy Q, [the] result of striking down P may [be] to produce a federal statute that mandates *both* P *and* Q." Consider the constitutionality of a federal ban on the possession of machine guns *anywhere*, not just near schools. Vermeule reports that the lower federal courts have upheld such a ban, some arguing that the aggregation principle supports a general ban even when it would not support a narrow one.

Page 202. At the end of section 5 of the Note, add the following:

Should the Court attempt to develop an interpretation of the commerce clause that takes account of subsequent *constitutional* developments? Should modern notions of equality lead the Court to find an activity within the scope of the power to regulate interstate commerce, even if that activity might not be regulable by Congress absent its implications for equality?

Page 203. At the end of the Note, add the following:

7. *The commerce clause after Reconstruction.* Consider the argument of Jackson, Holistic Interpretation: *Fitzpatrick v. Bitzer* and Our Bifurcated Constitution, 53 Stan. L. Rev. 1259 (2001), for a "holistic" interpretation of the Constitution, in which the adoption of the fourteenth amendment (and others) properly should affect the interpretation of the commerce clause. Jackson proposes that "where the special concern or 'central value' of the Fourteenth and subsequent equality-oriented

Amendments is at stake—a concern [with] overcoming barriers to full participation in public life, both economic and political, by groups traditionally disadvantaged by a history of government-sponsored discrimination—the federal government's powers across the Constitution should be interpreted in light of the now basic constitutional commitment to equality of treatment for all members of the polity." Id. at 1301-1302. Jackson suggests that this may provide the "articulable limit" the Court seeks on theories that require long chains of causation between the regulated subject and a substantial effect on interstate commerce.

Should we treat the Constitution as an integrated document even though portions were adopted at different times, in the absence of evidence that those who inserted the later portions intended to affect the interpretation of what had been adopted before? Jackson argues that "a sensible reconciliation of constitutionalism (in the sense of precommitment) with democracy is to give greater weight to the constitutional views [of] more contemporary supramajorities as compared with ratifiers who lived many more generations removed." Id. at 1290.

8. *Recent case.* Pierce County v. Guillen, 537 U.S. ___ (2003), upheld under the Commerce Clause a federal statute protecting reports and surveys compiled by state agencies after automobile accidents, as part of a federal program to identify potential accident sites, from discovery in lawsuits in state and federal courts. A federal statute gave state governments funds to improve highways, conditioned on, among other things, their compiling the information. States, fearing liability based on information in the reports, objected to the funding condition. "Congress could reasonably believe that adopting a measure eliminating an unforeseen side effect of the information-gathering requirement [would] result in more diligent efforts to collect the relevant information [and], ultimately, greater safety on our Nation's roads." The statute was "aimed at improving safety in the channels of commerce and increasing protection for the instrumentalities of interstate commerce." The Commerce Clause holding made it unnecessary for the Court to consider whether the statute could be upheld under the Spending Clause.

D. Other Powers of Congress: Are They More (or Less) Plenary than the Commerce Power?

Page 230.   After section 2 of the Note, add the following:

3. *The Court-Congress relation.*   Consider these observations:

Boerne assumes that the creation of constitutional meaning is divorced from political and social life. It imagines a world in which the Court pronounces constitutional values and the country merely obeys. . . .

[In contrast,] [i]n the aftermath of *Brown*, the Court invited Congress's participation in vindicating equality norms, both because Congress could secure popular acceptance of the Court's decisions [and] because representative branches of government were an important resource for the Court as it struggled to learn from and speak to the American people about the meaning of the Fourteenth Amendment's guarantee of "equal protection of the laws." In this era, the Court established a relationship with Congress that was fluid and dynamic, and that could not be comprehended by mechanical criteria like "congruence and proportionality." This institutional relationship enabled the Court to interpret the Equal Protection Clause in a manner that was attentive to evolving and contested social norms. The framework of the Court's recent Section 5 decisions represents a fundamental break with the forms of interaction that the Warren and Burger Courts cultivated with Congress.

Post and Siegel, Equal Protection by Law: Federal Antidiscrimination Legislation after *Morrison* and *Kimel*, 110 Yale L.J. 441, 519, 446 (2000). Can "the forms of interaction" used by the Warren and Burger Courts be reconciled with the theory underlying Cooper v. Aaron?

4.   *Changing times and prophylactic rules.*   Suppose that Congress has before it sufficient evidence to justify adoption of a remedy under section 5 that is proportional to and congruent with constitutional violations but goes beyond providing a remedy for such violations only. Citing cases upholding the Voting Rights Act of 1965, *Boerne* asserts that such prophylactic rules are constitutional. What if, after time passes, the number of direct constitutional violations drops, either because of widespread compliance with the congressional statute or because of changing social norms? Can a statute constitutionally valid when adopted later become disproportionate or incongruent and therefore unconstitutional?

The Supreme Court has held that the fifteenth amendment, guaranteeing a right to vote without regard to race, is violated only by actions that intentionally deprive persons of a right to vote on the basis of race. Section 2 of the Voting Rights Act as amended in 1982 allows relief where voting practices are shown to have a disparate effect on different racial groups. It therefore goes beyond the Constitution's direct requirements. The Court in *Boerne* did not indicate a view on the present constitutionality of section 2 of the Voting Rights Act. For a discussion of section 2's constitutionality after *Boerne*, see Karlan, Two Section Twos and Two Section Fives: Voting Rights and Remedies after *Boerne*, 39 Wm. & Mary L. Rev. 725 (1998); Gerken, Understanding the Right to an Undiluted Vote, 114 Harv. L. Rev. 1663, 1737 (2001).

At the same time, in a series of cases discussed infra at page 552 of the main text, the Court has suggested that compliance with the Act might serve as a compelling state interest sufficient to justify purposefully using race to draw legislative districts. In this light, consider Karlan, Easing the Spring: Strict Scrutiny and Affirmative Action After the Redistricting Cases, 43 Wm. & Mary L. Rev. 1569, 1586 (2002):

> In suggesting that compliance with sections 2 and 5 of the Voting Rights Act can constitute a compelling state interest [sufficient to justify race-specific districting], the Court has raised the possibility that congressional or executive understandings of equality that go beyond what the Constitution itself requires can provide a justification for race-conscious state action.

5. *Garrett.* Board of Trustees of the University of Alabama v. Garrett, 531 U.S. 356 (2000), held that Congress lacked power under section 5 to require that state governments pay monetary damages for their failure to comply with the requirement of the Americans With Disabilities Act that employers take steps to reasonably accommodate employees with disabilities. According to the Court "the legislative record available to Congress did not demonstrate sufficiently widespread violations of the constitutional requirement that states not act arbitrarily in their decisions about persons with disabilities." The record included findings by a congressionally appointed task force that identified instances of disability discrimination, but many of those instances involved discrimination by local governments, not by state governments. Justice Breyer, for four dissenters, criticized the Court for "[r]eviewing the congressional record as if it were an administrative agency record," and noted that there were 300 instances of state government discrimination enumerated in the task force report. Chief Justice Rehnquist's opinion for the Court replied that many of the examples showed a failure to accommodate, but that such failures might not be arbitrary and therefore might not involve constitutional violations.

Page 231.   At the end of the second paragraph, add the following:

Nevada Dept. of Human Resources v. Hibbs, 538 U.S. ___ (2003), rejected a constitutional challenge to the money damages provision of the Family and Medical Leave Act of 1993 as applied to states. Chief Justice Rehnquist wrote the Court's opinion, finding that the history of state-law discrimination based on "invalid gender stereotypes in the employment context" justified a "prophylactic" remedy "that proscribes facially constitutional conduct, in order to prevent and deter unconstitutional conduct." The FMLA satisfied the requirements of congruence and proportionality in part because state laws that discriminate on the basis of gender must survive a higher standard of review than those that discriminate on the basis of age or disability — implying that it is "easier [to] show a pattern of state constitutional violations" — and in part because of limitations on the remedy provided by the FMLA.

3

JUDICIAL EFFORTS TO PROTECT THE EXPANSION OF THE MARKET AGAINST ASSERTIONS OF LOCAL POWER

A.   The Fundamental Framework

Page 261.   At the end of Note 1a, add the following:

Regan, Judicial Review of Member-State Regulation of Trade Within a Federal or Quasi-Federal System: Protectionism and Balancing, *Da Capo*, 99 Mich. L. Rev. 1853, 1889 (2001):

> [P]roviding a neutral perspective [is] what we have judges for. If we had no neutral dispute-settlement organs, then how the regulation appeared to affected foreigners would determine their diplomatic or legislative reaction. [Even] the *appearance* of protectionism would tend to undermine future cooperation. But if there are courts in place, the situation is changed. Trust in the central institutions can to some extent replace trust in the other parties. [The] courts should decide for themselves what the regulating legislature's subjective intent was, not how it appears to the other parties.

C.　Facially Neutral Statutes with Effects on Commerce

Page 321.　After section 8 of the Note, add the following:

9. *Regulating the Internet.* A state enacts a statute requiring that all "spam" (multi-receiver, unsolicited commercial) e-mail messages to persons located in the state contain the letters "ADVERT" in the subject line. Does the statute violate the dormant commerce clause? Does such a statute "directly" regulate out-of-state businesses? Does it create a risk of multiple burdens? Are its burdens on interstate commerce excessive relative to its benefits to local e-mail users? See Goldsmith & Sykes, The Internet and the Dormant Commerce Clause, 110 Yale L.J. 785 (2001).

Page 327.　At the end of the last paragraph of Section 3 of the Note, add the following:

See also American Insurance Ass'n v. Garamendi, 539 U.S. ___ (2003) (holding that the California Holocaust Victim Insurance Relief Act, which required that insurers licensed to operate in the state disclose the details of insurance policies issued in Europe between 1920 and 1945, was preempted because it conflicted with an executive agreement concluded between the President and Germany, establishing a foundation to compensate victims).

4
THE DISTRIBUTION OF NATIONAL POWERS

A. Introduction

Page 334.   At the end of section 2 of the Note, add the following:

Do the efficiency promoting and liberty protecting functions of separation of powers doctrine conflict with each other? Consider Barber, Prelude to the Separation of Powers, 60 Cambridge L. J. 59, 64-65 (2001):

> A reading of the debates of the Federal Convention [does] not support [the] view that the purpose of separation of powers was to slow down government. Madison recognized the need for a division of powers in order to protect the people from tyrannical government; but it should not be assumed that the separation of powers was treated merely as a brake on power. [A] central function of the state was seen to be the promotion of liberty, and the constitution was therefore drafted in a manner that would facilitate this purpose. [The] efficient allocation of functions to institutions was the allocation that best served to protect, and to promote, liberty.

Page 334.   At the end of section 3 of the Note, add the following:

For a subtle and interesting criticism of contemporary separation of powers doctrine, see Magill, The Real Separation in Separation of Powers Law, 86 Va. L. Rev. 1127 (2000). Magill argues that despite superficial disagreement, courts and commentators have coalesced around the idea that separation of powers doctrine is designed to prevent a single institution of government from accumulating too much political power. This goal is achieved in two ways: by maintaining "separation of functions" among the three branches, and by maintaining a "balance of power" among them. Magill claims that the standard view is that these two techniques fit together well because the separation of functions will achieve a balance of power. In fact, however,

> Treating these two conceptions as related to one another is a mistake. [The] balance-of-power formulation suggests that courts should invalidate arrangements that undermine a balance among the departments. [Courts] are to be wary of efforts that would dilute tension and competition among the branches. The separation-of-functions conception [suggests] that courts should identify and enforce the allocation of the three functions of government among the departments. [These] doctrinal concerns [can] yield conflicting results.

Id. at 1130-31. Moreover, in Magill's view, when examined individually, neither of these conceptions will withstand analysis.

> The exact reasons why we might wish to keep the exercise of legislative, executive, and judicial power in different departments — reasons other than the failed connection to balancing government power — are rarely specified. When justifications for separated functions are offered, they are inadequate. [Subjecting] the balance-of-power conception to independent analysis likewise reveals serious difficulties with the idea: The meaning of "balance" is obscure and the way in which that balance is maintained is inadequate.

Id. See also Magill, Beyond Powers and Branches in Separation of Powers Law, 150 U. Pa. L. Rev. 603 (2001) (arguing, inter alia, that concern about balance of powers between the branches is misguided because there is no way to measure the distribution of power at any given time and, in any event, intra-branch fragmentation prevents a concentration of power). As you read the rest of the material in this chapter, consider whether these criticisms are justified. How might separation of powers doctrine be reformulated so as to take account of them?

Page 347.   Before section 3 of the Note, add the following:

Consider in this connection Bellia, Executive Power in Youngstown's Shadows, 19 Const. Comm. 87, 93 (2002) ("To the extent that Justice Jackson's approach suggests that law has little role to play when Congress is silent, that approach contains the seeds of a misplaced political question doctrine, allowing courts to skirt questions of executive power even when other justiciability requirements are met.").

B.   A Case Study: Presidential Seizure

Page 352.   Before Section C, add the following:

Note: Presidential Authority to Establish Military Tribunals

One week after the destruction of the World Trade Center, Congress enacted a Joint Resolution authorizing the President to

> use all necessary and appropriate force against those nations, organizations, or persons he determines planned, authorized, committed, or aided the terrorist attacks that occurred on September 11, 2001, or harbored such organizations or persons, in order to prevent any future acts of international terrorism against the United States by such nations, organizations or persons.

Joint Resolution of Congress Authorizing the Use of Force, Pub. L. No. 107-40, 115 Stat. 224 (2001).

About a month later, President Bush signed an executive order establishing military tribunals with jurisdiction to try anyone who was not an American citizen and whom the President determined that there was reason to believe was a member of al Qaida, or had "engaged in, aided or abetted, or conspired to commit, acts of international terrorism, or acts in preparation therefor," or who had knowingly harbored such individuals. The order provided for conviction and sentencing upon concurrence of two-thirds of the members of the tribunal with review of the final decision vested solely in the President or the Secretary of Defense. The order further provided that defendants before the tribunal "shall not be privileged to seek any remedy or maintain any proceeding [in any] court of the United States, or any State thereof."

Does the President's order exceed his powers under Article II? Consider the following:

1. *The President's claimed legal authority.* In support of the order, President Bush cited his power as "President and as Commander in Chief of the Armed Forces," the Joint Resolution quoted above, and 10 U.S.C. §§821 and 836. Section 821 provides that the statutory jurisdiction for courts martial does not "deprive military commissions [of] concurrent jurisdiction with respect to offenders or offenses that [by] the law of war may be tried by military commissions." Section 836 authorizes the President to prescribe "procedures [for] cases arising under this chapter triable in [military] commissions and other military tribunals." Are any of these measures sufficient to justify the order without more specific congressional acquiescence?

2. *The Commander in Chief Power.* In Ex parte Milligan, 71 U.S. (1 Wall.) 2 (1866), the Court invalidated the conviction of a civilian United States citizen for conspiracy against the United States. The conviction was obtained before a military commission established in Indiana during the Civil War. In a famous passage, the Court held that "[martial] rule can never exist where the courts are open, and in the proper and unobstructed exercise of their jurisdiction." The Court went on to state the following:

> Certainly no part of the judicial power of the country was conferred on [the military commission]; because the Constitution expressly vests it "in one supreme court and such inferior courts as the Congress may from time to time ordain and establish," and it is not pretended that the commission was a court ordained and established by Congress. They cannot justify on the mandate of the President; because he is controlled by law, and has his appropriate sphere of duty, which is to execute, not to make the laws; and there is no unwritten criminal code to which resort can be had as a source of jurisdiction.

Compare Milligan to Ex parte Quirin, 317 U.S. 1 (1942), where the Court upheld the conviction before a military tribunal of eight Nazi saboteurs, including a United States citizen, who landed in the United States armed with explosives. The Court noted that the detention and trial "ordered by the President in the declared exercise of his powers as Commander in Chief of the Army in time of war and of grave public danger [are] not to be set aside by the courts without the clear conviction that they are in conflict with the Constitution or laws of Congress constitutionally enacted." It also observed that

> The Constitution [invests] the President as Commander in Chief with the power to wage war which Congress has declared, and to carry into effect all laws passed by Congress for the conduct of war and for the government and regulation of the Armed Forces and all laws defining and punishing offences against the law of nations, including those which pertain to the conduct of war.

However, the Court found it "unnecessary for present purposes to determine to what extent the President as Commander in Chief has constitutional power to create military commissions without the support of Congressional legislation. For here Congress has authorized trial of offenses against the law of war before such commissions." (For a discussion of this part of the opinion, see section 4 of this Note.) The Court distinguished *Milligan* on the ground that there, the defendant "was not an enemy belligerent either entitled to the status of a prisoner of war or subject to the penalties imposed upon unlawful belligerents." See also In re Yamashita, 327 U.S. 1 (1946) (upholding the use of a military commission to try the commander of Japanese forces in the Philippines for violation of the laws of war).

In light of *Milligan* and *Quirin*, is the President's Commander in Chief power sufficient to justify President Bush's order? Consider Bradley & Goldsmith, The Constitutional Validity of Military Commissions, 5 Green Bag 2d 249, 252 (2002):

> A strong argument can be made that President Bush has independent power, as Commander in Chief, to establish military commissions to try war crimes violations, even in the absence of affirmative congressional authorization. Presidents have long claimed that their constitutional authority to manage the war effort includes the power to create military commissions, and they have exercised such power throughout U.S. history. The Supreme Court in *Quirin* appeared to agree with this claim in [dicta].

Compare Katyal & Tribe, Waging War, Deciding Guilt: Trying the Military Tribunals, 111 Yale L. J. 1259, 1270 (2002):

> The moment the President moves beyond detaining enemy combatants as war prisoners to actually adjudicating their guilt and meting out punishment [he] has moved outside the perimeter of his role as Commander in Chief of our armed forces and entered a zone that involves judging and punishing alleged violations of the [laws]. In that adjudicatory and punitive zone, the fact that the President entered wearing his military garb should not blind us to the fact that he is now pursuing a different goal—assessing guilt and meting out retrospective justice rather than waging war.

See also Fletcher, On Justice and War: Contradictions in the Proposed Military Tribunals, 25 Harv. J. of L. & Pub. Pol. 635, 637 (2002) (arguing that President Bush's order reflects our "state of collective confusion" about whether our response to September 11 should be grounded in "the ideas of justice or the principles of war").

Does it follow from the position advanced by Katyal and Tribe that the Constitution permits the President to hold a suspect indefinitely as a prisoner of war with no process at all, but not to establish a military tribunal before which the suspect can plead his or her case? In June 2002, the government arrested an American citizen, Jose Padilla, suspected of preparing a "dirty bomb" for explosion in the United States. Because of his citizenship, the suspect was ineligible for trial before a military tribunal. At first, the government held the suspect as a material witness, but shortly before a hearing at which it would have been required to present evidence against him, the government placed him in military custody and asserted the authority to hold him indefinitely as an "enemy combatant."

The government has also asserted authority to hold indefinitely another United States citizen arrested in Afghanistan. So far, neither detainee has been successful in judicial challenges to his incarceration. See Hamdi v. Rumsfeld, 316 F. 3d 450 (4th Cir. 2003) (denying right of U.S. citizen seized within combat zone to hearing to contest status as "enemy combatant"); Padilla v. Bush, 233 F. Supp. 2d 564

(S.D.N.Y. 2002) (permitting detention of U.S. citizen as "enemy combatant" if "some evidence" supports designation). See also Al Odah v. United States, 321 F. 3d 1134 (2d Cir. 2003) (holding that U.S. courts lack jurisdiction over aliens held in military custody in Guantanamo Bay, Cuba).

3. *The Relevance of the Joint Resolution.* Does the Joint Resolution support President Bush's actions? Consider Bradley & Goldsmith, *supra,* at 254:

> A congressional declaration of war is not necessary in order for the President to exercise his independent or statutorily delegated war powers, including the power to establish military commissions. At most, all that is required is congressional authorization of the war effort. Congress provided President Bush with such authorization in its [Joint] Resolution.

Compare Katyal & Tribe, *supra* at 1248-49:

> In *Quirin,* [Congress] had declared war and had underscored the government's total commitment to the war effort. . . .
> Nothing even close to that World War II authorization or a wartime emergency in which Congress's consent cannot be obtained, is present today. Significantly, the Resolution [permits] only the use of "force," applies only to persons or other entities involved in some way in the September 11 attacks, and then extends only to the "prevent[ion of] . . . future acts of international [terrorism]." [But] the Order, unlike Congress's Resolution, in no way confines its reach to those involved in the September 11 attacks. [No] matter how broadly the statutes and precedents are stretched, there is no constitutional warrant for expanding the military tribunals' authority in just the way Congress refused to expand presidential power—to cover individuals completely unconnected to the September 11 attacks.

4. *Statutory authorization.* Did President Bush have adequate statutory authority for creation of the tribunals? In *Quirin,* the Court relied in part on the predecessor of 10 U.S.C. §821, quoted above, in support of President Roosevelt's order. But cf. Duncan v. Kahanamoku, 327 U.S. 304 (1946) (narrowly construing federal statute that authorized the Governor of Hawaii, with the concurrence of the President, to declare "martial law," so as not to authorize military tribunals for ordinary crimes). Note that by its terms, §821 seems to do no more than protect the jurisdiction of military commissions that have already been established. Consider Katyal & Tribe, supra at 1290-92:

> [To] the extent that *Quirin* did provide the President with broad authority [there] is reason to discount the case itself as statutory precedent. After all, just two years after *Quirin,* the same Supreme Court upheld government orders that imposed severe curtailments of liberty on Japanese Americans during World War II in the in-

famous *Korematsu* case. [*Korematsu* is excerpted on pp. 501-505 of the main volume.] Justice Frankfurter, with characteristic understatement, called *Quirin* "not a happy precedent." [A] principal reason for authorization of these military tribunals was the government's wish to cover up the evidence of the FBI's bungling of the case. And it also appears that some highly questionable ex parte arm-twisting by the executive may have spurred the Supreme Court's unanimous decision.

In which of the Justice Jackson's *Youngstown* categories does President Bush's order fall?

5. *The relevance of constitutional law.* In *Korematsu,* supra, Justice Jackson dissented from the Court's judgment upholding the conviction of a defendant who had disobeyed the order excluding Japanese Americans from the West Coast during World War II. Unlike the other dissenters, however, Justice Jackson did not argue that the exclusion should not have taken place. Jackson wrote that it would be

impracticable and dangerous idealism to expect or insist that each specific military command in an area of probable operations will conform to conventional tests of constitutionality. When an area is so beset that it must be put under military control at all, the paramount consideration is that its measures be successful rather than legal.

For Jackson, the crucial question was not whether the exclusion should have taken place, but whether the courts should endorse the exclusion.

I should hold that a civil court cannot be made to enforce an order which violates constitutional limitations even if it is a reasonable exercise of military authority. The courts can exercise only the judicial power, can apply only law, and must abide by the Constitution, for the case to be civil courts and become instruments of military policy.

Note also Jackson's distinction in *Youngstown* between the President's "paper powers" and "real powers." How would Justice Jackson have ruled on a petition for habeas corpus presented to a civilian court by a defendant convicted by a military tribunal authorized by President Bush's order?

Compare Justice Jackson's approach to Gross, Chaos and Rules: Should Responses to Violent Crises Always Be Constitutional?, 112 Yale L.J. 1011, 1022-23 (2003):

[We] need to reexamine a [fundamental] assumption that underlies the traditional models of emergency powers. The *assumption of constitutionality* tells us that whatever responses are made to the challenges of a particular exigency, such responses are to be found and limited within the confines of the constitution. . . .

[There] may be circumstances where the appropriate method of tackling grave dangers and threats entails going outside the constitutional order, at times even violating otherwise accepted constitutional principles, rules, and norms. . . .

This [model informs] public officials that they may act extralegally when they believe that such action is necessary for protecting the nation and the public in the face of calamity, provided that they openly and publicly acknowledge the nature of their actions. It is then up to the people to decide, either directly or indirectly (e.g., through their elected representatives in the legislature), how to respond to such actions. The people may decide to hold the actor to the wrongfulness of her actions, demonstrating commitment to the violated principles and values. [Alternatively,] the people may approve, ex post, the extralegal actions of the public official.

C. Domestic Affairs

Page 365.   Before the Note, add the following:

Consider the possibility that separation of powers doctrine is designed, in part at least, to protect the states from federal overreaching by making it more difficult for branches of the federal government to act, and that the formalism/functionalism debate is influenced by this concern. In Clark, Separation of Powers as a Safeguard of Federalism, 79 Tex. L. Rev. 1321, 1326 (2001), the author argues that the

debate over formalism and functionalism [affects] the division of power between the federal government and the states. Many of the Court's most prominent decisions employing a formal approach involve enforcement of constitutionally prescribed lawmaking procedures designed to safeguard federalism. Formalism in this context operates to preserve state governance prerogatives by making federal law more difficult to adopt. Decisions taking a functional approach [by] contrast, typically involve potential interference by one branch with the constitutional functions of another rather than attempts to evade federal lawmaking procedures.

Page 367.   At the end of section 4a of the Note, add the following:

For a detailed textual argument in favor of the nondelegation doctrine, see Lawson, Delegation and Original Meaning, 88 Va. L. Rev. 327 (2002). Consider Posner &

Vermeule, Interring the Nondelegation Doctrine, 69 U. Chi. L. Rev. 1721, 1722-23 (2002):

> [There] just is no constitutional nondelegation rule, nor has there ever been. The nondelegation position lacks any foundation in constitutional text and structure, in standard originalist sources, or in sound economic and political theory. . . .
>
> [We] agree that the Constitution bars the "delegation of legislative power." In our view, however, the content of that prohibition is the following: Neither Congress nor its members may delegate to anyone else the authority to vote on federal statutes or to exercise other de jure powers of federal legislators. [A] statutory grant of authority to the executive isn't a transfer of legislative power, but an exercise of legislative power. Conversely, agents acting within the terms of such a source of statutory grant are exercising executive power, not legislative power.

Page 369. At the end of section 4 of the Note, add the following:

e.   In Whitman v. American Trucking Assn., Inc., 531 U.S. 457 (2001), the Court emphatically rejected a nondelegation challenge to the Clean Air Act. Section 109(b)(1) of the act instructs the Environmental Protection Administration (EPA) to set ambient air quality standards "the attainment and maintenance of which [are] requisite to protect the public health [with] an adequate margin of safety." The court of appeals held that the EPA's interpretation of this provision was unconstitutional because it provided no "intelligible principle to guide the agency's exercise of authority." However, instead of holding the provision unconstitutional, the court remanded the matter to the agency in order to allow it to adopt a different construction of the provision.

The Supreme Court, in a unanimous opinion written by Justice Scalia, rejected this approach:

> We have never suggested that an agency can cure an unlawful delegation of legislative power by adopting in its discretion a limiting construction of the statute. [The] idea that an agency can cure an unconstitutionally standardless delegation of power by declining to exercise some of that power seems to us internally contradictory. The very choice of which portion of the power to exercise [would] *itself* be an exercise of the forbidden legislative authority.

The Court then held that the

> scope of discretion § 109(b)(1) allows is [well] within the outer limits of our nondelegation precedents. In the history of the Court we have found the requisite "in-

telligible principle" lacking in only two statutes, one of which provided literally no guidance for the exercise of our discretion, and the other of which conferred authority to regulate the entire economy on the basis of no more precise a standard than stimulating the economy by assuring "fair competition." [In] short, we have "almost never felt qualified to second-guess Congress regarding the permissible degree of policy judgment that can be left to those executing or applying the law." [Mistretta v. United States, 488 U.S. 361, 416 (1989) (Scalia, J., dissenting).] [Even] in sweeping regulatory schemes we have never demanded, as the Court of Appeals did here, that statutes provide a "determinate criterion" for saying "how much [of the regulated harm] is too much."

Justice Thomas wrote a short concurring opinion:

I am not convinced that the intelligible principle doctrine serves to prevent all cessions of legislative power. I believe that there are cases in which the principle is intelligible and yet the significance of the delegated decision is simply too great for the decision to be called anything other than "legislative."

Justice Stevens, joined by Justice Souter, also concurred:

The Court has two choices. We could choose to articulate our ultimate disposition of this issue by frankly acknowledging that the power delegated to the EPA is "legislative" but nevertheless conclude that the delegation is constitutional because adequately limited by the terms of the authorizing statute. Alternatively, we could pretend, as the Court does, that the authority delegated to EPA is somehow not "legislative power." Despite the fact that there is language in our opinions that supports the Court's articulation of our holding, I am persuaded that it would be both wiser and more faithful to what we have actually done in delegation cases to admit that agency rulemaking authority is "legislative power."

Page 378.   At the bottom of the page, add the following:

In Kagan, Presidential Administration, 114 Harv. L. Rev. 2245, 2248-2251 (2001), the author argues that "presidential control of [administrative agencies] expanded dramatically" in recent years. She claims that the expanded use of presidential authority to dictate how administrative agencies should exercise their delegated authority is inconsistent with the "conventional view" that "Congress can insulate discretionary decisions of even removable (that is, executive branch) officials from presidential dictation—and, indeed, that Congress has done so whenever (as is usual) it has delegated power not to the President, but to a specified agency official."

In place of this view, she claims that "Congress has left more power in presidential hands than is generally recognized" and that "statutory delegation to an executive agency official—although not to an independent agency head—usually should be read as allowing the President to assert directive authority [over] the exercise of the delegated discretion."

Page 397.   At the end of section 2 of the Note, add the following:

Consider the following synthesis:

Chadha is significant not so much for its emphasis on the requirements of bicameralism and presentment as for its implicit recognition of a constitutional principle against congressional self-aggrandizement: Congress may not, by statute, draw to itself, nor confer upon any part of itself, or upon any of its agents, powers that Congress does not already have by virtue of the Constitution. Understanding *Chadha* as embodying a rule against congressional self-aggrandizement explains the mystery of why Congress may delegate to others powers that it may not confer upon its own houses; it also explains why the rule applies even to attempts by Congress to grant itself extra power that it may exercise only through bicameralism and presentment.

Siegel, The Use of Legislative History in a System of Separated Powers, 53 Vand. L. Rev. 1457, 1467-1468 (2000).

D.   Foreign Affairs

Page 403.   Before Section 1, add the following:

For an argument that "modern scholarship should stop assuming that the Constitution's text says little about foreign affairs and stop treating foreign affairs powers as 'up for grabs' to be resolved by hasty resort to extratextual sources," see Prakash & Ramsey, The Executive Power over Foreign Affairs, 111 Yale L. J. 231, 233 (2001). The authors derive four basic principles from the constitutional text:

First, and most importantly, the President enjoys a "residual" foreign affairs power under Article II, Section 1's grant of "the executive Power." [The] ordinary eighteenth-century meaning of executive power [included] foreign affairs power. . . .

Second, the President's executive power over foreign affairs is limited by specific allocations of foreign affairs power to other entities — such as the allocation of the power to declare war to Congress. [Third], Congress in addition to its specific foreign affairs powers has a derivative power to legislate in support of the President's executive power over foreign affairs and its own foreign affairs powers. But [Congress] does not have a general and independent authority over all foreign affairs matters. [Fourth], the President's executive power over foreign affairs does not extend to matters that were not part of the traditional executive power, even where they touch upon foreign affairs. In particular, the President cannot claim power over appropriations and lawmaking, even in the foreign affairs arena, by virtue of the executive power.

Page 410.   After section 4c of the Note, add the following:

d. *The "war" against terrorism.* On September 18, 2001, Congress enacted a joint resolution, granting the President authority to

use all necessary and appropriate force against those nations, organizations, or persons he determines planned, authorized, committed, or aided the terrorist attacks that occurred on September 11, 2001, or harbored such organizations or persons, in order to prevent any future acts of international terrorism against the United States by such nations, organizations or persons.

Joint Resolution of Congress Authorizing the Use of Force, Pub. L. No. 107-40, 115 Stat. 224 (2001).

Is the Joint Resolution the constitutional equivalent of a declaration of war? If so, why did Congress fail to adopt an official declaration of war? Compare Turner, The War on Terrorism and the Modern Relevance of the Congressional Power to "Declare War," 25 Harv. J. of Law & Pol. 519, 521 (2002) (quoting Senate Foreign Relations Committee Chairman Joseph Biden as stating that the resolution was "the constitutional equivalent of a declaration of war") with Katyal & Tribe, Waging War, Deciding Guilt: Trying the Military Tribunals, 111 Yale L. J. 1259, 1285 (2002) (quoting Representative Conyers as stating that "[by] not declaring war the resolution preserves our precious civil liberties" and that "[this] is important because declarations of war trigger broad statutes that not only criminalize interference with troops and recruitment but also authorize the President to apprehend 'alien enemies'").

If the Resolution is the equivalent of a declaration of war, whom is the war being waged against? Traditionally, wars are ended by treaties, subject to ratification by the Senate. Is there some comparable event that will demarcate the end of the war against terrorism? How will we know when the war is over? Consider Paulsen, Youngstown Goes to War, 19 Const. Com. 215 (2002). The author acknowledges that the Joint Resolution constitutes "a truly extraordinary congressional grant to the President of extraordinary discretion in the use of military power for an indefinite period of time." Yet the author also concludes that Congress's position articulated in the Resolution is within the "twilight zone" described in Justice Jackson's *Youngstown* concurrence. Across a broad range of circumstances, Congress's interpretation of the Constitution in support of presidential constitutional power—its view, enacted as part of the 9-18-01 Resolution that 'the President has authority under the Constitution to take action to deter and prevent acts of international terrorism against the United States'—is a legitimate and constitutionally proper one."

Notice that the Resolution authorizes military action only with respect to those involved in the destruction of the World Trade Center. Does the President have constitutional authority to conduct a broader "war" against alleged terrorists not associated with that attack? For an argument that the war power was meant to apply solely to offensive wars and that it is therefore anachronistic under modern conditions, see Turner, supra. See also Delahunty & Yoo, The President's Constitutional Authority to Conduct Military Operations against Terrorist Organizations and the Nations that Harbor or Support Them, 25 Harv. J. of Law & Pol. 488 (2002) (arguing that the President has broad, unilateral authority to act against terrorists). Compare Telman, A Truism that Isn't True? The Tenth Amendment and Executive War Power, 51 Cath. U. L. Rev. 135 (2001) (suggesting that the Tenth Amendment argues against inherent executive authority to wage war without congressional authorization); Ramsey, Textualism and War Powers, 69 U. Chi. L. Rev. 1543 (2002) (concluding that in the eighteenth century the phrase "declare war" was understood to include an armed attack, even without a formal proclamation, and that this understanding "refutes the claim that the President can order military attacks upon foreign powers without Congress's approval so long as no formal declaration is involved") For criticism of Professor Ramsey's view, see Yoo, War and the Constitutional Text, 69 U. Chi. L. Rev. 1639 (2002) (arguing that "the Constitution vests the executive and legislative branches with different powers involving war, which the President and Congress may use to cooperate or to compete for control over war making").

Page 413.   At the bottom of the page, add the following:

In Currie, Rumors of Wars: Presidential and Congressional War Powers, 1809-1829, 67 U. Chi. L. Rev. 1 (2000), the author concludes that "the express position of every President to address the subject [of warmaking power] during the first forty years of the present Constitution was entirely in line with [the War Powers Resolution]: The President may introduce troops into hostilities only pursuant to a congressional declaration of war or other legislative authorization, or in response to an attack on the United States."

Page 414.   At the end of section 2 of the Note, add the following:

Consider the following evaluation in Paulsen, Youngstown Goes to War, 19 Const. Com. 215, 247-48 (2002):

> [In] a constitutional regime in which congressional and presidential war powers are recognized as overlapping and in some respects concurrent, [the] lawfulness of presidential military action [is] affected by Congress's constitutional interpretation of the scope of the President's authority. In this respect, the War Powers Resolution operates, somewhat ironically and probably unintentionally, to provide a constitutional "safe harbor" for certain unilateral presidential actions involving the use of military force—a zone of nearly unchallengeable exercise of presidential power within the zone of twilight marked by the overlap of congressional and presidential war powers, where Congress has by statute explicitly chosen to accept presidential military initiatives, and where it is not clear that the Constitution of its own force renders such presidential action unlawful.

Page 415.   At the end of the Note on the War Powers Resolution, add the following:

4. *The War in Iraq.* On October 16, 2002, Congress enacted the following resolution:

(a) AUTHORIZATION. — The President is authorized to use the Armed Forces of the United States as he determines to be necessary and appropriate in order to —

(1) defend the national security of the United States against the continuing threat posed by Iraq; and

(2) enforce all relevant United Nations Security Council resolutions regarding Iraq.

(b) PRESIDENTIAL DETERMINATION.—In connection with the exercise of the authority granted in subsection (a) to use force the President shall, prior to such exercise or as soon thereafter as may be feasible, but no later than 48 hours after exercising such authority, make available to the Speaker of the House of

Representatives and the President pro tempore of the Senate his determination that—

(1) reliance by the United States on further diplomatic or other peaceful means alone either (A) will not adequately protect the national security of the United States against the continuing threat posed by Iraq or (B) is not likely to lead to enforcement of all relevant United Nations Security Council resolutions regarding Iraq; and

(2) acting pursuant to this joint resolution is consistent with the United States and other countries continuing to take the necessary actions against international terrorist and terrorist organizations, including those nations, organizations, or persons who planned, authorized, committed or aided the terrorist attacks that occurred on September 11, 2001.

(c) WAR POWERS RESOLUTION REQUIREMENTS.—

(1) SPECIFIC STATUTORY AUTHORIZATION.—Consistent with section [1547(A)(1)] of the War Powers Resolution, the Congress declares that this section is intended to constitute specific statutory authorization within the meaning of section [1544(B)] of the War Powers Resolution.

(2) APPLICABILITY OF OTHER REQUIREMENTS.—Nothing in this joint resolution supersedes any requirement of the War Powers Resolution.

Authorization for Use of Military Force against Iraq Resolution of 2002, PL 107-243, 116 Stat. 1498 (2002).

Months later, acting pursuant to this authority, the President committed American military forces to Iraq. Does a congressional authorization for military action at some point in the indefinite future constitute a declaration of war within the meaning of Article I §8? Consider in this regard the material on the nondelegation doctrine at page 365 of the main volume and the implications of United States v. Curtiss-Wright Corp., excerpted at page 403 of the main volume. If the Use of Military Force Resolution is not a declaration of war, does the War Powers Resolution make the President's actions legal? Consider in this regard the effect of §(c)(2) of the Use of Military Force Resolution in conjunction with §1547(D)(2) of the War Powers Resolution.

Page 418.   Before section 3 of the Note, add the following:

For the Court's latest decision on the constitutional effect of executive agreements, see American Insurance Association v. Garamendi, 539 U.S. ___ (2003). In a 5-4 decision the Court, per Justice Souter, invalidated a California statute that required insurers doing business in the state to disclose details of insurance policies issued to persons in Europe which were in effect between 1920 and 1945. The statute was enacted to assist Holocaust victims and their descendants in their efforts to collect the proceeds of insurance policies that were either unpaid by the companies or seized by the Nazi government. The Court held that the state law was preempted by an executive agreement between the United States and Germany. Although the executive agreement did not expressly deal with California's disclosure requirement, the Court held that the agreement's approach, which emphasized voluntary cooperation and settlement of claims through a special fund established by the German government, conflicted with the statute.

With regard to the constitutional power of the President to reach binding executive agreements with foreign states, the Court said the following:

> There is, of course, no question that at some point an exercise of state power that touches on foreign relations must yield to the National Government's [policy]. . . .
>
> Nor is there any question generally that there is executive authority to decide what that policy should be. Although the source of the President's power to act in foreign affairs does not enjoy any textual detail, the historical gloss on the "executive Power" vested in Article II of the Constitution has recognized the President's "vast share of responsibility for the conduct of our foreign relations." [*Youngstown* (Frankfurter, J., concurring)]. While Congress holds express authority to regulate public and private dealings with other nations in its war and foreign commerce powers, in foreign affairs the President has a degree of independent authority to act. . . .
>
> At a more specific level, our cases have recognized that the President has authority to make "executive agreements" with other countries, requiring no ratification by the Senate or approval by Congress, this power having been exercised since the early years of the Republic. See [*Dames & Moore*]. [Making] executive agreements to settle claims of American nationals against foreign governments is a particularly longstanding [practice]. Given the fact that the practice goes back over 200 years to the first Presidential administration, and has received congressional acquiescence throughout its history, the conclusion "[t]hat the President's control of foreign relations includes the settlement of claims is indisputable."

In which of Justice Jackson's three categories does the German-American executive agreement fall? Recall that in *Dames & Moore*, the Court stated that it was "crucial" to its decision that "Congress [had] implicitly approved the practice of claim settlement by executive agreement" through the International Claims Settlement Act. Given *Garamendi*, is this fact still "crucial"?

Would a federal statute that specifically disapproved of the executive agreement relied upon in *Garamendi* be constitutional? The *Garamendi* petitioner argued that Congress had authorized state laws of the sort California had enacted, but the Court held that it "need [not] consider the possible significance for preemption doctrine of tension between an Act of Congress and Presidential foreign policy, cf. generally [*Youngstown* (Jackson, J., concurring)]" because the federal statute did not grant such authorization.

Indeed, it is worth noting that Congress has done nothing to express disapproval of the President's policy. Legislation along the lines of [the California statute] has been introduced in Congress repeatedly, but none of the bills has come close to making it into law.

In sum, Congress has not acted on the matter addressed here. Given the President's independent authority "in the areas of foreign policy and national security, . . . congressional silence is not to be equated with congressional disapproval."

Page 419. At the end of section 3 of the Note, add the following:

For a criticism of both the Tribe and Ackerman-Golove positions, see Spiro, Treaties, Executive Agreements, and Constitutional Method, 79 Tex. L. Rev. 961 (2001). Spiro argues that Tribe's conclusion is "refuted by the broad national acceptance of the manner in which the NAFTA and [World Trade Organization] agreements were effected. [This] constitutional acceptance exposes the flaws of a methodology that does not account for history and practice." Id. at 963. Spiro finds that Ackerman and Golove overstate their case in claiming that there is "full interchangeability" between treaties and congressional-executive agreements. "There remain some types of international agreements for which the treaty process is constitutionally required, and perhaps some for which the congressional-executive agreement is now the only permitted route to international undertakings." Id. at 964.

5
EQUALITY AND THE CONSTITUTION

B. Equal Protection Methodology: Rational Basis Review

Page 483.   After the first paragraph, add the following:

Consider, for example, Fitzgerald v. Racing Association of Central Iowa, 539 U.S. ___ (2003). Iowa law imposed a higher tax on revenues gained from slot machines at racetracks than from slot machines on excursion riverboats. The Iowa Supreme Court held that this differential violated the equal protection clause. It reasoned that the "differential tax completely defeats the [statute's] alleged purpose [of helping] racetracks recover from economic distress" and that there could therefore be "no rational reason for this differential tax." In an opinion written by Justice Breyer, the Supreme Court unanimously reversed:

> [The] Iowa law, like most laws, might predominately serve one general objective, say, helping racetracks, while containing subsidiary provisions that seek to achieve other desirable (perhaps even contrary) ends as well, thereby producing a law that balances objectives but still serves the general objective when seen as a whole. . . .
> [The statute's] grant to the racetracks of authority to operate slot machines should help the racetracks economically to some degree—even if its simultaneous imposition of a tax on slot machine adjusted revenue means that the law provides less help than respondents might like. . . .
> [The] difference [in taxation rates], harmful to the racetracks, is helpful to the riverboats, which [were] also facing financial peril.

Page 494.   Before section 2 of the Note, add the following:

In connection with the "expressions of animosity" theory, consider the exchange between Justices O'Connor and Scalia in Lawrence v. Texas, 539 U.S. ___ (2003).

At issue was the constitutionality of a Texas criminal statute that prohibited homosexual, but not heterosexual sodomy. The Court's majority invalidated the law on due process grounds. (This portion of the opinion is discussed in the Supplement to page 901 of the main text.) Justice O'Connor concurred in the result on the ground that the distinction between heterosexual and homosexual sodomy violated equal protection:

> We have consistently held [that] some objectives, such as a "bare . . . desire to harm a politically unpopular group" are not legitimate state interests. [*Moreno*; *Cleburne*; *Romer*] When a law exhibits such a desire to harm a politically unpopular group, we have applied a more searching form of rational basis review to strike down such laws under the Equal Protection Clause. . . .
>
> Moral disapproval of [homosexuals], like a bare desire to harm the group, is an interest that is insufficient to satisfy rational basis review under the Equal Protection Clause. . . .
>
> Moral disapproval of a group cannot be a legitimate governmental interest under the Equal Protection Clause because legal classifications must not be "drawn for the purpose of disadvantaging the group burdened by the law." [*Romer*]. Texas' invocation of moral disapproval as a legitimate interest proves nothing more than Texas' desire to criminalize homosexual sodomy. But the Equal Protection Clause prevents a State from creating "a classification of persons undertaken for its own sake." [*Romer*]. . . .
>
> That this law as applied to private, consensual conduct is unconstitutional under the Equal Protection Clause does not mean that other laws distinguishing between heterosexuals and homosexuals would similarly fail under rational basis review. Texas cannot assert any legitimate state interest here, such as national security or preserving the traditional institution of marriage. Unlike the moral disapproval of same-sex relations—the asserted state interest in this case—other reasons exist to promote the institution of marriage beyond mere moral disapproval of an excluded group.

Compare Justice Scalia's response in his dissenting opinion:

> [Justice O'Connor's] reasoning leaves on pretty shaky grounds state laws limiting marriage to opposite-sex couples. [She] seeks to preserve them by the conclusory statement that "preserving the traditional institution of marriage" is a legitimate state interest. But "preserving the traditional institution of marriage" is just a kinder way of describing the State's *moral disapproval* of same-sex couples. Texas's interest in [its anti-sodomy statute] could be recast in similarly euphemistic terms: "preserving the traditional sexual mores of our society." In the jurisprudence Justice O'Connor has seemingly created, judges can validate laws by characterizing them as "preserving the traditions of society" (good); or invalidate them by characterizing them as "expressing moral disapproval" (bad).

Page 497.   At the bottom of the page, add the following:

The Court again distinguished *Allegheny Pittsburgh* in Fitzgerald v. Racing Association of Central Iowa, 539 U.S. ___ (2003). Iowa law imposed a heavier tax on revenues gained from slot machines located at racetracks than from slot machines located on riverboats. A unanimous Supreme Court, in an opinion by Justice Breyer, rejected an equal protection challenge to this different treatment.

In [*Allegheny Pittsburgh*] the Court held that substantial differences in [property tax assessments] violated the Federal Equal Protection Clause. [But the] Court in *Nordlinger* [held] that "*Allegheny Pittsburgh* was the rare case where the facts precluded any plausible inference that the reason for the unequal assessment practice was to achieve the benefits of an acquisition-value scheme." Here, "the facts" do not "preclud[e]" an inference that the reason for the different tax rates was to help the riverboat industry or the river communities.

C. Equal Protection Methodology: Heightened Scrutiny and the Problem of Race

Page 505.   After the first paragraph of the Note, add the following:

In Gudridge, Remember Endo?, 116 Harv. L. Rev. 1933 (2003), the author argues that *Korematsu* should be read together with its companion case, Ex parte Endo, 323 U.S. 283 (1944), which held that the detention (as opposed to the exclusion from the West Coast) of loyal Americans of Japanese descent was illegal. Although formally no more than an interpretation of the power granted by the underlying executive order, the Court's interpretation was influenced by its belief that the detention "touch[ed] the sensitive area of rights specifically guaranteed by the Constitution" and by the Court's practice of favoring "that interpretation of legislation which gives it the greater chance of surviving the test of constitutionality."

Gudridge argues that when *Endo* and *Korematsu* are read together, they produce a "doubled legal consciousness."

Korematsu posited a gap open to military [improvisers]. *Endo* did not close the gap, but rather ignored it, proceeded as though there was no possibility that constitutional law was a less than universal language. *Endo* shows *Korematsu* to be marginal—even as, of course, *Korematsu* also shows *Endo* to be marginal. . . .

Especially in circumstances in which judicial review is unavailable, reluctant, or likely to be too late to be relevant, executive or legislative appreciation and expression of this alternation may be the only telling manifestation of constitutional law. Thus, in a Justice Department or Defense Department under stress, challenged, doubled perspectives evident in instruments or acts, signs that both emergency responses and ordinary senses of limitation are or were subject to question, may be the only readable signs of the continuing impact of constitutional sensibility, of at least the elementary patterns of constitutional law.

Page 510.   Before section 7 of the Note, add the following:

What implications does the antisubordination argument hold regarding strict scrutiny of racial classifications? In Harris, Equality Trouble: Sameness and Difference in Twentieth-Century Law, 88 Cal. L. Rev. 1923 (2000), the author argues that twentieth-century race law has moved from a conception of constitutional equality that encompassed the notion of inherent racial difference to a conception that made racial sameness "the foundation of common sense." However,

> [both] equality as sameness and equality as difference have a way of obscuring questions such as "who sets the standard for equality?" The fact that both equality as sameness and equality as difference can coexist with relations of dominance begins to explain why many of today's antiracists denounce colorblindness. It also begins to explain how we may not have made as much progress over the past century as it might initially appear.

Id. at 1929.

Page 512.   After the first two lines on the page, add the following:

8. *A synthesis.*   For a detailed and insightful "unified framework" for strict scrutiny, see Rubin, Reconnecting Doctrine and Purpose: A Comprehensive Approach to Strict Scrutiny after *Adarand* and *Shaw*, 149 U. Penn. L. Rev. 1 (2000). Rubin provides a taxonomy of the risks and harms that may accompany the use of race as a classificatory principle:

1. The risk that race is being used "to harm an unpopular group [or] to indicate that the members of that group are unfit to partake of something given to others [and] to convey in this way the community's judgment about the inherent worth of people of different kinds."
2. The risk that the classification "reflects nothing more than racial politics, a desire to reward the members of [one's] own racial group."

3. The risk that a racial classification "[reflects] nothing more than erroneous stereotypes."
4. The risk that racial classifications, even if related to a legitimate purpose, may perpetuate a negative racial stereotype.
5. The risk that decisionmaking based on race may "[deny] a person treatment as an individual in a way that other sorting mechanisms do not."
6. The risk that "the very use of race to identify people [will] [have] some divisive effect on the races by reinforcing the belief in inherent racial differences, regardless of [correlation] with traditional stereotypes."
7. The risk that the use of race will "cause a dignitary harm to individuals [regardless] of whether anyone is disadvantaged on the basis of their racial identity."

Id. at 20-23. Rubin goes on to argue in considerable detail that "strict scrutiny must be flexible enough to recognize that different uses of race pose different risks and impose different harms. To determine what risks and harms are present requires a careful examination of the factual circumstances and social contexts in which the use of race by government has taken place." Id. at 25-26. Consider the extent to which this flexibility undermines the advantages of having formally distinct levels of review in the first place.

9. *Abandoning special scrutiny?* Although in recent years, the Supreme Court has continued to insist upon strict scrutiny for racial classifications, it has also suggested that this scrutiny need not be "fatal in fact." Adarand Constructors Inc. v. Pena, 515 U.S. 200, 202 (1995). Thus, in the context of affirmative action it has suggested that narrowly tailored measures designed to remedy specific acts of prior discrimination might satisfy strict scrutiny. See id. Similarly, in the context of racial districting, the Court has held that the use of race is permissible so long as it is not "the predominant factor motivating the legislature's decision to place a significant number of voters within or without a particular district." Miller v. Johnson, 515 U.S. 900, 916 (1995). (These cases are considered in more detail at pp. 545 and 574 of the main volume.) Consider whether these decisions constitute a dilution or abandonment of strict scrutiny, in fact if not in name. Karlan, Easing the Spring: Strict Scrutiny and Affirmative Action After the Redistricting Cases, 43 Wm. & Mary L. Rev. 1569 (2002), argues that these cases suggest that "strict scrutiny may be strict in theory, but . . . rather pliable in practice." Id. at 1573.

In Griffin, Judicial Supremacy and Equal Protection in a Democracy of Rights, 4 U. Pa. J. of Con. L. 281 (2002), the author argues that the Court should formally abandon strict scrutiny for racial classifications. From a strategic point of view, Professor Griffin contends, recent decisions make clear that minorities gain little from such scrutiny. As Griffin puts it, "if you are a member of a racial minority, the Supreme Court is not your friend." Id. at 282. Moreover, "the protection against unjust discrimination all Americans receive from civil rights statutes is plainly superior to the protection provided by the Equal Protection Clause." Id. The abandonment of strict scrutiny is also normatively desirable: This is so, Griffin argues, because we presently live in a "democracy of rights," which "connects rights with democratic deliberation." In a democracy of this sort, "government actors take it for granted that it is desirable to create, enforce, and promote individual constitutional and legal rights. Hence, the political branches of government (not just the courts) are seeking constantly to maintain and extend the system of rights they have created through democratic means." Id. Do you agree? If the Supreme Court announced tomorrow that racial classifications were no longer subject to strict scrutiny, would the announcement make any practical difference?

Page 551. At the end of section 1 of the Note, add the following:

Does the Court's conception of harm match its restrictive standing rule? Compare Ely, Standing to Challenge Pro-Minority Gerrymanders, 111 Harv. L. Rev. 576, 594 (1997) (arguing that white voters "have standing basically because they've been deprived of a meaningful shot at helping to elect a representative whose race is the same as theirs") with Issacharoff & Karlan, Standing and Misunderstanding in Voting Rights Law, 111 Harv. L. Rev. 2276 (1998) (arguing that the Court's standing doctrine is completely incoherent because it fails to explain the dividing line between those voters who have standing and those who lack standing and that the plaintiffs in the race-specific districting cases deliberately declined to claim vote dilution or the inability to elect their preferred candidates).

For a particularly dramatic example of the formal bite and substantive emptiness of the Court's standing doctrine, consider Sinkfield v. Kelley, 531 U.S. 28 (2000). The plaintiffs lived in several majority-white state legislative districts that were adjacent to deliberately-created majority black legislative districts. Taking *Hays* at its word, they challenged the majority-white districts in which they lived: an inevitable consequence of having to redraw those districts would be the need also to redraw the adjacent majority-black districts. The Supreme Court, in a per curiam opinion, directed the district court to dismiss the complaint for lack of standing.

"[The voters'] position here is essentially indistinguishable from that of the appellees in *Hays*. Appellees are challenging their own majority-white districts as the product of unconstitutional racial gerrymandering under a redistricting plan whose purpose was the creation of majority-minority districts, some of which border appellees' districts. Like the appellees in *Hays*, they have neither alleged nor produced any evidence that any of them was assigned to his or her district as a direct result of having 'personally been subjected to a racial classification.' . . .

"The shapes of appellees' districts, however, were necessarily influenced by the shapes of the majority-minority districts upon which they border, and appellees have produced no evidence that anything other than the deliberate creation of those majority-minority districts is responsible for the districting lines of which they complain. Appellees' suggestion thus boils down to the claim that an unconstitutional use of race in drawing the boundaries of majority-minority districts necessarily involves an unconstitutional use of race in drawing the boundaries of neighboring majority-white districts. We rejected that argument in *Hays* . . . ."

Page 552.   At the end of section 2 of the Note, add the following:

EASLEY v. CROMARTIE, 532 U.S. 234 (2001). This case involved a challenge to a redrawn version of North Carolina's Twelfth Congressional District, the district challenged originally in Shaw v. Reno, 509 U.S. 630 (1993) (discussed supra page 544 of the main text), and struck down as unjustifiably race conscious in Shaw v. Hunt, 517 U.S. 899 (1996). This time around, the Court held that the district court had erred in finding that race, rather than politics, drove the legislature's districting decision.

Justice Breyer's opinion for the Court sharpened the distinction between race "simply hav[ing] been '*a* motivation for the drawing of a majority minority district'" —which would be permissible—and race being the "predominant factor," the showing that would trigger strict scrutiny. Justice Breyer cautioned against concluding that race was the predominant factor in situations "where the State has articulated a legitimate political explanation for its districting decision, and the voting population is one in which race and political affiliation are highly correlated."

Justice Breyer's opinion performed a painstakingly thorough review of the record, going beyond the district court's findings to examine the entire testimony of the expert witness on whom the trial court had relied. It also discounted the direct evidence relied on by the district court. One of the leaders of the redistricting process, State Senator Roy Cooper, testified before the legislative committee considering the plan "'overall it provides for a fair, geographic, racial and partisan balance throughout the State of North Carolina. . . .'" Justice Breyer "agree[d] that one can read the statement about 'racial . . . balance' as the District Court read it—to refer to the current congressional delegation's racial balance. But even as so read, the phrase shows that the legislature considered race, along with other partisan and geographic considerations; and as so read it says little or nothing about whether race played a predominant role comparatively speaking. . . .

"We can put the matter more generally as follows: In a case such as this one where majority-minority districts (or the approximate equivalent) are at issue and where racial identification correlates highly with political affiliation, the party attacking the legislatively drawn boundaries must show at the least that the legislature could have achieved its legitimate political objectives in alternative ways that are comparably consistent with traditional districting principles. That party must also show that those districting alternatives would have brought about significantly greater racial balance."

Justice Thomas, joined by the Chief Justice and Justices Scalia and Kennedy, dissented: "The issue for this Court is simply whether the District Court's factual finding—that racial considerations [predominated in drawing the district]—was clearly erroneous. . . . [P]erhaps the best evidence that the Court has emptied clear error review of meaningful content in the redistricting context . . . is the Court's foray into the minutiae of the record. I do not doubt this Court's ability to sift through volumes of facts or to argue its interpretation of those facts persuasively. But I do doubt the wisdom, efficiency, increased accuracy, and legitimacy of an extensive review that is any more searching than clear error review. . . .

"If I were the District Court, I might have reached the same conclusion that the Court does, that 'the evidence taken together . . . does not show that racial considerations predominated in the drawing of District 12's boundaries.' But I am not the trier of fact, and it is not my role to weigh evidence in the first instance. The only question that this Court should decide is whether the District Court's finding of racial predominance was clearly erroneous. In light of the direct evidence of racial motive and the inferences that may be drawn from the circumstantial evidence, I am satisfied that the District Court's finding was permissible, even if not compelled by the record."

And Justice Thomas "assume[d] because the District Court did, that the goal of protecting incumbents is legitimate, even where, as here, individuals are incumbents by virtue of their election in an unconstitutional racially gerrymandered district. No doubt this assumption is a questionable proposition. Because the issue was not presented in this action, however, I do not read the Court's opinion as addressing it."

In light of *Easley*, consider Karlan, Easing the Spring: Strict Scrutiny and Affirmative Action After the Redistricting Cases, 43 Wm. & Mary L. Rev. 1569, 1586, 1602-03 (2002):

[The Supreme Court's recognition that] the legislature "considered" race is, of course, not precisely the same thing as saying that the legislature was "aware" of race—the state of mind described in Shaw v. Reno and *Miller*.] The former at least suggests some level of volition as to the consequences of its decision, whereas the latter need not. Put in *Feeney* terms, it seems quite clear that the Supreme Court is prepared to conclude that North Carolina selected the challenged plan "at least in part 'because of,' not merely 'in spite of,'" the racial composition of the districts. Yet the Court did not apply strict scrutiny. . . .

[T]he redistricting cases suggest there is definitely more than one kind of strict scrutiny. Faced with the prospect of applying a form of strict scrutiny that threatened to resegregate state legislatures and congressional delegations, the Supreme Court has been unwilling to apply strict scrutiny strictly. It has constricted the domain in which strict scrutiny comes into play, permitting race to be taken into account when it is one factor among many and its inclusion produces districts that do not deviate too obviously from the sorts of districts created for other groups. It has also broadened the interests that can justify race-conscious redistricting, by holding that compliance with the Voting Rights Act's results tests can serve as a compelling state interest. The understanding of political equality embodied in the Act goes beyond what the Constitution itself demands. It requires states to arrange their electoral institutions to minimize the lingering effects of prior un-constitutional discrimination not otherwise chargeable to them, as well as to mitigate the impact of racially polarized voting that involves otherwise constitutionally protected private choice. In short, the theory of strict scrutiny yielded to the need for an electoral system that is equally open to members of minority groups.

Page 552.   Before section 3 of the Note, add the following:

Might some government actions be shielded from improper purpose review because they are "mandatory" or "ministerial" rather than "discretionary"? Consider City of Cuyahoga Falls, Ohio v. Buckeye Community Hope Foundation, 538 U.S. ___ (2003). The City Council enacted legislation authorizing construction of a low-income housing complex to be built by Buckeye. Before construction began, opponents of the project mounted a referendum petition campaign. At public meetings, some of the opponents claimed that the project would cause crime and drug activity to escalate, that families with children would move in, and that the complex would attract a population similar to the one in the City's only African-American neighborhood.

The campaign culminated in a formal petition filed with the City requesting that the ordinance be repealed or submitted to a popular vote. Pursuant to a provision of the City Charter, the filing stayed the implementation of the project. Buckeye thereupon sought relief from a state court, claiming that the proposed referendum violated the Ohio Constitution. While this lawsuit was pending, Buckeye's request for a building permit was denied on the ground that the City Council ordinance could not take effect because of the petition. Eventually, Ohio voters passed the referendum, but the Ohio Supreme Court agreed with Buckeye that the referendum violated state law. Although Buckeye was then allowed to begin construction, it filed suit in federal court arguing that the City had violated the equal protection clause by delaying the project. The court of appeals held that Buckeye had produced enough evidence to survive summary judgment on the allegation that the City, by allowing the referendum petition to stay construction, gave effect to racial bias reflected in public opposition to the project. The Supreme Court, in an opinion by Justice O'Connor, unanimously reversed:

> [The court of appeals] erred in relying on cases in which we have subjected enacted, discretionary measures to equal protection scrutiny and treated decisionmakers' statements as evidence of such intent. . . .
> By placing the referendum on the ballot, the City did not enact the referendum and therefore cannot be said to have given effect to voters' allegedly discriminatory [motives]. Similarly, the city engineer, in refusing to issue the building permits while the referendum was pending, performed a nondiscretionary, ministerial act. [Respondents] point to no evidence suggesting that these official acts were themselves motivated by racial animus.

According to the Court, the fact that individuals who supported the petition drive may have done so for racially motivated reasons did not change this conclusion:

> [Statements] made by private individuals in the course of a citizen-driven petition drive, while sometimes relevant to equal protection analysis [do] not, in and of themselves, constitute state action for the purpose of the Fourteenth Amendment. . . .
> [By] adhering to charter procedures, city officials enabled public debate on the referendum to take place, thus advancing significant First Amendment interests. [Our] well established First Amendment admonition that "government may not prohibit the expression of an idea simply because society finds the idea itself offensive or disagreeable," [citing Texas v. Johnson, discussed at page 1314 of the main text] dovetails with the notion that all citizens, regardless of the content of their ideas, have the right to petition their government.

If the Ohio Court had allowed the referendum result to stand, would discriminatory motives by private citizens who supported it make it vulnerable to constitutional challenge? According to Justice O'Connor, "statements by decisionmakers or referendum sponsors during deliberation over the referendum may constitute relevant evidence of discriminatory intent in a challenge to an ultimately enacted initiative. [But] respondents do not challenge an enacted referendum." Can this observation be reconciled with the First Amendment concerns quoted above? If it could be shown that voters supported a candidate for public office for racially discriminatory reasons, is the candidate's election unconstitutional? If the discriminatory motives of referendum sponsors can vitiate the legal effect of the enacted referendum (e.g., a permanent prohibition of the proposed project), why do not similar motives on the

part of petition sponsors vitiate the legal effect of the petition (e.g., a temporary prohibition of the proposed project)?

In connection with equal protection standards appropriate when evaluating the results of referenda, consider Washington v. Seattle School District No. 1 at page 535
of the main text and Romer v. Evans at page 638 of the main text.

Page 552.   At the end of section 3a of the Note, add the following:

Consider Karlan, Easing the Spring: Strict Scrutiny and Affirmative Action After
the Redistricting Cases, 43 Wm. & Mary L. Rev. 1569, 1586 (2002):

> In suggesting that compliance with sections 2 and 5 of the Voting Rights Act can
> constitute a compelling state interest [sufficient to justify race-specific districting],
> the Court has raised the possibility that congressional or executive understandings
> of equality that go beyond what the Constitution itself requires can provide a justi-
> fication for race-conscious state action.

Is this suggestion consistent with the Court's current approach to section 5 of the
fourteenth amendment (discussed supra at pages 224-30 of the main text)?

Page 590.   At the end of subsection b of the Note, add the following:

For criticism of the diversity argument, see Lawrence, Two Views of the River: A
Critique of the Liberal Defense of Affirmative Action, 101 Colum. 928 (2001). Professor Lawrence argues that

> liberal supporters of affirmative action have used the diversity argument to defend
> affirmative action at elite universities and law schools without questioning the
> ways that traditional admissions criteria continue to perpetuate race and class
> privilege. [As] diversity has emerged as the dominant defense of affirmative ac-
> tion in the university setting, it has pushed other more radical substantive defenses
> to the background. These more radical arguments focus on the need to remedy
> past discrimination, address present discriminatory practices, and reexamine
> traditional notions of merit and the role of universities in the reproduction of
> elites.

Page 590.   Before subsection c of the Note, add the following:

GRUTTER v. BOLLINGER
539 U.S. ___ (2003)

JUSTICE O'CONNOR delivered the opinion of the Court.

This case requires us to decide whether the use of race as a factor in student admissions by the University of Michigan Law School [is] unlawful.

I

[The Law School's admission policy required admissions officials to evaluate each applicant based upon the entire file, including a personal statement, letters of recommendation, and an essay. Admissions officers were directed to take into account undergraduate grades and LSAT scores, but the policy made clear that no score led to either automatic admission or rejection. Instead, officials also looked to "soft variables" such as the enthusiasm of recommenders or the areas and difficulty of undergraduate course selection. The policy also emphasized diversity of various sorts. In this connection, the policy reaffirmed the Law School's commitment to "one particular type of diversity" that is "racial and ethnic diversity with special reference to the inclusion of students from groups which have been historically discriminated against, like African-Americans, Hispanics and Native Americans, who without this commitment might not be represented in our student body in meaningful numbers."

[Grutter, a white Michigan resident whose application to the Law School was denied, claimed that she was rejected because the Law School used race as a predominant factor in violation of the equal protection clause. The trial court heard testimony from the Law School's director of admissions, who said that he did not direct his staff to admit a particular percentage or number of minority students, but rather to consider an applicant's race along with all other factors. He further testified that at the height of the admissions season, he would frequently consult the "daily reports" indicating the racial and ethnic composition of the class in order to ensure that a "critical mass" of underrepresented minority students would be reached so as to realize the educational benefits of a diverse student body. He stressed, however, that he did not seek to admit any particular number or percentage of minority students.

[The Dean of the Law School also testified. He stated that "critical mass" meant numbers such that underrepresented minority students did not feel isolated or like spokespersons for their race. When asked about the extent to which race was considered, he stated that it varied from one applicant to another. In some cases, an applicant's race might play no role, while in others it might be a determinative factor.

[An expert witness testifying for Grutter examined data obtained from the Law School and concluded that membership in certain minority groups "is an extremely strong factor in the decision for acceptance" and that applicants from these groups "are given an extremely large allowance for admission." An expert testifying for the Law School predicted that if race were eliminated as a factor, the change would have a "very dramatic" negative effect on minority admissions.

[The District Court concluded that the Law School's use of race was unlawful, but the Court of Appeals reversed].

II

A

We last addressed the use of race in public higher education over 25 years ago. In the landmark *Bakke* case, we reviewed a racial set-aside program that reserved 16 out of 100 seats in a medical school class for members of certain minority groups. . . .

Since this Court's splintered decision in *Bakke*, Justice Powell's opinion announcing the judgment of the Court has served as the touchstone for constitutional analysis of race-conscious admissions policies. Public and private universities across the Nation have modeled their own admissions programs on Justice Powell's views on permissible race-conscious policies. . . .

[For] the reasons set out below, today we endorse Justice Powell's view that student body diversity is a compelling state interest that can justify the use of race in university admissions.

B

We have held that all racial classifications imposed by government "must be analyzed by a reviewing court under strict scrutiny." [*Adarand*]. . . .

Although all governmental uses of race are subject to strict scrutiny, not all are invalidated by it. [When] race-based action is necessary to further a compelling governmental interest, such action does not violate the constitutional guarantee of equal protection so long as the narrow-tailoring requirement is also satisfied.

Context matters when reviewing race-based governmental action under the Equal Protection Clause. [Not] every decision influenced by race is equally objectionable and strict scrutiny is designed to provide a framework for carefully examining the importance and the sincerity of the reasons advanced by the governmental decision-maker for the use of race in that particular context.

71

III

A

With these principles in mind, we turn to the question whether the Law School's use of race is justified by a compelling state interest. [The] Law School asks us to recognize, in the context of higher education, a compelling state interest in student body diversity.

We first wish to dispel the notion that the Law School's argument has been foreclosed, either expressly or implicitly, by our affirmative-action cases decided since *Bakke*. [We] have never held that the only governmental use of race that can survive strict scrutiny is remedying past discrimination. Nor, since *Bakke*, have we directly addressed the use of race in the context of public higher education. Today, we hold that the Law School has a compelling interest in attaining a diverse student body.

The Law School's educational judgment that such diversity is essential to its educational mission is one to which we defer. The Law School's assessment that diversity will, in fact, yield educational benefits is substantiated by respondents and their *amici*. Our scrutiny of the interest asserted by the Law School is no less strict for taking into account complex educational judgments in an area that lies primarily within the expertise of the university. Our holding today is in keeping with our tradition of giving a degree of deference to a university's academic decisions, within constitutionally prescribed limits.

We have long recognized that, given the important purpose of public education and the expansive freedoms of speech and thought associated with the university environment, universities occupy a special niche in our constitutional tradition.

As part of its goal of "assembling a class that is both exceptionally academically qualified and broadly diverse," the Law School seeks to "enroll a 'critical mass' of minority students." The Law School's interest is not simply "to assure within its student body some specified percentage of a particular group merely because of its race or ethnic origin." [*Bakke* (opinion of Powell, J.)]. That would amount to outright racial balancing, which is patently unconstitutional. . . . Rather, the Law School's concept of critical mass is defined by reference to the educational benefits that diversity is designed to produce.

These benefits are substantial. As the District Court emphasized, the Law School's admissions policy promotes "cross-racial understanding," helps to break down racial stereotypes, and "enables [students] to better understand persons of different races." These benefits are "important and laudable," because "classroom discussion is livelier, more spirited, and simply more enlightening and interesting" when the students have "the greatest possible variety of backgrounds."

The Law School's claim of a compelling interest is further bolstered by its *amici*, who point to the educational benefits that flow from student body diversity. . . .

These benefits are not theoretical but real, as major American businesses have made clear that the skills needed in today's increasingly global marketplace can only be developed through exposure to widely diverse people, cultures, ideas, and viewpoints. Brief for 3M et al. as *Amici Curiae*; Brief for General Motors Corp. as *Amicus Curiae*. What is more, high-ranking retired officers and civilian leaders of the United States military assert that, "[b]ased on [their] decades of experience,"a "highly qualified, racially diverse officer corps . . . is essential to the military's ability to fulfill its principle mission to provide national security." Brief for Julius W. Becton, Jr. et al. as *Amici Curiae*. The primary sources for the Nation's officer corps are the service academies and the Reserve Officers Training Corps (ROTC) the latter comprising students already admitted to participating colleges and universities. At present, "the military cannot achieve an officer corps that is *both* highly qualified *and* racially diverse unless the service academies and the ROTC used limited race-conscious recruiting and admissions policies." (emphasis in original). . . .

We have repeatedly acknowledged the overriding importance of preparing students for work and citizenship, describing education as pivotal to "sustaining our political and cultural heritage" with a fundamental role in maintaining the fabric of society. Plyler v. Doe, 457 U.S. 202, 221 (1982). . . .

Moreover, universities, and in particular, law schools, represent the training ground for a large number of our Nation's leaders. Sweatt v. Painter, 339 U.S. 629, 634 (1950) (describing law school as a "proving ground for legal learning and practice"). Individuals with law degrees occupy roughly half the state governorships, more than half the seats in the United States Senate, and more than a third of the seats in the United States House of Representatives. The pattern is even more striking when it comes to highly selective law schools. A handful of these schools accounts for 25 of the 100 United States Senators, 74 United States Courts of Appeals judges, and nearly 200 of the more than 600 United States District Court judges.

In order to cultivate a set of leaders with legitimacy in the eyes of the citizenry, it is necessary that the path to leadership be visibly open to talented and qualified individuals of every race and ethnicity. All members of our heterogeneous society must have confidence in the openness and integrity of the educational institutions that provide this training. As we have recognized, law schools "cannot be effective in isolation from the individuals and institutions with which the law interacts." See *Sweatt v. Painter*. Access to legal education (and thus the legal profession) must be inclusive of talented and qualified individuals of every race and ethnicity, so that all members of our heterogeneous society may participate in the educational institutions that provide the training and education necessary to succeed in America.

The Law School does not premise its need for critical mass on "any belief that minority students always (or even consistently) express some characteristic minority viewpoint on any issue." To the contrary, diminishing the force of such stereotypes is both a crucial part of the Law School's mission, and one that it cannot accomplish with only token numbers of minority students. Just as growing up in a particular

73

region or having particular professional experiences is likely to affect an individual's views, so too is one's own, unique experience of being a racial minority in a society, like our own, in which race unfortunately still matters. The Law School has determined, based on its experience and expertise, that a "critical mass" of underrepresented minorities is necessary to further its compelling interest in securing the educational benefits of a diverse student body.

B

To be narrowly tailored, a race-conscious admissions program cannot use a quota system—it cannot "insulat[e] each category of applicants with certain desired qualifications from competition with all other applicants." *Bakke* (opinion of Powell, J.). Instead, a university may consider race or ethnicity only as a " 'plus' in a particular applicant's file, without 'insulat[ing]' the individual from comparison with all other candidates for the available seats." *Id.* In other words, an admissions program must be "flexible enough to consider all pertinent elements of diversity in light of the particular qualifications of each applicant, and to place them on the same footing for consideration, although not necessarily according them the same weight." *Ibid.*

We find that the Law School's admissions program bears the hallmarks of a narrowly tailored plan. . . .

We are satisfied that the Law School's admissions program, like the Harvard plan described by Justice Powell, does not operate as a quota. Properly understood, a "quota" is a program in which a certain fixed number or proportion of opportunities are "reserved exclusively for certain minority groups." Richmond v. J. A. Croson Co., (plurality opinion). [In] contrast, "a permissible goal . . . require[s] only a good-faith effort . . . to come within a range demarcated by the goal itself," and permits consideration of race as a "plus" factor in any given case while still ensuring that each candidate "compete[s] with all other qualified applicants". . . .

The Law School's goal of attaining a critical mass of underrepresented minority students does not transform its program into a quota. As the Harvard plan described by Justice Powell recognized, there is of course "some relationship between numbers and achieving the benefits to be derived from a diverse student body, and between numbers and providing a reasonable environment for those students admitted." [*Bakke*]. "[S]ome attention to numbers," without more, does not transform a flexible admissions system into a rigid quota. *Ibid.* Nor, as Justice Kennedy posits, does the Law School's consultation of the "daily reports," which keep track of the racial and ethnic composition of the class (as well as of residency and gender), "suggest[ ] there was no further attempt at individual review save for race itself" during the final stages of the admissions process. To the contrary, the Law School's admissions officers testified without contradiction that they never gave race any more or less weight based on the information contained in these reports. Moreover, as Justice Kennedy concedes, between 1993 and 2000, the number of African-American, Latino, and

74

Native-American students in each class at the Law School varied from 13.5 to 20.1 percent, a range inconsistent with a quota.

The Chief Justice believes that the Law School's policy conceals an attempt to achieve racial balancing, and cites admissions data to contend that the Law School discriminates among different groups within the critical mass. But, as The Chief Justice concedes, the number of underrepresented minority students who ultimately enroll in the Law School differs substantially from their representation in the applicant pool and varies considerably for each group from year to year.

That a race-conscious admissions program does not operate as a quota does not, by itself, satisfy the requirement of individualized consideration. When using race as a "plus" factor in university admissions, a university's admissions program must remain flexible enough to ensure that each applicant is evaluated as an individual and not in a way that makes an applicant's race or ethnicity [dispositive].

Here, the Law School engages in a highly individualized, holistic review of each applicant's file, giving serious consideration to all the ways an applicant might contribute to a diverse educational environment. The Law School affords this individualized consideration to applicants of all races. There is no policy, either *de jure* or *de facto*, of automatic acceptance or rejection based on any single "soft" variable. Unlike the program at issue in *Gratz v. Bollinger*, the Law School awards no mechanical, predetermined diversity "bonuses" based on race or ethnicity. . . .

We also find that, like the Harvard plan Justice Powell referenced in *Bakke*, the Law School's race-conscious admissions program adequately ensures that all factors that may contribute to student body diversity are meaningfully considered alongside race in admissions decisions. With respect to the use of race itself, all underrepresented minority students admitted by the Law School have been deemed qualified. By virtue of our Nation's struggle with racial inequality, such students are both likely to have experiences of particular importance to the Law School's mission, and less likely to be admitted in meaningful numbers on criteria that ignore those experiences.

The Law School does not, however, limit in any way the broad range of qualities and experiences that may be considered valuable contributions to student body diversity. To the contrary, the 1992 policy makes clear "[t]here are many possible bases for diversity admissions," and provides examples of admittees who have lived or traveled widely abroad, are fluent in several languages, have overcome personal adversity and family hardship, have exceptional records of extensive community service, and have had successful careers in other fields. . . .

What is more, the Law School actually gives substantial weight to diversity factors besides race. The Law School frequently accepts nonminority applicants with grades and test scores lower than underrepresented minority applicants (and other nonminority applicants) who are rejected.

Petitioner and the United States argue that the Law School's plan is not narrowly tailored because race-neutral means exist to obtain the educational benefits of student body diversity that the Law School seeks. We disagree. Narrow tailoring does not require exhaustion of every conceivable race-neutral alternative. Nor does it require a university to choose between maintaining a reputation for excellence or fulfilling a commitment to provide educational opportunities to members of all racial groups. Narrow tailoring does, however, require serious, good faith consideration of workable race-neutral alternatives that will achieve the diversity the university seeks.

We agree with the Court of Appeals that the Law School sufficiently considered workable race-neutral alternatives. The District Court took the Law School to task for failing to consider race-neutral alternatives such as "using a lottery system" or "decreasing the emphasis for all applicants on undergraduate GPA and LSAT scores." But these alternatives would require a dramatic sacrifice of diversity, the academic quality of all admitted students, or both.

The Law School's current admissions program considers race as one factor among many, in an effort to assemble a student body that is diverse in ways broader than race. Because a lottery would make that kind of nuanced judgment impossible, it would effectively sacrifice all other educational values, not to mention every other kind of diversity. So too with the suggestion that the Law School simply lower admissions standards for all students, a drastic remedy that would require the Law School to become a much different institution and sacrifice a vital component of its educational mission. The United States advocates "percentage plans," recently adopted by public undergraduate institutions in Texas, Florida, and California to guarantee admission to all students above a certain class-rank threshold in every high school in the State. The United States does not, however, explain how such plans could work for graduate and professional schools. Moreover, even assuming such plans are race-neutral, they may preclude the university from conducting the individualized assessments necessary to assemble a student body that is not just racially diverse, but diverse along all the qualities valued by the university. We are satisfied that the Law School adequately considered race-neutral alternatives currently capable of producing a critical mass without forcing the Law School to abandon the academic selectivity that is the cornerstone of its educational mission. . . .

We are mindful, however, that "[a] core purpose of the Fourteenth Amendment was to do away with all governmentally imposed discrimination based on race." *Palmore v. Sidoti*. Accordingly, race-conscious admissions policies must be limited in time. This requirement reflects that racial classifications, however compelling their goals, are potentially so dangerous that they may be employed no more broadly than the interest demands. Enshrining a permanent justification for racial preferences would offend this fundamental equal protection principle. We see no reason to exempt race-conscious admissions programs from the requirement that all governmental use of race must have a logical end point. The Law School, too, concedes that all "race-conscious programs must have reasonable durational limits."

In the context of higher education, the durational requirement can be met by sunset provisions in race-conscious admissions policies and periodic reviews to determine whether racial preferences are still necessary to achieve student body diversity. Universities in California, Florida, and Washington State, where racial preferences in admissions are prohibited by state law, are currently engaged in experimenting with a wide variety of alternative approaches. Universities in other States can and should draw on the most promising aspects of these race-neutral alternatives as they develop.

The requirement that all race-conscious admissions programs have a termination point "assure[s] all citizens that the deviation from the norm of equal treatment of all racial and ethnic groups is a temporary matter, a measure taken in the service of the goal of equality itself." *Richmond v. J. A. Croson Co.* (plurality opinion).

We take the Law School at its word that it would "like nothing better than to find a race-neutral admissions formula" and will terminate its race-conscious admissions program as soon as practicable. It has been 25 years since Justice Powell first approved the use of race to further an interest in student body diversity in the context of public higher education. Since that time, the number of minority applicants with high grades and test scores has indeed increased. We expect that 25 years from now, the use of racial preferences will no longer be necessary to further the interest approved today.

IV

In summary, the Equal Protection Clause does not prohibit the Law School's narrowly tailored use of race in admissions decisions to further a compelling interest in obtaining the educational benefits that flow from a diverse student body. [The] judgment of the Court of Appeals for the Sixth Circuit, accordingly, is affirmed.

JUSTICE GINSBURG, with whom JUSTICE BREYER joins, concurring. . . .

The Court [observes] that "[i]t has been 25 years since Justice Powell [first] approved the use of race to further an interest in student body diversity in the context of public higher education." For at least part of that time, however, the law could not fairly be described as "settled," and in some regions of the Nation, overtly race-conscious admissions policies have been proscribed. Moreover, it was only 25 years before *Bakke* that this Court declared public school segregation unconstitutional, a declaration that, after prolonged resistance, yielded an end to a law-enforced racial caste system, itself the legacy of centuries of slavery.

It is well documented that conscious and unconscious race bias, even rank discrimination based on race, remain alive in our land, impeding realization of our highest values and ideals. As to public education, data for the years 2000-2001 show that 71.6% of African-American children and 76.3% of Hispanic children attended a school in which minorities made up a majority of the student body. And schools in predominantly minority communities lag far behind others measured by the educational resources available to them.

However strong the public's desire for improved education systems may be, it remains the current reality that many minority students encounter markedly inadequate and unequal educational opportunities. Despite these inequalities, some minority students are able to meet the high threshold requirements set for admission to the country's finest undergraduate and graduate educational institutions. As lower school education in minority communities improves, an increase in the number of such students may be anticipated. From today's vantage point, one may hope, but not firmly forecast, that over the next generation's span, progress toward nondiscrimination and genuinely equal opportunity will make it safe to sunset affirmative action.

CHIEF JUSTICE REHNQUIST, with whom JUSTICE SCALIA, JUSTICE KENNEDY, and JUSTICE THOMAS join, dissenting.

I agree with the Court that, "in the limited circumstance when drawing racial distinctions is permissible," the government must ensure that its means are narrowly tailored to achieve a compelling state interest. I do not believe, however, that the University of Michigan Law School's [means] are narrowly tailored to the interest it asserts. The Law School claims it must take the steps it does to achieve a "critical mass" of underrepresented minority students. But its actual program bears no relation to this asserted goal. Stripped of its "critical mass" veil, the Law School's program is revealed as a naked effort to achieve racial balancing. . . .

Although the Court recites the language of [strict] scrutiny analysis, its application of that review is unprecedented in its deference. . . .

In practice, the Law School's program bears little or no relation to its asserted goal of achieving "critical mass." Respondents explain that the Law School seeks to accumulate a "critical mass" of *each* underrepresented minority group. But the record demonstrates that the Law School's admissions practices with respect to these groups differ dramatically and cannot be defended under any consistent use of the term "critical mass."

From 1995 through 2000, the Law School admitted between 1,130 and 1,310 students. Of those, between 13 and 19 were Native American, between 91 and 108 were African-Americans, and between 47 and 56 were Hispanic. If the Law School is admitting between 91 and 108 African-Americans in order to achieve "critical mass," thereby preventing African-American students from feeling "isolated or like spokespersons for their race," one would think that a number of the same order of magnitude would be necessary to accomplish the same purpose for Hispanics and Native Americans. Similarly, even if all of the Native American applicants admitted in a given year matriculate, which the record demonstrates is not at all the case, how can this possibly constitute a "critical mass" of Native Americans in a class of over 350 students? In order for this pattern of admission to be consistent with the Law School's explanation of "critical mass," one would have to believe that the objectives of "critical mass" offered by respondents are achieved with only half the number of

Hispanics and one-sixth the number of Native Americans as compared to African-Americans. But respondents offer no race-specific reasons for such disparities. Instead, they simply emphasize the importance of achieving "critical mass," without any explanation of why that concept is applied differently among the three underrepresented minority groups.

These different numbers, moreover, come only as a result of substantially different treatment among the three underrepresented minority groups, as is apparent in an example offered by the Law School and highlighted by the Court: The school asserts that it "frequently accepts nonminority applicants with grades and test scores lower than underrepresented minority applicants (and other nonminority applicants) who are rejected." Specifically, the Law School states that "[s]ixty-nine minority applicants were rejected between 1995 and 2000 with at least a 3.5 [Grade Point Average (GPA)] and a [score of] 159 or higher on the [Law School Admissions Test (LSAT)]" while a number of Caucasian and Asian-American applicants with similar or lower scores were admitted.

Review of the record reveals only 67 such individuals. Of these 67 individuals, 56 were Hispanic, while only 6 were African-American, and only 5 were Native American. This discrepancy reflects a consistent practice. . . .

[Respondents] have *never* offered any race-specific arguments explaining why significantly more individuals from one underrepresented minority group are needed in order to achieve "critical mass" or further student body diversity. They certainly have not explained why Hispanics, who they have said are among "the groups most isolated by racial barriers in our country," should have their admission capped out in this manner. [The] Law School's disparate admissions practices with respect to these minority groups demonstrate that its alleged goal of "critical mass" is simply a sham. [Surely] strict scrutiny cannot permit these sort of disparities without at least some explanation.

Only when the "critical mass" label is discarded does a likely explanation for these numbers emerge. . . .

[The] correlation between the percentage of the Law School's pool of applicants who are members of the three minority groups and the percentage of the admitted applicants who are members of these same groups is far too precise to be dismissed as merely the result of the school paying "some attention to [the] numbers." [From] 1995 through 2000 the percentage of admitted applicants who were members of these minority groups closely tracked the percentage of individuals in the school's applicant pool who were from the same groups. . . .

For example, in 1995, when 9.7% of the applicant pool was African-American, 9.4% of the admitted class was African-American. By 2000, only 7.5% of the applicant pool was African-American, and 7.3% of the admitted class was African-American. This correlation is striking. [The] tight correlation between the percentage of applicants and admittees of a given race, therefore, must result from careful race based planning by the Law School. It suggests a formula for admission based on the aspirational assumption that all applicants are equally qualified academically, and therefore that the proportion of each group admitted should be the same as the proportion of that group in the applicant pool.

Not only do respondents fail to explain this phenomenon, they attempt to obscure it. See [the Law School's brief] ("The Law School's minority enrollment percentages . . . diverged from the percentages in the applicant pool by as much as 17.7% from 1995-2000"). But the divergence between the percentages of underrepresented minorities in the applicant pool and in the *enrolled* classes is not the only relevant comparison. In fact, it may not be the most relevant comparison. The Law School cannot precisely control which of its admitted applicants decide to attend the university. But it can and, as the numbers demonstrate, clearly does employ racial preferences in extending offers of admission. Indeed, the ostensibly flexible nature of the Law School's admissions program that the Court finds appealing, appears to be, in practice, a carefully managed program designed to ensure proportionate representation of applicants from selected minority groups. . . .

Finally, I believe that the Law School's program fails strict scrutiny because it is devoid of any reasonably precise time limit on the Law School's use of race in admissions. . . .

The Court suggests a possible 25-year limitation on the Law School's current program. Respondents, on the other hand, remain more ambiguous, explaining that "the Law School of course recognizes that race-conscious programs must have reasonable durational limits, and the Sixth Circuit properly found such a limit in the Law School's resolve to cease considering race when genuine race-neutral alternatives become available." These discussions of a time limit are the vaguest of assurances. In truth, they permit the Law School's use of racial preferences on a seemingly permanent basis. Thus, an important component of strict scrutiny—that a program be limited in time—is casually subverted.

The Court, in an unprecedented display of deference under our strict scrutiny analysis, upholds the Law School's program despite its obvious flaws. We have said that when it comes to the use of race, the connection between the ends and the means used to attain them must be precise. But here the flaw is deeper than that; it is not merely a question of "fit" between ends and means. Here the means actually used are forbidden by the Equal Protection Clause of the Constitution.

JUSTICE KENNEDY, dissenting.

The separate opinion by Justice Powell in *Regents of Univ. of Cal. v. Bakke* is based on the principle that a university admissions program may take account of race as one, nonpredominant factor in a system designed to consider each applicant as an individual, provided the program can meet the test of strict scrutiny by the judiciary. This is a unitary formulation. If strict scrutiny is abandoned or manipulated to distort its real and accepted meaning, the Court lacks authority to approve the use of race even in this modest, limited way. . . .

It is unfortunate, however, that the Court takes the first part of Justice Powell's rule but abandons the second. Having approved the use of race as a factor in the admissions process, the majority proceeds to nullify the essential safeguard Justice Powell insisted upon as the precondition of the approval. The safeguard was rigorous judicial review, with strict scrutiny as the controlling standard. . . .

The Court, in a review that is nothing short of perfunctory, accepts the University of Michigan Law School's assurances that its admissions process meets with constitutional requirements. The majority fails to confront the reality of how the Law School's admissions policy is implemented. The dissenting opinion by The Chief Justice, which I join in full, demonstrates beyond question why the concept of critical mass is a delusion used by the Law School to mask its attempt to make race an automatic factor in most instances and to achieve numerical goals indistinguishable from quotas. . . .

The Law School has not demonstrated how individual consideration is, or can be, preserved [given] the instruction to attain what it calls critical mass. In fact the evidence shows otherwise. There was little deviation among admitted minority students during the years from 1995 to 1998. The percentage of enrolled minorities fluctuated only by 0.3%, from 13.5% to 13.8%. The number of minority students to whom offers were extended varied by just a slightly greater magnitude of 2.2%, from the high of 15.6% in 1995 to the low of 13.4% in 1998.

[Admittedly,] there were greater fluctuations among enrolled minorities in the preceding years, 1987-1994, by as much as 5 or 6%. The percentage of minority offers, however, at no point fell below 12%, historically defined by the Law School as the bottom of its critical mass range. The greater variance during the earlier years, in any event, does not dispel suspicion that the school engaged in racial balancing. The data would be consistent with an inference that the Law School modified its target only twice, in 1991 (from 13% to 19%), and then again in 1995 (back from 20% to 13%). The intervening year, 1993, when the percentage dropped to 14.5%, could be an aberration, caused by the school's miscalculation as to how many applicants with offers would accept or by its redefinition, made in April 1992, of which minority groups were entitled to race-based preference. . . .

The narrow fluctuation band raises an inference that the Law School subverted individual determination, and strict scrutiny requires the Law School to overcome the inference. . . .

The Court's refusal to apply meaningful strict scrutiny will lead to serious consequences. By deferring to the law schools' choice of minority admissions programs, the courts will lose the talents and resources of the faculties and administrators in devising new and fairer ways to ensure individual consideration. Constant and rigorous judicial review forces the law school faculties to undertake their responsibilities as state employees in this most sensitive of areas with utmost fidelity to the mandate of the Constitution. Dean Allan Stillwagon, who directed the Law School's Office of Admissions from 1979 to 1990, explained the difficulties he encountered in defining racial groups entitled to benefit under the School's affirmative action policy. He testified that faculty members were "breathtakingly cynical" in deciding who would qualify as a member of underrepresented minorities. An example he offered was faculty debate as to whether Cubans should be counted as Hispanics: One professor objected on the grounds that Cubans were Republicans. Many academics at other law schools who are "affirmative action's more forthright defenders readily concede that diversity is merely the current rationale of convenience for a policy that they prefer to justify on other grounds." Schuck, Affirmative Action: Past, Present, and Future, 20 Yale L. & Pol'y Rev. 1, 34 (2002) (citing Levinson, Diversity, 2 U. Pa. J. Const. L. 573, 577-578 (2000); Rubenfeld, Affirmative Action, 107 Yale L. J. 427, 471 (1997)). This is not to suggest the faculty at Michigan or other law schools do not pursue aspirations they consider laudable and consistent with our constitutional traditions. It is but further evidence of the necessity for scrutiny that is real, not feigned, where the corrosive category of race is a factor in decisionmaking. . . .

It is difficult to assess the Court's pronouncement that race-conscious admissions programs will be unnecessary 25 years from now. If it is intended to mitigate the damage the Court does to the concept of strict scrutiny, neither petitioners nor other rejected law school applicants will find solace in knowing the basic protection put in place by Justice Powell will be suspended for a full quarter of a century. Deference is antithetical to strict scrutiny, not consistent with it.

As to the interpretation that the opinion contains its own self-destruct mechanism, the majority's abandonment of strict scrutiny undermines this objective. Were the courts to apply a searching standard to race-based admissions schemes, that would force educational institutions to seriously explore race-neutral alternatives. The Court, by contrast, is willing to be satisfied by the Law School's profession of its own good faith. . . .

It is regrettable the Court's important holding allowing racial minorities to have their special circumstances considered in order to improve their educational opportunities is accompanied by a suspension of the strict scrutiny which was the predicate of allowing race to be considered in the first place. If the Court abdicates its constitutional duty to give strict scrutiny to the use of race in university admissions, it negates my authority to approve the use of race in pursuit of student diversity. The Constitution cannot confer the right to classify on the basis of race even in this special context absent searching judicial review. For these reasons, though I reiterate my approval of giving appropriate consideration to race in this one context, I must dissent in the present case.

JUSTICE SCALIA, with whom JUSTICE THOMAS joins, concurring in part and dissenting in part. . . .

The "educational benefit" that the University of Michigan seeks to achieve by racial discrimination consists, according to the Court, of "cross-racial understanding," and "better prepar[ation of] students for an increasingly diverse workforce and society," all of which is necessary not only for work, but also for good "citizenship," This is not, of course, an "educational benefit" on which students will be graded on their Law School transcript (Works and Plays Well with Others: B+) or tested by the bar examiners (Q: Describe in 500 words or less your cross-racial understanding). For it is a lesson of life rather than law—essentially the same lesson taught to (or rather learned by, for it cannot be "taught" in the usual sense) people three feet shorter and twenty years younger than the full-grown adults at the University of Michigan Law School, in institutions ranging from Boy Scout troops to public-school kindergartens. If properly considered an "educational benefit" at all, it is surely not one that is either uniquely relevant to law school or uniquely "teachable", in a formal educational setting. *And therefore:* If it is appropriate for the University of Michigan Law School to use racial discrimination for the purpose of putting together a "critical mass" that will convey generic lessons in socialization and good citizenship, surely it is no less appropriate—indeed, *particularly* appropriate—for the civil service system of the State of Michigan to do so. There, also, those exposed to "critical masses" of certain races will presumably become better Americans, better Michiganders, better civil servants. And surely private employers cannot be criticized—indeed, should be praised—if they also "teach" good citizenship to their adult employees through a patriotic, all-American system of racial discrimination in hiring. The nonminority individuals who are deprived of a legal education, a civil service job, or any job at all by reason of their skin color will surely understand.

Unlike a clear constitutional holding that racial preferences in state educational institutions are impermissible, or even a clear anticonstitutional holding that racial preferences in state educational institutions are OK, today's *Grutter-Gratz* split double header seems perversely designed to prolong the controversy and the litigation. Some future lawsuits will presumably focus on whether the discriminatory scheme in question contains enough evaluation of the applicant "as an individual," and sufficiently avoids "separate admissions tracks" to fall under *Grutter* rather than *Gratz.* Some will focus on whether a university has gone beyond the bounds of a "good faith effort" and has so zealously pursued its "critical mass" as to make it an unconstitutional *de facto* quota system, rather than merely "a permissible goal." Other lawsuits may focus on whether, in the particular setting at issue, any educational benefits flow from racial diversity. (That issue was not contested in *Grutter*; and while the opinion accords "a degree of deference to a university's academic decisions," "deference does not imply abandonment or abdication of judicial review," Miller-El v. Cockrell, 537 U.S. 322, 340 (2003).) Still other suits may challenge the bona fides of the institution's expressed commitment to the educational benefits of diversity that immunize the discriminatory scheme in *Grutter*. (Tempting targets, one would suppose, will be those universities that talk the talk of multiculturalism and racial diversity in the courts but walk the walk of tribalism and racial segregation on their campuses—through minority-only student organizations, separate minority housing opportunities, separate minority student centers, even separate minority-only graduation ceremonies.) And still other suits may claim that the institution's racial preferences have gone below or above the mystical *Grutter*-approved "critical mass." Finally, litigation can be expected on behalf of minority groups intentionally short changed in the institution's composition of its generic minority "critical mass." I do not look forward to any of these cases. The Constitution proscribes government discrimination on the basis of race, and state-provided education is no exception.

JUSTICE THOMAS, with whom JUSTICE SCALIA joins as to Parts I-VII, concurring in part and dissenting in part.

Frederick Douglass, speaking to a group of abolitionists almost 140 years ago, delivered a message lost on today's majority:

> [I]n regard to the colored people, there is always more that is benevolent, I perceive, than just, manifested towards us. What I ask for the negro is not benevolence, not pity, not sympathy, but simply *justice*. The American people have always been anxious to know what they shall do with us. . . . I have had but one answer from the beginning. Do nothing with us! Your doing with us has already played the mischief with us. Do nothing with us! If the apples will not remain on the tree of their own strength, if they are worm-eaten at the core, if they are early ripe and disposed to fall, let them fall! . . . And if the negro cannot stand on his own legs, let him fall also. All I ask is, give him a chance to stand on his own legs! Let him alone! . . . [Y]our interference is doing him positive injury.

What the Black Man Wants: An Address Delivered in Boston, Massachusetts, on 26 January 1865, reprinted in 4 The Frederick Douglass Papers 59, 68 (J. Blassingame & J. McKivigan eds. 1991) (emphasis in original).

Like Douglass, I believe blacks can achieve in every avenue of American life without the meddling of university administrators. Because I wish to see all students succeed whatever their color, I share, in some respect, the sympathies of those who sponsor the type of discrimination advanced by the University of Michigan Law School (Law School). The Constitution does not, however, tolerate institutional devotion to the status quo in admissions policies when such devotion ripens into racial discrimination. Nor does the Constitution countenance the unprecedented deference the Court gives to the Law School, an approach inconsistent with the very concept of "strict scrutiny."

No one would argue that a university could set up a lower general admission standard and then impose heightened requirements only on black applicants. Similarly, a university may not maintain a high admission standard and grant exemptions to favored races. The Law School, of its own choosing, and for its own purposes, maintains an exclusionary admissions system that it knows produces racially disproportionate results. Racial discrimination is not a permissible solution to the self-inflicted wounds of this elitist admissions policy.

The majority upholds the Law School's racial discrimination not by interpreting the people's Constitution, but by responding to a faddish slogan of the cognoscenti. Nevertheless, I concur in part in the Court's opinion. First, I agree with the Court insofar as its decision, which approves of only one racial classification, confirms that further use of race in admissions remains unlawful. Second, I agree with the Court's holding that racial discrimination in higher education admissions will be illegal in 25 years. I respectfully dissent from the remainder of the Court's opinion and the judgment, however, because I believe that the Law School's current use of race violates the Equal Protection Clause and that the Constitution means the same thing today as it will in 300 months.

I

The majority agrees that the Law School's racial discrimination should be subjected to strict scrutiny. Before applying that standard to this case, I will briefly revisit the Court's treatment of racial classifications. [Justice Thomas summarizes the Court's cases upholding and invalidating racial classifications based on strict scrutiny.] . . .

Where the Court has accepted only national security, [*Korematsu*] and rejected even the best interests of a child, [Palmore v. Sidoti] as a justification for racial discrimination, I conclude that only those measures the State must take to provide a bulwark against anarchy, or to prevent violence, will constitute a "pressing public necessity."

The Constitution abhors classifications based on race, not only because those classifications can harm favored races or are based on illegitimate motives, but also because every time the government places citizens on racial registers and makes race relevant to the provision of burdens or benefits, it demeans us all. . . . .

II

Unlike the majority, I seek to define with precision the interest being asserted by the Law School before determining whether that interest is so compelling as to justify racial discrimination. The Law School maintains that it wishes to obtain "educational benefits that flow from student body diversity." This statement must be evaluated carefully, because it implies that both "diversity" and "educational benefits" are components of the Law School's compelling state interest. Additionally, the Law School's refusal to entertain certain changes in its admissions process and status indicates that the compelling state interest it seeks to validate is actually broader than might appear at first glance.

Undoubtedly there are other ways to "better" the education of law students aside from ensuring that the student body contains a "critical mass" of underrepresented minority students. . . .

One must also consider the Law School's refusal to entertain changes to its current admissions system that might produce the same educational benefits. The Law School adamantly disclaims any race-neutral alternative that would reduce "academic selectivity," which would in turn "require the Law School to become a very different institution, and to sacrifice a core part of its educational mission." In other words, the Law School seeks to improve marginally the education it offers without sacrificing too much of its exclusivity and elite status.

The proffered interest that the majority vindicates today, then, is not simply "diversity." Instead the Court upholds the use of racial discrimination as a tool to advance the Law School's interest in offering a marginally superior education while maintaining an elite institution. Unless each constituent part of this state interest is of pressing public necessity, the Law School's use of race is unconstitutional. I find each of them to fall far short of this standard.

III. . . .

B

Under the proper standard, there is no pressing public necessity in maintaining a public law school at all and, it follows, certainly not an elite law school. Likewise, marginal improvements in legal education do not qualify as a compelling state interest.

1

While legal education at a public university may be good policy or otherwise laudable, it is obviously not a pressing public necessity when the correct legal standard is applied. Additionally, circumstantial evidence as to whether a state activity is of pressing public necessity can be obtained by asking whether all States feel compelled to engage in that activity. [In] this sense, the absence of a public, American Bar Association (ABA) accredited, law school in Alaska, Delaware, Massachusetts, New Hampshire, and Rhode Island, provides further evidence that Michigan's maintenance of the Law School does not constitute a compelling state interest.

2

[Still,] even assuming that a State may, under appropriate circumstances, demonstrate a cognizable interest in having an elite law school, Michigan has failed to do so here.

This Court has limited the scope of equal protection review to interests and activities that occur within that State's jurisdiction. . . .

The only cognizable state interests vindicated by operating a public law school are, therefore, the education of that State's citizens and the training of that State's lawyers. . . .

The Law School today, however, does precious little training of those attorneys who will serve the citizens of Michigan. [Less] than 16% of the Law School's graduating class elects to stay in Michigan after law school. . . .

It does not take a social scientist to conclude that it is precisely the Law School's status as an elite institution that causes it to be a way-station for the rest of the country's lawyers, rather than a training ground for those who will remain in Michigan. The Law School's decision to be an elite institution does little to advance the welfare of the people of Michigan or any cognizable interest of the State of Michigan. . . .

IV. . . .

With the adoption of different admissions methods, such as accepting all students who meet minimum qualifications, the Law School could achieve its vision of the racially aesthetic student body without the use of racial discrimination. The Law School concedes this, but the Court holds, implicitly and under the guise of narrow tailoring, that the Law School has a compelling state interest in doing what it wants to do. I cannot agree. First, under strict scrutiny, the Law School's assessment of the benefits of racial discrimination and devotion to the admissions status quo are not entitled to any sort of deference, grounded in the First Amendment or anywhere else. Second, even if its "academic selectivity" must be maintained at all costs along with racial discrimination, the Court ignores the fact that other top law schools have succeeded in meeting their aesthetic demands without racial discrimination.

A

The Court bases its unprecedented deference to the Law School—a deference antithetical to strict scrutiny—on an idea of "educational autonomy" grounded in the First Amendment. In my view, there is no basis for a right of public universities to do what would otherwise violate the Equal Protection Clause. . . .

B

1

The Court's deference to the Law School's conclusion that its racial experimentation leads to educational benefits will, if adhered to, have serious collateral consequences. The Court relies heavily on social science evidence to justify its deference. The Court never acknowledges, however, the growing evidence that racial (and other sorts) of heterogeneity actually impairs learning among black students. [Justice

Thomas cites studies showing that black students attending historically black colleges (HBCs) report higher academic achievement than those attending predominantly white colleges.] . . . .

The majority grants deference to the Law School's "assessment that diversity will, in fact, yield educational benefits." It follows, therefore, that an HBC's assessment that racial homogeneity will yield educational benefits would similarly be given deference. An HBC's rejection of white applicants in order to maintain racial homogeneity seems permissible, therefore, under the majority's view of the Equal Protection Clause. But see United States v. Fordice. (Thomas, J., concurring) ("Obviously, a State cannot maintain . . . traditions by closing particular institutions, historically white or historically black, to particular racial groups"). Contained within today's majority opinion is the seed of a new constitutional justification for a concept I thought long and rightly rejected—racial segregation. . . .

C

The sky has not fallen at Boalt Hall at the University of California, Berkeley. Prior to Proposition 209's adoption of Cal. Const., Art. 1, §31(a), which bars the State from "grant[ing] preferential treatment . . . on the basis of race . . . in the operation of . . . public education," Boalt Hall enrolled 20 blacks and 28 Hispanics in its first-year class for 1996. In 2002, without deploying express racial discrimination in admissions, Boalt's entering class enrolled 14 blacks and 36 Hispanics. Total underrepresented minority student enrollment at Boalt Hall now exceeds 1996 levels. Apparently the Law School cannot be counted on to be as resourceful. The Court is willfully blind to the very real experience in California and elsewhere, which raises the inference that institutions with "reputation[s] for excellence," rivaling the Law School's have satisfied their sense of mission without resorting to prohibited racial discrimination.

V

Putting aside the absence of any legal support for the majority's reflexive deference, there is much to be said for the view that the use of tests and other measures to "predict" academic performance is a poor substitute for a system that gives every applicant a chance to prove he can succeed in the study of law. The rallying cry that in the absence of racial discrimination in admissions there would be a true meritocracy ignores the fact that the entire process is poisoned by numerous exceptions to "merit." For example, in the national debate on racial discrimination in higher education admissions, much has been made of the fact that elite institutions utilize a so-called "legacy" preference to give the children of alumni an advantage in admissions. This, and other, exceptions to a "true" meritocracy give the lie to protestations that merit admissions are in fact the order of the day at the Nation's universities. The

Equal Protection Clause does not, however, prohibit the use of unseemly legacy preferences or many other kinds of arbitrary admissions procedures. What the Equal Protection Clause does prohibit are classifications made on the basis of race. So while legacy preferences can stand under the Constitution, racial discrimination cannot. I will not twist the Constitution to invalidate legacy preferences or otherwise impose my vision of higher education admissions on the Nation. The majority should similarly stay its impulse to validate faddish racial discrimination the Constitution clearly forbids.

In any event, there is nothing ancient, honorable, or constitutionally protected about "selective" admissions. The University of Michigan should be well aware that alternative methods have historically been used for the admission of students, for it brought to this country the German certificate system in the late-19th century . . . Under this system, a secondary school was certified by a university so that any graduate who completed the course offered by the school was offered admission to the university. The certification regime supplemented, and later virtually replaced (at least in the Midwest), the prior regime of rigorous subject-matter entrance examinations. The facially race-neutral "percent plans" now used in Texas, California, and Florida are in many ways the descendents of the certificate system.

Certification was replaced by selective admissions in the beginning of the 20th century, as universities sought to exercise more control over the composition of their student bodies. Since its inception, selective admissions has been the vehicle for racial, ethnic, and religious tinkering and experimentation by university administrators. The initial driving force for the relocation of the selective function from the high school to the universities was the same desire to select racial winners and losers that the Law School exhibits today. Columbia, Harvard, and others infamously determined that they had "too many" Jews, just as today the Law School argues it would have "too many" whites if it could not discriminate in its admissions process.

Columbia employed intelligence tests precisely because Jewish applicants, who were predominantly immigrants, scored worse on such tests. Thus, Columbia could claim (falsely) that "[w]e have not eliminated boys because they were Jews and do not propose to do so. We have honestly attempted to eliminate the lowest grade of applicant [through the use of intelligence testing] and it turns out that a good many of the low grade men are New York City Jews." In other words, the tests were adopted with full knowledge of their disparate impact.

Similarly no modern law school can claim ignorance of the poor performance of blacks, relatively speaking, on the Law School Admissions Test (LSAT). Nevertheless, law schools continue to use the test and then attempt to "correct" for black underperformance by using racial discrimination in admissions so as to obtain their aesthetic student body. The Law School's continued adherence to measures it knows produce racially skewed results is not entitled to deference by this Court. The Law School itself admits that the test is imperfect, as it must, given that it regularly admits students who score at or below 150 (the national median) on the test. . . .

Having decided to use the LSAT, the Law School must accept the constitutional burdens that come with this decision. The Law School may freely continue to employ the LSAT and other allegedly merit-based standards in whatever fashion it likes. What the Equal Protection Clause forbids, but the Court today allows, is the use of these standards hand-in-hand with racial discrimination. An infinite variety of admissions methods are available to the Law School. Considering all of the radical thinking that has historically occurred at this country's universities, the Law School's intractable approach toward admissions is striking. . . .

VI

The absence of any articulated legal principle supporting the majority's principal holding suggests another rationale. I believe what lies beneath the Court's decision today are the benighted notions that one can tell when racial discrimination benefits (rather than hurts) minority groups, and that racial discrimination is necessary to remedy general societal ills. This Court's precedents supposedly settled both issues, but clearly the majority still cannot commit to the principle that racial classifications are *per se* harmful and that almost no amount of benefit in the eye of the beholder can justify such classifications.

Putting aside what I take to be the Court's implicit rejection of *Adarand*'s holding that beneficial and burdensome racial classifications are equally invalid, I must contest the notion that the Law School's discrimination benefits those admitted as a result of it. The Court spends considerable time discussing the impressive display of *amicus* support for the Law School in this case from all corners of society. But nowhere in any of the filings in this Court is any evidence that the purported "beneficiaries" of this racial discrimination prove themselves by performing at (or even near) the same level as those students who receive no preferences.

The silence in this case is deafening to those of us who view higher education's purpose as imparting knowledge and skills to students, rather than a communal, rubber-stamp, credentialing process. The Law School is not looking for those students who, despite a lower LSAT score or undergraduate grade point average, will succeed in the study of law. The Law School seeks only a facade—it is sufficient that the class looks right, even if it does not perform right.

The Law School tantalizes unprepared students with the promise of a University of Michigan degree and all of the opportunities that it offers. These overmatched students take the bait, only to find that they cannot succeed in the cauldron of competition. And this mismatch crisis is not restricted to elite institutions. Indeed, to cover the tracks of the aestheticists, this cruel farce of racial discrimination must continue—in selection for the Michigan Law Review, see University of Michigan Law School Student Handbook 2002-2003, pp. 39-40 (noting the presence of a "diversity plan" for admission to the review), and in hiring at law firms and for judicial clerkships—until the "beneficiaries" are no longer tolerated. While these students may graduate with law degrees, there is no evidence that they have received a qualitatively better legal education (or become better lawyers) than if they had gone to a less "elite" law school for which they were better prepared. And the aestheticists will never address the real problems facing "underrepresented minorities," instead continuing their social experiments on other people's children. . . .

It is uncontested that each year, the Law School admits a handful of blacks who would be admitted in the absence of racial discrimination. Who can differentiate between those who belong and those who do not? The majority of blacks are admitted to the Law School because of discrimination, and because of this policy all are tarred as undeserving. This problem of stigma does not depend on determinacy as to whether those stigmatized are actually the "beneficiaries" of racial discrimination. When blacks take positions in the highest places of government, industry, or academia, it is an open question today whether their skin color played a part in their advancement. The question itself is the stigma—because either racial discrimination did play a role, in which case the person may be deemed "otherwise unqualified," or it did not, in which case asking the question itself unfairly marks those blacks who would succeed without discrimination. Is this what the Court means by "visibly open"? . . .

VII . . . .

For the immediate future, [the] majority has placed its *imprimatur* on a practice that can only weaken the principle of equality embodied in the Declaration of Independence and the Equal Protection Clause. "Our Constitution is color-blind, and neither knows nor tolerates classes among citizens." *Plessy v. Ferguson* (Harlan, J., dissenting). It has been nearly 140 years since Frederick Douglass asked the intellectual ancestors of the Law School to "[d]o nothing with us!" and the Nation adopted the Fourteenth Amendment. Now we must wait another 25 years to see this principle of equality [vindicated].

GRATZ v. BOLLINGER, 539 U.S. ___ (2003). In this companion case to *Grutter,* the Court invalidated the affirmative action plan used by the undergraduate college of liberal arts and sciences at the University of Michigan. The University ranked college applicants according to a 150 point scale. Students receiving over 100 points were generally admitted, while those receiving under 75 points were generally delayed or rejected. Applicants received points based upon factors like high school grade point average, standardized test scores, the academic quality of an applicant's high school, in-state residency and alumni relationships. Up to 110 points could be assigned for academic performance, and up to 40 points could be assigned for the other, nonacademic factors. Michigan residents, for example, received 10 points, and children of alumni received 4. Counselors could assign an outstanding essay up to 3 points and could award up to 5 points for an applicant's personal achievement, leadership, or public service. An applicant automatically received a 20 point bonus if he or she possesses any one of the following "miscellaneous" factors: membership in an underrepresented minority group; attendance at a predominantly minority or disadvantaged high school; or recruitment for athletics.

This point system was supplemented by the review of some applications by an Admissions Review Committee (ARC). Under this system, some applications were "flagged" for review by the Committee if it was determined that the applicant was academically prepared to succeed at the University, had received a minimum index score, and possessed characteristics important to the University's composition of its freshman class, such as high class rank, unique life experiences, challenges, circumstances, interests or talents, socioeconomic disadvantage, and underrepresented race, ethnicity, or geography. The Committee reviewed "flagged" applications and determined whether to admit or deny each applicant.

Chief Justice Rehnquist delivered the opinion of the Court: "Justice Powell's opinion in *Bakke* emphasized the importance of considering each particular applicant as an individual, assessing all of the qualities that individual possesses, and in turn, evaluating that individual's ability to contribute to the unique setting of higher education. . . .

"The [challenged] policy does not provide such individualized consideration. The [policy] automatically distributes 20 points to every single applicant from an 'underrepresented minority' group, as defined by the University. The only consideration that accompanies this distribution of points is a factual review of an application to determine whether an individual is a member of one of these minority groups. Moreover, unlike Justice Powell's example, where the race of a 'particular black applicant' could be considered without being decisive, see *Bakke*, the [University's] automatic distribution of 20 points has the effect of making 'the factor of race . . . decisive' for virtually every minimally qualified underrepresented minority applicant.

"Respondents emphasize the fact that the [college] has created the possibility of an applicant's file being flagged for individualized consideration by the ARC. . . .

"But the fact that the 'review committee can look at the applications individually and ignore the points,' once an application is flagged, is of little comfort under our strict scrutiny analysis. The record does not reveal precisely how many applications are flagged for this individualized consideration, but it is undisputed that such consideration is the exception and not the [rule]. Additionally, this individualized review is only provided *after* admissions counselors automatically distribute the University's version of a 'plus' that makes race a decisive factor for virtually every minimally qualified underrepresented minority applicant.

"Respondents contend that '[t]he volume of applications and the presentation of applicant information make it impractical for [the College] to use the . . . admissions system' upheld by the Court today in *Grutter*. But the fact that the implementation of a program capable of providing individualized consideration might present administrative challenges does not render constitutional an otherwise problematic system."

Justice O'Connor wrote a concurring opinion: "Although the Office of Undergraduate Admissions does assign 20 points to some 'soft' variables other than race, the points available for other diversity contributions, such as leadership and service, personal achievement, and geographic diversity, are capped at much lower levels. Even the most outstanding national high school leader could never receive more than five points for his or her accomplishments—a mere quarter of the points automatically assigned to an underrepresented minority solely based on the fact of his or her race. Of course, as Justice Powell made clear in *Bakke*, a university need not 'necessarily accor[d]' all diversity factors 'the same weight,' and the 'weight attributed to a particular quality may vary from year to year depending on the "mix" both of the student body and the applicants for the incoming class.' But the selection index, by setting up automatic, predetermined point allocations for the soft variables, ensures that the diversity contributions of applicants cannot be individually assessed. This policy stands in sharp contrast to the law school's admissions plan, which enables admissions officers to make nuanced judgments with respect to the contributions each applicant is likely to make to the diversity of the incoming class."

Justices Thomas and Breyer also wrote concurring opinions.

Justice Souter, joined by Justice Ginsburg, dissented: "The record does not describe a system with a quota like the one struck down in *Bakke*, which 'insulate[d]' all nonminority candidates from competition from certain seats. [The] *Bakke* plan 'focused *solely* on ethnic diversity' and effectively told nonminority applicants that '[n]o matter how strong their qualifications, quantitative and extracurricular, including their own potential for contribution to educational diversity, they are never afforded the chance to compete with applicants from the preferred [groups].'

"The plan here, in contrast, lets all applicants compete for all places and values an applicant's offerings for any place not solely on the grounds of [race]. A nonminority applicant who scores highly in [other] categories can readily garner a selection index exceeding that of a minority applicant who gets the 20-point bonus. . . .

"The very nature of a college's permissible practice of awarding value to racial diversity means that race must be considered in a way that increases some applicants' chances for admission. Since college admission is not left entirely to inarticulate intuition, it is hard to see what is inappropriate in assigning some stated value to a relevant characteristic, whether it be reasoning ability, writing style, running speed, or minority race. [The] college simply does by a numbered scale what the law school accomplishes in its 'holistic review'; the distinction does not imply that applicants to the undergraduate college are denied individualized consideration or a fair chance to compete on the basis of all the various merits their applications may disclose. . . .

"[In] contrast to the college's forthrightness in saying just what plus factor it gives for membership in an underrepreseted minority, it is worth considering the character of one alternative thrown up as preferable, because supposedly not based on race. Drawing on admissions systems used at public universities in California, Florida, and Texas, the United States contends that Michigan could get student diversity [by] guaranteeing admission to a fixed percentage of the top students from each high school in Michigan.

"While there is nothing unconstitutional about such a practice, it nonetheless suffers from a serious disadvantage. It is the disadvantage of deliberate obfuscation. The 'percentage plans' are just as race conscious as the point system (and fairly so), but they get their racially diverse results without saying directly what they are doing or why they are doing it. In contrast, Michigan states its purpose directly and, if this were a doubtful case for me, I would be tempted to give Michigan an extra point of its own for its frankness. Equal protection cannot become an exercise in which the winners are the ones who hide the ball."

Justice Ginsburg, joined by Justice Souter, also dissented: "The stain of generations of racial oppression is still visible in our society, and the determination to hasten its removal remains vital. One can reasonably anticipate, therefore, that colleges and universities will seek to maintain their minority enrollment—and the networks and opportunities thereby opened to minority graduates—whether or not they can do so in full candor through adoption of affirmative action plans of the kind here at issue. Without recourse to such plans, institutions of higher education may resort to camouflage. For example, schools may encourage applicants to write of their cultural traditions in the essays they submit, or to indicate whether English is their second language. Seeking to improve their chances for admission, applicants may highlight the minority group associations to which they belong, or the Hispanic surnames of their mothers or grandparents. In turn, teachers' recommendations may emphasize who a student is as much as what he or she has accomplished. If honesty is the best policy, surely Michigan's accurately described, fully disclosed College affirmative action program is preferable to achieving similar numbers through winks, nods, and disguises."

In an opinion joined by Justice Souter, Justice Stevens dissented on the ground that the plaintiffs lacked standing.

Page 592.   Before section 3 of the Note, add the following:

Consider in this connection Katz, Race and the Right to Vote after *Rice v. Cayetano*, 99 Mich. L. Rev. 491, 503 (2000):

Rice [accepts] the Indian analogy but nevertheless insists that the OHA's electoral restriction rests on a racial classification. It holds that aboriginal Hawaiians may well enjoy a special legal or political status when receiving employment preferences or other benefits. [But] once Hawaii's native people compose an exclusive electorate for a state agency [they] are transformed (at least for purposes of judicial review) into a racial group. . . .

The decision accordingly conceives of race not as an immutable physical characteristic, but instead as a legal conclusion reached when the State organizes a group for some activities, but not others.

For an examination of the equal protection problems posed by defining membership in Indian tribes based upon racial criteria, see Gould, Mixing Bodies and Beliefs: The Predicament of Tribes, 101 Colum. L. Rev. 702 (2001).

D. Equal Protection Methodology: Heightened Scrutiny and the Problem of Gender

Page 608.   At the end of section 2c of the Note, add the following:

For a criticism of the Court's reliance on the race analogy, see Siegel, She the People: The Nineteenth Amendment, Sex Equality, Federalism, and the Family, 115 Harv. L. Rev. 949, 960 (2002). Siegel argues that seeing gender discrimination through the lens of race

[obscures] the extent to which gender status regulation had its own constitutional and common law history and distinctive social forms. Doctrinal effacement of this history [has] two important consequences. By enjoining sex discrimination on the ground that it resembled race discrimination prohibited by the Fourteenth Amendment, the Court suggested that the new body of sex discrimination doctrine lacked independent grounding in our constitutional history. At the same time, the Court's effort to reason by analogy deflected attention from the ways that race and gender status regulation intersect and [differ].

Instead of focusing on the fourteenth amendment alone, Siegel advocates a "synthetic" approach that reads the fourteenth amendment against the backdrop of the struggle to attain women's suffrage, which culminated in the nineteenth amendment. (For a more general defense of an approach that attempts to integrate language from different parts of the constitutional text, see Amar, Intratextualism, 112 Harv. L. Rev. 748 (1999).) Of course, on its face, the nineteenth amendment does no more than guarantee women the right to vote. But Siegel argues that its adoption constituted a rejection of two interrelated arguments: that men adequately represented women within the family, and that the family, as so understood, was immune from federal regulation. Rejection of these arguments, in turn, should be read back into the fourteenth amendment conception of equality.

What practical difference would this regrounding of gender discrimination doctrine make? Siegel argues that her approach would extend equal protection review beyond suspicion of gender-based classifications:

> [Sex] discrimination doctrine grounded in a synthetic interpretation of the Fourteenth and Nineteenth Amendments, and in an understanding of the history of the woman suffrage campaign might accord heightened scrutiny to state action regulating the family that denies women "full citizenship stature" or that perpetuates the "legal, social, and economic inferiority of women."

Id. at 1044 (quoting United States v. Virginia, 518 U.S. 532, 534 (1996)).

Given that the language of the Nineteenth Amendment more nearly tracks the language of the Fifteenth Amendment, which has been given an extremely narrow reading (protecting against racial discrimination only in formal participation in the political process), does reading the Nineteenth Amendment in tandem with the Fourteenth Amendment instead raise interpretive problems?

Page 610.   At the end of section 3 of the Note, add the following:

May a state permit the establishment of a gender-segregated charter school? For an analysis, see Brown-Nagin, Toward a Pragmatic Understanding of Status-Consciousness: The Case of Deregulated Education, 50 Duke L.J. 753, 802-831 (2000).

Page 619.   At the end of section 1 of the Note, add the following:

In Hasday, The Principle and Practice of Women's "Full Citizenship": A Case Study of Sex-Segregated Public Education, 101 Mich. L. Rev. 755, 757-58 (2002), the author points out that "[the] practice of sex-segregated public education [has] historically been entangled in both racial and class stratification" and suggests that "a decisionmaker regulating single-sex public schools [would] be well-advised to consider whether some or all of those schools have different consequences for different groups of women." The author also argues that historically "the differences [between] sex-segregated and coeducational public education [may be] relatively unimportant in terms of their substantive impact on women's status." If this remains true, "it is hard to see why a jurisprudence committed to women's 'full citizenship' would want to emphasize form by absolutely prohibiting sex-segregated public schooling, or how transferring all public school students to coeducational schools would advance women's 'full citizenship stature' and fight their 'inferiority.'"

Page 624.   Before the Note, add the following:

In the case that follows, the Court answered the question that *Miller* left unresolved.

NGUYEN v. IMMIGRATION AND NATURALIZATION SERVICE, 533 U.S. 33 (2001). Nguyen was a nonmarital child, born in Vietnam to his father, who was a U.S. citizen, and his mother, a citizen of Vietnam. When he was six, he came to the United States, became a lawful permanent resident, and was raised by his father. At age 22, he was convicted of two counts of sexual assault on a child. The Immigration and Naturalization Service thereupon initiated deportation proceedings against him as an alien who had been convicted of crimes of moral turpitude. While the matter was pending, the father obtained an order of parentage from state court based on a DNA test that conclusively demonstrated paternity. The Board of Immigration Appeals nonetheless rejected Nguyen's claim to U.S. citizenship because he failed to meet the requirements of citizenship for nonmarital children born abroad to a citizen father and noncitizen mother. (The requirements are set out on pages 621-622 of the main volume.) Both Nguyen and his father challenged the constitutionality of this determination.

In a five-to-four decision, the Court, in an opinion written by Justice Kennedy, held that the statute was consistent with the constitutional guarantee of equal protection.

Justice Kennedy began his analysis by noting the familiar requirements that gender-based classifications serve important governmental objectives and be substantially related to the achievement of those objectives. "The first governmental interest to be served [by the statute] is the importance of assuring that a biological parent-child relationship exists. In the case of the mother, the relation is verifiable from the birth itself. . . .

"In the case of the father, the uncontestable fact is that he need not be present at the birth. If he is present, furthermore, that circumstance is not incontrovertible proof of fatherhood. . . .

"Petitioners argue that the requirement of [the statute] that a father provide clear and convincing evidence of parentage is sufficient to achieve the end of establishing paternity, given the sophistication of modern DNA tests. [The statute] does not actually mandate a DNA test, however. The Constitution, moreover, does not require that Congress elect one particular mechanism from among many possible methods of establishing paternity, even if that mechanism arguably might be the most scientifically advanced method. With respect to DNA testing, the expense, reliability, and availability of such testing in various parts of the world may have been a particular concern of Congress. . . .

"[To] require Congress to speak without reference to the gender of the parent with regard to its objective of ensuring a blood tie between parent and child would be to insist on a hollow neutrality.

"[Congress] could have required both mothers and fathers to provide parenthood within 30 days or, for that matter, 18 years, of the child's birth. Given that the mother is always present at birth, but that the father need not be, the facially neutral rule would sometimes require fathers to take additional affirmative steps which would not be required of [mothers]. Just as neutral terms can mark discrimination that is unlawful, gender specific terms can mark a permissible distinction. [Here,] the use of gender specific terms takes into account a biological difference between the parents. The differential treatment is inherent in a sensible statutory scheme, given the unique relationship of the mother to the event of birth.

"The second important governmental interest furthered in a substantial manner by [the statute] is the determination to ensure that the child and the citizen parent have some demonstrated opportunity or potential to develop not just a relationship that is recognized, as a formal matter, by the law, but one that consists of the real, everyday ties that provide a connection between child and citizen parent and, in turn, the United States. In the case of a citizen mother and a child born overseas, the opportunity for a meaningful relationship between citizen parent and child inheres in the very event of birth, an event so often critical to our constitutional and statutory understandings of citizenship. The mother knows that the child is in being and is hers and has an initial point of contact with him. There is at least an opportunity for mother and child to develop a real, meaningful relationship.

"The same opportunity does not result from the event of birth, as a matter of biological inevitability, in the case of the unwed father. Given the 9-month interval between conception and birth, it is not always certain that a father will know that a child was conceived, nor is it always clear that even the mother will be sure of the father's identity. This fact takes on particular significance in the case of a child born overseas and out of wedlock. One concern in this context has always been with young people, men for the most part, who are on duty with the Armed Forces in foreign countries.

"[The] passage of time has produced additional and even more substantial grounds to justify the statutory distinction. The ease of travel and the willingness of Americans to visit foreign countries have resulted in numbers of trips abroad that must be of real concern when we contemplate the prospect of accepting petitioners' argument, which would mandate, contrary to Congress' wishes, citizenship by male parentage subject to no condition save the father's previous length of residence in this country. . . .

"The importance of the governmental interest at issue here is too profound to be satisfied merely by conducting a DNA test. [Scientific] proof of biological paternity does nothing, by itself, to ensure contact between father and child during the child's minority. . . .

"[This] difference does not result from some stereotype, defined as a frame of mind resulting from irrational or uncritical analysis. There is nothing irrational or improper in the recognition that at the moment of birth—the critical event in the statutory scheme and in the whole tradition of citizenship law—the mother's knowledge of the child and the fact of parenthood have been established in a way not guaranteed in the case of the unwed father. This is not a stereotype. . . .

"[The] question remains whether the means Congress chose to further its objective—the imposition of certain additional requirements upon an unwed father—substantially relate to [the ends of the statute].

"[It] should be unsurprising that Congress decided to require that an opportunity for a parent-child relationship occur during the formative years of the child's minority. . . .

"[Petitioners] assert that, although a mother will know of her child's birth, 'knowledge that one is a parent, no matter how it is acquired, does not guarantee a relationship with one's child.' They thus maintain that imposition of the additional requirements of [the statute] only on the children of citizen fathers must reflect a stereotype that women are more likely than men to actually establish a relationship with their children.

"[Congress] would of course be entitled to advance the interest of ensuring an actual, meaningful relationship in every case before citizenship is conferred. Or Congress could excuse compliance with the formal requirements when an actual father-child relationship is proved. It did neither here, perhaps because of the subjectivity, intrusiveness, and difficulties of proof that might attend an inquiry into any particular bond or tie. Instead, Congress enacted an easily administered scheme to promote the different but still substantial interest of ensuring at least an opportunity for a parent-child relationship to develop. . . .

"To fail to acknowledge even our most basic biological differences—such as the fact that a mother must be present at birth but the father need not be—risks making the guarantee of equal protection superficial, and so disserving it. Mechanistic classification of all our differences as stereotypes would operate to obscure those misconceptions and prejudices that are real. The distinction embodied in the statutory scheme here at issue is not marked by misconception and prejudice, nor does it show disrespect for either class. The difference between men and women in relation to the birth process is a real one, and the principle of equal protection does not forbid Congress to address the problem at hand in a manner specific to each gender."

Justice O'Connor, joined by Justices Souter, Ginsburg, and Breyer, dissented:

99

"While the Court invokes heightened scrutiny, the manner in which it explains and applies this standard is a stranger to our precedents. . . .

"Sex-based statutes, even when accurately reflecting the way most men or women behave, deny individuals opportunity. Such generalizations must be viewed not in isolation, but in the context of our nation's 'long and unfortunate history of sex discrimination' [quoting *Frontiero*]. . . .

"It is [difficult] to see how [the statute's] limitation of the time allowed for obtaining proof of paternity substantially furthers the assurance of a blood relationship. Modern DNA testing, in addition to providing accuracy unmatched by other methods of establishing a biological link, essentially negates the evidentiary significance of the passage of time. . . .

"[Petitioners'] argument does not depend on the idea that one particular method of establishing paternity is constitutionally required. Petitioners' argument rests instead on the fact that, if the goal is to obtain proof of paternity, the existence of a statutory provision governing such proof, coupled with the efficacy and availability of modern technology, is highly relevant to the sufficiency of the tailoring between [the statute's] sex-based classification and the asserted end. . . .

"In our prior cases, the existence of comparable or superior sex-neutral alternatives has been a powerful reason to reject a sex-based classification. The majority, however, turns this principle on its head by denigrating as 'hollow' the very neutrality that the law requires. While the majority trumpets the availability of superior sex-neutral alternatives as confirmation of [the statute's] validity, our precedents demonstrate that this fact is a decided strike against the law. Far from being 'hollow,' the avoidance of gratuitous sex-based distinctions is the hallmark of equal protection. . . .

"The [majority's] discussion [demonstrates] that, at most, differential impact will result from the fact that '[f]athers and mothers are not similarly situated with regard to the proof of biological parenthood.' [But] facially neutral laws that have a disparate impact are a different animal for purposes of constitutional analysis than laws that specifically provide for disparate treatment. . . .

"Assuming as the majority does, that Congress was actually concerned about ensuring a 'demonstrated opportunity' for a relationship, it is questionable whether such an opportunity qualifies as an 'important' governmental interest apart from the existence of an actual relationship. [It] is difficult to see how [anyone] profits from a 'demonstrated opportunity' for a relationship in the absence of the fruition of an actual tie. . . .

"Even if it is important 'to require that an opportunity for a parent-child relationship occur during the formative years of the child's minority,' it is difficult to see how the requirement that proof of such opportunity be obtained before the child turns 18 substantially furthers the asserted interest. . . .

"Moreover, available sex-neutral alternatives would at least replicate, and could easily exceed, whatever fit there is between [the statute's] discriminatory means and the majority's asserted end. [Congress] could simply substitute for [the statute] a requirement that the parent be present at birth or have knowledge of birth. Congress could at least allow proof of such presence or knowledge to be one way of demonstrating an opportunity for a relationship. [Indeed], the idea that a mother's presence at birth supplies adequate assurance of an opportunity to develop a relationship while a father's presence at birth does not would appear to rest only on an overbroad sex-based generalization. . . .

"The claim that [the statute] substantially relates to the achievement of the goal of a 'real practical relationship' thus finds support not in biological differences but instead in a stereotype. . . .

"The majority asserts that a 'stereotype' is 'defined as a frame of mind resulting from irrational or uncritical analysis.' This Court has long recognized, however, that an impermissible stereotype may enjoy empirical support and thus be in a sense 'rational.' . . .

"Nor do stereotypes consist only of those overbroad generalizations that the reviewing court considers to 'show disrespect' for a class. [Indeed], arbitrary distinction between the sexes may rely on no identifiable generalization at all but may simply be a denial of opportunity out of pure caprice. Such a distinction, of course, would nonetheless be a classic equal protection violation."

Page 625.   At the conclusion of section 1 of the Note, add the following:

With regard to the "naturalness" of gender differences, consider the possibility that current constitutional doctrine does not deal adequately with "people for whom gender and anatomical birth sex in some way diverge." Flynn, *Trans*forming the Debate: Why We Need to Include Transgender Rights in the Struggles for Sex and Sexual Orientation Equality, 101 Colum. L. Rev. 392, 394 (2001). Flynn argues that this problem leads to the

> failure to remedy much of the discrimination experienced by women and sexual minorities, specifically the discrimination based on gender nonconformity. This failure is premised on a prevalent juridical assumption that the law should target discrimination based on sex (i.e., whether a person is anatomically male or female), rather than gender (i.e., whether a person has qualities that society considers masculine or feminine). In both law and life, though, conceptions of sex and gender are so firmly cemented together that courts' frequent refusals to address gender-based inequalities mean that much discrimination against women and sexual minorities goes unremedied.

Id. at 394-395. For a discussion of the relationship between gender discrimination and discrimination based on sexual orientation, see page 656 of the main volume.

Page 626.   Before section 3 of the Note, add the following:

In connection with these issues, consider Nevada Department of Human Resources v. Hibbs, 538 U.S. ___ (2003). At issue was whether Congress could constitutionally authorize private suits for damages against state governments under the Family and Medical Leave Act. The act authorized eligible employees to take up to 12 weeks of unpaid leave annually for the onset of a "serious health condition" in the employee's spouse, child, or parent. Congress used its powers under §5 of the fourteenth amendment to apply this prohibition to state governments. Section 5 authorizes Congress to enforce the amendment with appropriate legislation. In previous cases, the Court had held that Congress could not use its §5 powers to change substantive equal protection rights, but that it could adopt prophylactic remedial measures that proscribed facially constitutional conduct in order to prevent and deter unconstitutional conduct so long as these remedial measures were "congruent and proportional." (For a discussion of these cases, see page 220 of the main text.)

In a 6-3 decision, the Court, per Chief Justice Rehnquist, used this test to uphold Hibbs' claim for damages.

> According to evidence that was before Congress, [States] continue to rely on invalid gender stereotypes in the employment context, specifically in the administration of leave benefits. . . .
>
> Congress [heard] testimony that "[p]arental leave for fathers . . . is rare. Even . . . [w]here child-care leave policies do exist, men, *both in the public and private sectors*, receive notoriously discriminatory treatment in their requests for such leave." [Many] States offer women extended "maternity" leave that far exceeded the typical 4- to 8-week period of physical disability due to pregnancy and childbirth, but very few States grant men a parallel [benefit]. This and other differential leave policies were not attributable to any differential physical needs of men and women, but rather to the pervasive sex-role stereotype that caring for family members is women's work.

Given the social roles commonly played by men and women, are the state practices upon which the Court relies evidence of gender discrimination or are they, instead, efforts to respond to gender discrimination? According to Chief Justice Rehnquist,

> [Mutually] reenforcing stereotypes [that women have domestic responsibilities and men do not] created a self-fulfilling cycle of discrimination that forced women to continue to assume the role of primary family caregiver, and fostered employers' stereotypical views about women's commitment to work and their value as employees . . . .
>
> By creating an across-the-board routine employment benefit for all eligible employees, Congress sought to ensure that family-care leave would no longer be

stigmatized as an inordinate drain on the workplace caused by female employees, that the employers could not evade leave obligations simply by hiring men.

In the Court's view, a simple requirement that states administer leave benefits in a gender neutral fashion would not solve this problem:

> Such a law would allow States to provide for no family leave at all. Where "[t]wo thirds of the nonprofessional caregivers for older, chronically ill, or disabled persons are working women" and state practices continue to reinforce the stereotype of women as caregivers, such a policy would exclude far more women than men from the workplace.

Why is this fact relevant? Isn't this mode of analysis in tension with the Court's own conclusion that official recognition of different social roles performed by men and women serves to reenforce stereotypes about those roles? In light of the statistics cited by the Court, would it be constitutional for Congress to mandate caretaker leave for women but not for men?

E. Equal Protection Methodology: The Problem of Sexual Orientation

Page 652.   Before subsection b of the Note, add the following:

The Court overruled *Bowers* in Lawrence v. Texas, 539 U.S. ___ (2003). The opinion is excerpted at the Supplement to page 901 of the main text.

Page 657.   At the end of section 4 of the Note, add the following:

For a skeptical examination of the gender discrimination argument, see Stein, Evaluating the Sex Discrimination Argument for Lesbian and Gay Rights, 49 UCLA L. Rev. 471 (2001).

In Flynn, *Trans*forming the Debate: Why We Need to Include Transgender Rights in the Struggles for Sex and Sexual Orientation Equality, 101 Colum. L. Rev. 392 (2001), the author argues that the law should focus on "transgendered" individuals. People are "transgendered" when their "appearance, behavior, or other personal characteristics differ from traditional gender norms." Id. at 392. Flynn argues that focusing on transgender discrimination

addresses a rather astonishing gap in sex and sexual orientation equality jurisprudence: The failure to remedy much of the discrimination experienced by women
and sexual minorities [based] on gender nonconformity. [Transgender] rights
cases [challenge] the sex system by presenting the courts with people for whom
gender and anatomical birth sex in some way diverge. The typical conceptualiza-
tion of sex, a doctor's peek at a newborn's genitals, is simply a form of shorthand
that [is] [an] oversimplification that fails to capture the multitude of factors that
constitute sex. Most crucially, this shorthand overlooks a person's gender identification, one's internal sense of being male or female.

Id. at 394.

F.   Equal Protection Methodology: Other Candidates for Heightened Scrutiny

Page 668.   At the end of section 1 of the Note, add the following:

In the wake of September 11, the President ordered the establishment of military
tribunals with jurisdiction to try aliens, but not American citizens, for, inter alia, engaging in acts of "international terrorism." (The order is discussed at greater length
in the supplement to page 352 of the main volume). In light of *Mathews*, is there a
plausible argument that the order unconstitutionally discriminates against nonciti-
zens? Consider Katyal & Tribe, Waging War, Deciding Guilt: Trying the Military
Tribunals, 111 Yale L. J. 1259, 1300-01 (2002):

> [Deferential] review of federal distinctions between citizens and aliens [has] its
> roots in the wide berth accorded the political branches "in the area of immigration
> and naturalization" [citing *Mathews*]. When a categorical preference for American
> citizens cannot be justified in terms of immigration and naturalization policy or as
> an adjunct to our international bargaining posture, the basis for relaxing the scru-
> tiny otherwise applicable to discrimination against aliens as a class [evaporates].
>   Even more important, the decisions manifesting relaxed [scrutiny] of federal
> discrimination [have] involved nothing beyond the preferential availability to our
> own citizens of government employment or other socioeconomic benefits that do
> not touch the raw never of equal justice under [law]. Crucially, the Military Order
> curtails rights that, at least when made available to others similarly situated, have
> long been deemed too fundamental to be dispensed with on a merely rational ba-
> sis. For a more general criticism of the government's treatment of aliens in the

wake of the World Trade Center attack, see Cole, Enemy Aliens, 54 Stan. L. Rev. 953 (2002).

Page 683.   At the end of section 2 of the Note, add the following:

Consider the accuracy of the following description of how the Court goes about deciding which groups to protect:

> [The] present Court [is] reluctant to strike down particular discriminations so long as the minority group is totally marginalized and powerless. [Once] an historically excluded group shows political clout and cultural and economic resonance, however, the Court becomes sensitive to discriminations against the group and increasingly willing to nullify some such discriminations at the retail level, but remains unenthusiastic about insisting on radical, or wholesale, revisions. Such revisions would be risky for the Court, because people whose status or values depend on discriminating against the minority group will be riled by any big constitutional entitlement for the group. The Court's current strategy is to send up trial balloons and to see what happens.

Eskridge, Destabilizing Due Process and Evolutive Equal Protection, 47 UCLA L. Rev. 1183, 1216-17 (2000).

Page 683.   Before section 3 of the Note, add the following:

Consider the suggestion in Dorf, Equal Protection Incorporation, 88 Va. L. Rev. 951 (2002), that the Court can give the strict scrutiny doctrine principled content by "incorporating" other provisions of the Constitution into equal protection analysis. Under this approach, the first, fourteenth and nineteenth amendments make discrimination based upon religion, race, color, previous condition of servitude, and sex presumptively unconstitutional. Moreover, the twenty sixth amendment raises important questions about the constitutionality of age discrimination. For another discussion of how the equal protection and due process clauses inform on another, see Karlan, Equal Protection, Due Process, and the Stereoscopic Fourteenth Amendment, 33 McGeorge L. Rev. 473 (2002).

6
IMPLIED FUNDAMENTAL RIGHTS

E. Fundamental Interests and the Equal Protection Clause

Page 744. At the end of the Note, add the following:

3a. *Bush v. Gore.* In connection with the putative "fundamental" character of the right to vote, consider the Supreme Court's decision that brought to a conclusion the disputed presidential election of 2000. (The decision is excerpted at greater length in the material supplementing page 135 of the main volume). With the presidential candidates separated by no more than a few hundred votes and the deadline for the casting of electoral ballots fast approaching, the Florida Supreme Court ordered a state-wide, manual recount of all ballots on which the voting machines had failed to detect a vote for president. In Bush v. Gore, 531 U.S. 98 (2000), the Supreme Court, in a five-to-four decision, reversed. In a per curiam opinion, joined by five justices, the Court held that the failure of the Florida Court to specify standards for determining which votes would count violated the equal protection clause:

When the state legislature vests the right to vote for President in its people, the right to vote as the legislature has prescribed is fundamental; and one source of its fundamental nature lies in the equal weight accorded to each vote and the equal dignity owned to each voter. . . .

The right to vote is protected in more than the initial allocation of the franchise. Equal protection applies as well to the manner of its exercise. Having once granted the right to vote on equal terms, the State may not, by later arbitrary and disparate treatment, value one person's vote over that of another. . . .

The recount mechanisms implemented in response to the decisions of the Florida Supreme Court do not satisfy the minimum requirement for non-arbitrary treatment of voters necessary to secure the fundamental right. [The] problem inheres in the absence of specific standards to ensure [equal] application. The formulation of uniform rules to determine intent based on [recurring] circumstances is practicable and, we conclude, necessary. . . .

Our consideration is limited to the present circumstances, for the problem of equal protection in election processes generally presents many complexities.

The question before the Court is not whether local entities, in the exercise of their expertise, may develop different systems for implementing elections. Instead, we are presented with a situation where a state court with the power to assure uniformity has ordered a statewide recount with minimal procedural safeguards. When a court orders a statewide remedy, there must be at least some assurance that the rudimentary requirements of equal treatment and fundamental fairness are satisfied.

The Court went on to hold that it was impossible to conduct a recount satisfying equal protection standards before the deadline specified in 3 U.S.C. §5, which made conclusive state resolutions of election controversies if the determination was made at least six days prior to the date for the casting of electoral votes. (By the time the Court rendered its decision, this deadline was only hours away). The Court also determined that the Florida legislature intended to take advantage of this "safe harbor." Accordingly, the Court held that the recount could not proceed. Chief Justice Rehnquist, joined by Justices Scalia and Thomas, wrote a concurring opinion. Justices Souter and Breyer both wrote opinions in which they agreed with the majority that the absence of uniform standards for the recount created constitutional difficulties. However, both would have remanded the case to the Florida court so that it could formulate such standards. Justices Ginsburg and Stevens also wrote dissenting opinions.

Page 763.   After Note 4, add the following:

5. *Bush v. Gore.* The Supreme Court's per curiam opinion in Bush v. Gore relies heavily on the Court's one-person, one-vote jurisprudence in holding that the recount ordered by the Florida Supreme Court violated the equal protection clause. (The decision is excerpted in the material supplementing page 135 of the main volume.) To what extent do these cases support the Court's result? Consider, for example, Karlan, Equal Protection: *Bush v. Gore* and the Making of a Precedent, in The Unfinished Election of 2000, at 159, 189 (J.N. Rakove ed., 2001) (suggesting that "the problem in *Gray* and *Reynolds* was not the random, one-time-only differential weighting of individuals' votes," in the context of an unprecedented and unanticipated recount that served to decrease, rather than heighten, inequalities in treatment, "but the systematic degradation of identifiable blocs of citizens' votes" and that the remedy of stopping the recount ignored the fundamental rights strand of the Court's earlier equal protection cases, which would have suggested that such a recount might

be required); Lund, The Unbearable Rightness of *Bush v. Gore*, 23 Cardozo L. Rev. 1219 (2002) (arguing that the situation in Florida resembled the "paradigmatic" and long-established equal protection violation that results from the stuffing of ballot boxes because there is no real distinction between adding illegal votes to the vote total and adding legal votes selectively as the recount ordered by the Florida Supreme Court would have done); Seidman, What's So Bad About Bush v. Gore? An Essay on Our Unsettled Election, 47 Wayne L. Rev. 953, 973, 984 (2001) (suggesting that the Court failed "to utilize any of the normal machinery of equal protection analysis" because it did not "[discuss] the relevant classes, [articulate] the appropriate level of review, . . . [determine] whether a "purpose" or "effects" test is appropriate, [or weigh] the countervailing state interest supporting the classification"); Tribe, eroG v. HsuB and Its Disguises: Freeing Bush v. Gore from Its Hall of Mirrors, 115 Harv. L. Rev. 170, 223 (2001) (arguing that the per curiam's analysis fails to comprehend that "*Reynolds* and its progeny have become increasingly sensitive to the political dimensions of the voting process, finding in the rough and tumble of party politicking over the composition of voting districts a set of 'neutral' justifications" and thus that "'one person, one vote' is not the place to find an antidote to partisanship [that would demand] . . . the sort of mechanistic, formula-driven methods of vote tabulation required by the Court in Bush v. Gore").

F. Modern Substantive Due Process

Page 901.   Before the Note, add the following:

LAWRENCE v. TEXAS
539 U.S. ___ (2003)

JUSTICE KENNEDY delivered the opinion of the Court.

Liberty protects the person from unwarranted government intrusions into a dwelling or other private places. In our tradition the State is not omnipresent in the home. And there are other spheres of our lives and existence, outside the home, where the State should not be a dominant presence. Freedom extends beyond spatial bounds. Liberty presumes an autonomy of self that includes freedom of thought, belief, expression, and certain intimate conduct. The instant case involves liberty of the person both in its spatial and more transcendent dimensions.

I

The question before the Court is the validity of a Texas statute making it a crime for two persons of the same sex to engage in certain intimate sexual conduct.

In Houston, Texas, officers of the Harris County Police Department were dispatched to a private residence in response to a reported weapons disturbance. They entered an apartment where one of the petitioners, John Geddes Lawrence, resided. The right of the police to enter does not seem to have been questioned. The officers observed Lawrence and another man, Tyron Garner, engaging in a sexual act. The two petitioners were arrested, held in custody overnight, and charged and convicted before a Justice of the Peace.

The complaints described their crime as "deviate sexual intercourse, namely anal sex, with a member of the same sex (man)." The applicable state law is Tex. Penal Code Ann. §21.06(a) (2003). It provides: "A person commits an offense if he engages in deviate sexual intercourse with another individual of the same sex." The statute defines "[d]eviate sexual intercourse" as follows:

> "(A) any contact between any part of the genitals of one person and the mouth or anus of another person; or
> "(B) the penetration of the genitals or the anus of another person with an object."
> §21.01(1). . . .

We granted certiorari, 537 U.S. 1044 (2002), to consider three questions:

> "1. Whether Petitioners' criminal convictions under the Texas "Homosexual Conduct" law—which criminalizes sexual intimacy by same-sex couples, but not identical behavior by different-sex couples—violate the Fourteenth Amendment guarantee of equal protection of laws?

> "2. Whether Petitioners' criminal convictions for adult consensual sexual intimacy in the home violate their vital interests in liberty and privacy protected by the Due Process Clause of the Fourteenth Amendment?

> "3. Whether Bowers v. Hardwick, 478 U.S. 186 (1986), should be overruled?"

The petitioners were adults at the time of the alleged offense. Their conduct was in private and consensual.

II

We conclude the case should be resolved by determining whether the petitioners were free as adults to engage in the private conduct in the exercise of their liberty under the Due Process Clause of the Fourteenth Amendment to the Constitution. For this inquiry we deem it necessary to reconsider the Court's holding in *Bowers*.

110

There are broad statements of the substantive reach of liberty under the Due Process Clause in earlier cases, including Pierce v. Society of Sisters, 268 U.S. 510 (1925), and Meyer v. Nebraska, 262 U.S. 390 (1923); but the most pertinent beginning point is our decision in Griswold v. Connecticut, 381 U.S. 479 (1965).

In *Griswold* the Court invalidated a state law prohibiting the use of drugs or devices of contraception and counseling or aiding and abetting the use of contraceptives. The Court described the protected interest as a right to privacy and placed emphasis on the marriage relation and the protected space of the marital bedroom.

After *Griswold* it was established that the right to make certain decisions regarding sexual conduct extends beyond the marital relationship. In *Eisenstadt v*. Baird, 405 U.S. 438 (1972), the Court invalidated a law prohibiting the distribution of contraceptives to unmarried persons. The case was decided under the Equal Protection Clause, but with respect to unmarried persons, the Court went on to state the fundamental proposition that the law impaired the exercise of their personal rights. It quoted from the statement of the Court of Appeals finding the law to be in conflict with fundamental human rights, and it followed with this statement of its own:

> It is true that in *Griswold* the right of privacy in question inhered in the marital relationship. . . . If the right of privacy means anything, it is the right of the *individual*, married or single, to be free from unwarranted governmental intrusion into matters so fundamentally affecting a person as the decision whether to bear or beget a child.

The opinions in *Griswold* and *Eisenstadt* were part of the background for the decision in *Roe v*. Wade, 410 U.S. 113 (1973). . . . *Roe* recognized the right of a woman to make certain fundamental decisions affecting her destiny and confirmed once more that the protection of liberty under the Due Process Clause has a substantive dimension of fundamental significance in defining the rights of the person.

In Carey v. Population Services Int'l, 431 U.S. 678 (1977), the Court confronted a New York law forbidding sale or distribution of contraceptive devices to persons under 16 years of age. Although there was no single opinion for the Court, the law was invalidated. Both *Eisenstadt* and *Carey*, as well as the holding and rationale in *Roe*, confirmed that the reasoning of *Griswold* could not be confined to the protection of rights of married adults. This was the state of the law with respect to some of the most relevant cases when the Court considered Bowers v. Hardwick. . . .

The Court began its substantive discussion in *Bowers* as follows: "The issue presented is whether the Federal Constitution confers a fundamental right upon homosexuals to engage in sodomy and hence invalidates the laws of the many States that still make such conduct illegal and have done so for a very long time." That statement, we now conclude, discloses the Court's own failure to appreciate the extent of the liberty at stake. To say that the issue in *Bowers* was simply the right to engage in certain sexual conduct demeans the claim the individual put forward, just as it would demean a married couple were it to be said marriage is simply about the right to have sexual intercourse. The laws involved in *Bowers* and there are, to be sure, statutes that purport to do no more than prohibit a particular sexual act. Their penalties and purposes, though, have more far-reaching consequences, touching upon the most private human conduct, sexual behavior, and in the most private of places, the home. The statutes do seek to control a personal relationship that, whether or not entitled to formal recognition in the law, is within the liberty of persons to choose without being punished as criminals.

This, as a general rule, should counsel against attempts by the State, or a court, to define the meaning of the relationship or to set its boundaries absent injury to a person or abuse of an institution the law protects. It suffices for us to acknowledge that adults may choose to enter upon this relationship in the confines of their homes and their own private lives and still retain their dignity as free persons. When sexuality finds overt expression in intimate conduct with another person, the conduct can be but one element in a personal bond that is more enduring. The liberty protected by the Constitution allows homosexual persons the right to make this choice.

Having misapprehended the claim of liberty there presented to it, and thus stating the claim to be whether there is a fundamental right to engage in consensual sodomy, the *Bowers* Court said: "Proscriptions against that conduct have ancient roots." In academic writings, and in many of the scholarly amicus briefs filed to assist the Court in this case, there are fundamental criticisms of [this statement.] We need not enter this debate in the attempt to reach a definitive historical judgment, but the following considerations counsel against adopting the definitive conclusions upon which *Bowers* placed such reliance.

At the outset it should be noted that there is no longstanding history in this country of laws directed at homosexual conduct as a distinct matter. Beginning in colonial times there were prohibitions of sodomy derived from the English criminal laws passed in the first instance by the Reformation Parliament of 1533. . . . The absence of legal prohibitions focusing on homosexual conduct may be explained in part by noting that according to some scholars the concept of the homosexual as a distinct category of person did not emerge until the late 19th century. See, e.g., J. Katz, The Invention of Heterosexuality 10 (1995); J. D'Emilio & E. Freedman, Intimate Matters: A History of Sexuality in America 121 (2d ed. 1997) ("The modern terms homosexuality and heterosexuality do not apply to an era that had not yet articulated these distinctions"). Thus early American sodomy laws were not directed at homosexuals as such but instead sought to prohibit nonprocreative sexual activity more generally. This does not suggest approval of homosexual conduct. It does tend to show that this particular form of conduct was not thought of as a separate category from like conduct between heterosexual persons.

Laws prohibiting sodomy do not seem to have been enforced against consenting adults acting in private. A substantial number of sodomy prosecutions and convictions for which there are surviving records were for predatory acts against those who could not or did not consent, as in the case of a minor or the victim of an assault. As to these, one purpose for the prohibitions was to ensure there would be no lack of coverage if a predator committed a sexual assault that did not constitute rape as defined by the criminal law. Thus the model sodomy indictments presented in a 19th-century treatise, addressed the predatory acts of an adult man against a minor girl or minor boy. Instead of targeting relations between consenting adults in private, 19th-century sodomy prosecutions typically involved relations between men and minor girls or minor boys, relations between adults involving force, relations between adults implicating disparity in status, or relations between men and animals.

To the extent that there were any prosecutions for the acts in question, 19th-century evidence rules imposed a burden that would make a conviction more difficult to obtain even taking into account the problems always inherent in prosecuting consensual acts committed in private. . . . In all events that infrequency makes it difficult to say that society approved of a rigorous and systematic punishment of the consensual acts committed in private and by adults. The longstanding criminal prohibition of homosexual sodomy upon which the *Bowers* decision placed such reliance is as consistent with a general condemnation of nonprocreative sex as it is with an established tradition of prosecuting acts because of their homosexual character.

The policy of punishing consenting adults for private acts was not much discussed in the early legal literature. We can infer that one reason for this was the very private nature of the conduct. Despite the absence of prosecutions, there may have been periods in which there was public criticism of homosexuals as such and an insistence that the criminal laws be enforced to discourage their practices. But far from possessing "ancient roots," *Bowers*, 478 U.S., at 192, American laws targeting same-sex couples did not develop until the last third of the 20th century. The reported decisions concerning the prosecution of consensual, homosexual sodomy between adults for the years 1880-1995 are not always clear in the details, but a significant number involved conduct in a public place.

It was not until the 1970's that any State singled out same-sex relations for criminal prosecution, and only nine States have done so. Post-*Bowers* even some of these States did not adhere to the policy of suppressing homosexual conduct. Over the course of the last decades, States with same-sex prohibitions have moved toward abolishing them.

In summary, the historical grounds relied upon in *Bowers* are more complex than the majority opinion and the concurring opinion by Chief Justice Burger indicate. Their historical premises are not without doubt and, at the very least, are overstated.

It must be acknowledged, of course, that the Court in *Bowers* was making the broader point that for centuries there have been powerful voices to condemn homosexual conduct as immoral. The condemnation has been shaped by religious beliefs, conceptions of right and acceptable behavior, and respect for the traditional family. For many persons these are not trivial concerns but profound and deep convictions

113

accepted as ethical and moral principles to which they aspire and which thus determine the course of their lives. These considerations do not answer the question before us, however. The issue is whether the majority may use the power of the State to enforce these views on the whole society through operation of the criminal law. . . .

Chief Justice Burger joined the opinion for the Court in *Bowers* and further explained his views as follows: "Decisions of individuals relating to homosexual conduct have been subject to state intervention throughout the history of Western civilization. Condemnation of those practices is firmly rooted in Judeao-Christian moral and ethical standards." As with Justice White's assumptions about history, scholarship casts some doubt on the sweeping nature of the statement by Chief Justice Burger as it pertains to private homosexual conduct between consenting adults. In all events we think that our laws and traditions in the past half century are of most relevance here. These references show an emerging awareness that liberty gives substantial protection to adult persons in deciding how to conduct their private lives in matters pertaining to sex. "[H]istory and tradition are the starting point but not in all cases the ending point of the substantive due process inquiry." County of Sacramento v. Lewis, 523 U.S. 833, 857 (1998) (Kennedy, J., concurring).

This emerging recognition should have been apparent when *Bowers* was decided. In 1955 the American Law Institute promulgated the Model Penal Code and made clear that it did not recommend or provide for "criminal penalties for consensual sexual relations conducted in private." ALI, Model Penal Code §213.2, Comment 2, p. 372 (1980). It justified its decision on three grounds: (1) The prohibitions undermined respect for the law by penalizing conduct many people engaged in; (2) the statutes regulated private conduct not harmful to others; and (3) the laws were arbitrarily enforced and thus invited the danger of blackmail. ALI, Model Penal Code, Commentary 277-280 (Tent. Draft No. 4, 1955). In 1961 Illinois changed its laws to conform to the Model Penal Code. Other States soon followed. . . .

The sweeping references by Chief Justice Burger to the history of Western civilization and to Judeo-Christian moral and ethical standards did not take account of other authorities pointing in an opposite direction. A committee advising the British Parliament recommended in 1957 repeal of laws punishing homosexual conduct. The Wolfenden Report: Report of the Committee on Homosexual Offenses and Prostitution (1963). Parliament enacted the substance of those recommendations 10 years later. Sexual Offences Act 1967, §1.

Of even more importance, almost five years before *Bowers* was decided the European Court of Human Rights considered a case with parallels to *Bowers* and to today's case. An adult male resident in Northern Ireland alleged he was a practicing homosexual who desired to engage in consensual homosexual conduct. The laws of Northern Ireland forbade him that right. He alleged that he had been questioned, his home had been searched, and he feared criminal prosecution. The court held that the laws proscribing the conduct were invalid under the European Convention on Human Rights. Dudgeon v. United Kingdom, 45 Eur. Ct. H. R. (1981) ¶52. Authoritative in all countries that are members of the Council of Europe (21 nations then, 45 nations now), the decision is at odds with the premise in *Bowers* that the claim put forward was insubstantial in our Western civilization.

In our own constitutional system the deficiencies in *Bowers* became even more apparent in the years following its announcement. The 25 States with laws prohibiting the relevant conduct referenced in the *Bowers* decision are reduced now to 13, of which 4 enforce their laws only against homosexual conduct. In those States where sodomy is still proscribed, whether for same-sex or heterosexual conduct, there is a pattern of nonenforcement with respect to consenting adults acting in private. The State of Texas admitted in 1994 that as of that date it had not prosecuted anyone under those circumstances.

Two principal cases decided after *Bowers* cast its holding into even more doubt. In *Planned Parenthood of Southeastern Pa. v. Casey*, 505 U.S. 833 (1992), the Court reaffirmed the substantive force of the liberty protected by the Due Process Clause. The *Casey* decision again confirmed that our laws and tradition afford constitutional protection to personal decisions relating to marriage, procreation, contraception, family relationships, child rearing, and education. In explaining the respect the Constitution demands for the autonomy of the person in making these choices, we stated as follows:

> These matters, involving the most intimate and personal choices a person may make in a lifetime, choices central to personal dignity and autonomy, are central to the liberty protected by the Fourteenth Amendment. At the heart of liberty is the right to define one's own concept of existence, of meaning, of the universe, and of the mystery of human life. Beliefs about these matters could not define the attributes of personhood were they formed under compulsion of the State.

Persons in a homosexual relationship may seek autonomy for these purposes, just as heterosexual persons do. The decision in *Bowers* would deny them this right.

The second post-*Bowers* case of principal relevance is *Romer v. Evans*, 517 U.S. 620 (1996). There the Court struck down class-based legislation directed at homosexuals as a violation of the Equal Protection Clause. . . .

As an alternative argument in this case, counsel for the petitioners and some amici contend that *Romer* provides the basis for declaring the Texas statute invalid under the Equal Protection Clause. That is a tenable argument, but we conclude the instant case requires us to address whether *Bowers* itself has continuing validity. Were we to hold the statute invalid under the Equal Protection Clause some might question whether a prohibition would be valid if drawn differently, say, to prohibit the conduct both between same-sex and different-sex participants.

Equality of treatment and the due process right to demand respect for conduct protected by the substantive guarantee of liberty are linked in important respects, and a decision on the latter point advances both interests. If protected conduct is made criminal and the law which does so remains unexamined for its substantive validity, its stigma might remain even if it were not enforceable as drawn for equal protection reasons. When homosexual conduct is made criminal by the law of the State, that declaration in and of itself is an invitation to subject homosexual persons to discrimination both in the public and in the private spheres. The central holding of *Bowers* has been brought in question by this case, and it should be addressed. Its continuance as precedent demeans the lives of homosexual persons.

The stigma this criminal statute imposes, moreover, is not trivial. The offense, to be sure, is but a class C misdemeanor, a minor offense in the Texas legal system. Still, it remains a criminal offense with all that imports for the dignity of the persons charged. The petitioners will bear on their record the history of their criminal convictions. . . . We are advised that if Texas convicted an adult for private, consensual homosexual conduct under the statute here in question the convicted person would come within the registration laws of at least four States were he or she to be subject to their jurisdiction. This underscores the consequential nature of the punishment and the state-sponsored condemnation attendant to the criminal prohibition. Furthermore, the Texas criminal conviction carries with it the other collateral consequences always following a conviction, such as notations on job application forms, to mention but one example.

The foundations of *Bowers* have sustained serious erosion from our recent decisions in *Casey* and *Romer*. When our precedent has been thus weakened, criticism from other sources is of greater significance. In the United States criticism of *Bowers* has been substantial and continuing, disapproving of its reasoning in all respects, not just as to its historical assumptions. The courts of five different States have declined to follow it in interpreting provisions in their own state constitutions parallel to the Due Process Clause of the Fourteenth Amendment.

To the extent *Bowers* relied on values we share with a wider civilization, it should be noted that the reasoning and holding in *Bowers* have been rejected elsewhere. The European Court of Human Rights has followed not *Bowers* but its own decision in Dudgeon v. United Kingdom. Other nations, too, have taken action consistent with an affirmation of the protected right of homosexual adults to engage in intimate, consensual conduct. The right the petitioners seek in this case has been accepted as an integral part of human freedom in many other countries. There has been no showing that in this country the governmental interest in circumscribing personal choice is somehow more legitimate or urgent.

The doctrine of stare decisis is essential to the respect accorded to the judgments of the Court and to the stability of the law. It is not, however, an inexorable command. In *Casey* we noted that when a Court is asked to overrule a precedent recognizing a constitutional liberty interest, individual or societal reliance on the existence of that liberty cautions with particular strength against reversing course. The holding in *Bowers*, however, has not induced detrimental reliance comparable to some instances where recognized individual rights are involved. Indeed, there has been no individual or societal reliance on *Bowers* of the sort that could counsel against over-turning its holding once there are compelling reasons to do so. *Bowers* itself causes uncertainty, for the precedents before and after its issuance contradict its central holding.

The rationale of *Bowers* does not withstand careful analysis. In his dissenting opinion in *Bowers* Justice Stevens came to these conclusions:

> Our prior cases make two propositions abundantly clear. First, the fact that the governing majority in a State has traditionally viewed a particular practice as im-moral is not a sufficient reason for upholding a law prohibiting the practice; nei-ther history nor tradition could save a law prohibiting miscegenation from constitutional attack. Second, individual decisions by married persons, concerning the intimacies of their physical relationship, even when not intended to produce offspring, are a form of "liberty" protected by the Due Process Clause of the Fourteenth Amendment. Moreover, this protection extends to intimate choices by unmarried as well as married persons.

Justice Stevens' analysis, in our view, should have been controlling in *Bowers* and should control here.

Bowers was not correct when it was decided, and it is not correct today. It ought not to remain binding precedent. Bowers v. Hardwick should be and now is over-ruled.

The present case does not involve minors. It does not involve persons who might be injured or coerced or who are situated in relationships where consent might not easily be refused. It does not involve public conduct or prostitution. It does not in-volve whether the government must give formal recognition to any relationship that homosexual persons seek to enter. The case does involve two adults who, with full and mutual consent from each other, engaged in sexual practices common to a ho-mosexual lifestyle. The petitioners are entitled to respect for their private lives. The State cannot demean their existence or control their destiny by making their private sexual conduct a crime. Their right to liberty under the Due Process Clause gives them the full right to engage in their conduct without intervention of the government. The Texas statute furthers no legitimate state interest which can justify its intrusion into the personal and private life of the individual.

Had those who drew and ratified the Due Process Clauses of the Fifth Amend-ment or the Fourteenth Amendment known the components of liberty in its manifold possibilities, they might have been more specific. They did not presume to have this insight. They knew times can blind us to certain truths and later generations can see that laws once thought necessary and proper in fact serve only to oppress. As the Constitution endures, persons in every generation can invoke its principles in their own search for greater freedom. . . .

JUSTICE O'CONNOR, concurring in the judgment.

The Court today overrules Bowers v. Hardwick, 478 U.S. 186 (1986). I joined *Bowers*, and do not join the Court in overruling it. Nevertheless, I agree with the Court that Texas' statute banning same-sex sodomy is unconstitutional. Rather than relying on the substantive component of the Fourteenth Amendment's Due Process Clause, as the Court does, I base my conclusion on the Fourteenth Amendment's Equal Protection Clause. . . .

This case raises a different issue than *Bowers*: whether, under the Equal Protection Clause, moral disapproval is a legitimate state interest to justify by itself a statute that bans homosexual sodomy, but not heterosexual sodomy. It is not. Moral disapproval of this group, like a bare desire to harm the group, is an interest that is insufficient to satisfy rational basis review under the Equal Protection Clause. Indeed, we have never held that moral disapproval, without any other asserted state interest, is a sufficient rationale under the Equal Protection Clause to justify a law that discriminates among groups of persons.

Moral disapproval of a group cannot be a legitimate governmental interest under the Equal Protection Clause because legal classifications must not be "drawn for the purpose of disadvantaging the group burdened by the law." Texas' invocation of moral disapproval as a legitimate state interest proves nothing more than Texas' desire to criminalize homosexual sodomy. But the Equal Protection Clause prevents a State from creating "a classification of persons undertaken for its own sake." And because Texas so rarely enforces its sodomy law as applied to private, consensual acts, the law serves more as a statement of dislike and disapproval against homosexuals than as a tool to stop criminal behavior. . . .

A State can of course assign certain consequences to a violation of its criminal law. But the State cannot single out one identifiable class of citizens for punishment that does not apply to everyone else, with moral disapproval as the only asserted state interest for the law. The Texas sodomy statute subjects homosexuals to "a lifelong penalty and stigma. . . .

A law branding one class of persons as criminal solely based on the State's moral disapproval of that class and the conduct associated with that class runs contrary to the values of the Constitution and the Equal Protection Clause, under any standard of review. I therefore concur in the Court's judgment that Texas' sodomy law banning "deviate sexual intercourse" between consenting adults of the same sex, but not between consenting adults of different sexes, is unconstitutional.

JUSTICE SCALIA, with whom THE CHIEF JUSTICE and JUSTICE THOMAS join, dissenting.

[I] begin with the Court's surprising readiness to reconsider a decision rendered a mere 17 years ago in Bowers v. Hardwick. I do not myself believe in rigid adherence to stare decisis in constitutional cases; but I do believe that we should be consistent rather than manipulative in invoking the doctrine. Today's opinions in support of reversal do not bother to distinguish—or indeed, even bother to mention—the paean to stare decisis coauthored by three Members of today's majority in Planned Parenthood v. Casey. . . .

Today's approach to stare decisis invites us to overrule an erroneously decided precedent (including an "intensely divisive" decision) if: (1) its foundations have been "eroded" by subsequent decisions; (2) it has been subject to "substantial and continuing" criticism; and (3) it has not induced "individual or societal reliance" that counsels against overturning. The problem is that *Roe* itself—which today's majority surely has no disposition to overrule—satisfies these conditions to at least the same degree as *Bowers*. . . .

I do not quarrel with the Court's claim that Romer v. Evans, 517 U.S. 620 (1996), "eroded" the "foundations" of *Bowers'* rational-basis holding. But *Roe* and *Casey* have been equally "eroded" by Washington v. Glucksberg, 521 U.S. 702, 721 (1997), which held that only fundamental rights which are "'deeply rooted in this Nation's history and tradition'" qualify for anything other than rational basis scrutiny under the doctrine of "substantive due process." *Roe* and *Casey*, of course, subjected the restriction of abortion to heightened scrutiny without even attempting to establish that the freedom to abort was rooted in this Nation's tradition.

Bowers, the Court says, has been subject to "substantial and continuing [criticism], disapproving of its reasoning in all respects, not just as to its historical assumptions." [Of] course, *Roe* too (and by extension *Casey*) had been (and still is) subject to unrelenting criticism, including criticism from the two commentators cited by the Court today.

That leaves, to distinguish the rock-solid, unamendable disposition of *Roe* from the readily overrulable *Bowers*, only the third factor. "[T]here has been," the Court says, "no individual or societal reliance on *Bowers* of the sort that could counsel against overturning its holding . . . ." It seems to me that the "societal reliance" on the principles confirmed in *Bowers* and discarded today has been overwhelming. Countless judicial decisions and legislative enactments have relied on the ancient proposition that a governing majority's belief that certain sexual behavior is "immoral and unacceptable" constitutes a rational basis for regulation. . . . State laws against bigamy, same-sex marriage, adult incest, prostitution, masturbation, adultery, fornication, bestiality, and obscenity are likewise sustainable only in light of *Bowers'* validation of laws based on moral choices. Every single one of these laws is called into question by today's decision; the Court makes no effort to cabin the scope of its decision to exclude them from its holding. The impossibility of distinguishing homosexuality from other traditional "morals" offenses is precisely why *Bowers* rejected the rational-basis challenge. . . .

What a massive disruption of the current social order, therefore, the overruling of *Bowers* entails. Not so the overruling of *Roe*, which would simply have restored the regime that existed for centuries before 1973, in which the permissibility of and restrictions upon abortion were determined legislatively State-by-State. . . .

To tell the truth, it does not surprise me, and should surprise no one, that the Court has chosen today to revise the standards of stare decisis set forth in *Casey*. It has thereby exposed *Casey*'s extraordinary deference to precedent for the result-oriented expedient that it is. . . .

Texas Penal Code Ann. §21.06(a) (2003) undoubtedly imposes constraints on liberty. So do laws prohibiting prostitution, recreational use of heroin, and, for that matter, working more than 60 hours per week in a bakery. But there is no right to "liberty" under the Due Process Clause, though today's opinion repeatedly makes that claim. The Fourteenth Amendment expressly allows States to deprive their citizens of "liberty," so long as "due process of law" is provided:

> No state shall . . . deprive any person of life, liberty, or property, *without due process of law*." Amdt. 14 (emphasis added).

Our opinions applying the doctrine known as "substantive due process" hold that the Due Process Clause prohibits States from infringing fundamental liberty interests, unless the infringement is narrowly tailored to serve a compelling state interest. We have held repeatedly, in cases the Court today does not overrule, that only fundamental rights qualify for this so-called "heightened scrutiny" protection—that is, rights which are "'deeply rooted in this Nation's history and tradition.'" All other liberty interests may be abridged or abrogated pursuant to a validly enacted state law if that law is rationally related to a legitimate state interest.

The Court's description of "the state of the law" at the time of *Bowers* only confirms that *Bowers* was right. The Court points to Griswold v. Connecticut, 381 U.S. 479, 481-482 (1965). But that case expressly disclaimed any reliance on the doctrine of "substantive due process," and grounded the so-called "right to privacy" in penumbras of constitutional provisions other than the Due Process Clause. Eisenstadt v. Baird, 405 U.S. 438 (1972), likewise had nothing to do with "substantive due process"; it invalidated a Massachusetts law prohibiting the distribution of contraceptives to unmarried persons solely on the basis of the Equal Protection Clause. Of course *Eisenstadt* contains well known dictum relating to the "right to privacy," but this referred to the right recognized in *Griswold*—a right penumbral to the specific guarantees in the Bill of Rights, and not a "substantive due process" right. . . .

After discussing the history of antisodomy laws, the Court proclaims that, "it should be noted that there is no longstanding history in this country of laws directed at homosexual conduct as a distinct matter." This observation in no way casts into doubt the "definitive [historical] conclusion," on which *Bowers* relied: that our Nation has a longstanding history of laws prohibiting sodomy in general—regardless of whether it was performed by same-sex or opposite-sex couples. . . .

It is (as *Bowers* recognized) entirely irrelevant whether the laws in our long national tradition criminalizing homosexual sodomy were "directed at homosexual conduct as a distinct matter." Whether homosexual sodomy was prohibited by a law targeted at same-sex sexual relations or by a more general law prohibiting both homosexual and heterosexual sodomy, the only relevant point is that it was criminalized—which suffices to establish that homosexual sodomy is not a right "deeply rooted in our Nation's history and tradition." The Court today agrees that homosexual sodomy was criminalized and thus does not dispute the facts on which *Bowers* actually relied.

Next the Court makes the claim, again unsupported by any citations, that "[l]aws prohibiting sodomy do not seem to have been enforced against consenting adults acting in private." The key qualifier here is "acting in private"—since the Court admits that sodomy laws were enforced against consenting adults (although the Court contends that prosecutions were "infrequent"). I do not know what "acting in private" means; surely consensual sodomy, like heterosexual intercourse, is rarely performed on stage. . . . *Bowers'* conclusion that homosexual sodomy is not a fundamental right "deeply rooted in this Nation's history and tradition" is utterly unassailable.

Realizing that fact, the Court instead says: "[W]e think that our laws and traditions in the past half century are of most relevance here. These references show *an emerging awareness* that liberty gives substantial protection to adult persons in deciding how to conduct their private lives *in matters pertaining to sex*." (emphasis added). Apart from the fact that such an "emerging awareness" does not establish a "fundamental right," the statement is factually false. States continue to prosecute all sorts of crimes by adults "in matters pertaining to sex": prostitution, adult incest, adultery, obscenity, and child pornography. Sodomy laws, too, have been enforced "in the past half century," in which there have been 134 reported cases involving prosecutions for consensual, adult, homosexual sodomy. . . .

In any event, an "emerging awareness" is by definition not "deeply rooted in this Nation's history and tradition[s]," as we have said "fundamental right" status requires. Constitutional entitlements do not spring into existence because some States choose to lessen or eliminate criminal sanctions on certain behavior. Much less do they spring into existence, as the Court seems to believe, because foreign nations decriminalize conduct. . . . The Court's discussion of these foreign views (ignoring, of course, the many countries that have retained criminal prohibitions on sodomy) is therefore meaningless dicta. . . .

I turn now to the ground on which the Court squarely rests its holding: the contention that there is no rational basis for the law here under attack. This proposition is so out of accord with our jurisprudence—indeed, with the jurisprudence of any society we know—that it requires little discussion.

The Texas statute undeniably seeks to further the belief of its citizens that certain forms of sexual behavior are "immoral and unacceptable"—the same interest furthered by criminal laws against fornication, bigamy, adultery, adult incest, bestiality, and obscenity. *Bowers* held that this was a legitimate state interest. The Court today reaches the opposite conclusion. The Texas statute, it says, "furthers no legitimate state interest which can justify its intrusion into the personal and private life of the individual." The Court embraces instead Justice Stevens' declaration in his *Bowers* dissent, that "the fact that the governing majority in a State has traditionally viewed a particular practice as immoral is not a sufficient reason for upholding a law prohibiting the practice." This effectively decrees the end of all morals legislation. If, as the Court asserts, the promotion of majoritarian sexual morality is not even a legitimate state interest, none of the above-mentioned laws can survive rational-basis review. . . .

Today's opinion is the product of a Court, which is the product of a law-profession culture, that has largely signed on to the so-called homosexual agenda, by which I mean the agenda promoted by some homosexual activists directed at eliminating the moral opprobrium that has traditionally attached to homosexual conduct. . . .

One of the most revealing statements in today's opinion is the Court's grim warning that the criminalization of homosexual conduct is "an invitation to subject homosexual persons to discrimination both in the public and in the private spheres." It is clear from this that the Court has taken sides in the culture war, departing from its role of assuring, as neutral observer, that the democratic rules of engagement are observed. Many Americans do not want persons who openly engage in homosexual conduct as partners in their business, as scoutmasters for their children, as teachers in their children's schools, or as boarders in their home. They view this as protecting themselves and their families from a lifestyle that they believe to be immoral and destructive. The Court views it as "discrimination" which it is the function of our judgments to deter. So imbued is the Court with the law profession's anti-anti-homosexual culture, that it is seemingly unaware that the attitudes of that culture are not obviously "mainstream"; that in most States what the Court calls "discrimination" against those who engage in homosexual acts is perfectly legal; that proposals to ban such "discrimination" under Title VII have repeatedly been rejected by Congress; that in some cases such "discrimination" is mandated by federal statute, see 10 U.S.C. §654(b)(1) (mandating discharge from the armed forces of any service member who engages in or intends to engage in homosexual acts); and that in some cases such "discrimination" is a constitutional right, see Boy Scouts of America v. Dale, 530 U.S. 640 (2000).

Let me be clear that I have nothing against homosexuals, or any other group, promoting their agenda through normal democratic means. Social perceptions of sexual and other morality change over time, and every group has the right to persuade its fellow citizens that its view of such matters is the best. That homosexuals have achieved some success in that enterprise is attested to by the fact that Texas is one of the few remaining States that criminalize private, consensual homosexual acts. But persuading one's fellow citizens is one thing, and imposing one's views in absence of democratic majority will is something else. I would no more require a State to criminalize homosexual acts—or, for that matter, display any moral disapprobation of them—than I would forbid it to do so. What Texas has chosen to do is well within the range of traditional democratic action, and its hand should not be stayed through the invention of a brand-new "constitutional right" by a Court that is impatient of democratic change. . . .

One of the benefits of leaving regulation of this matter to the people rather than to the courts is that the people, unlike judges, need not carry things to their logical conclusion. The people may feel that their disapprobation of homosexual conduct is strong enough to disallow homosexual marriage, but not strong enough to criminalize private homosexual acts—and may legislate accordingly. The Court today pretends that it possesses a similar freedom of action, so that we need not fear judicial imposition of homosexual marriage, as has recently occurred in Canada (in a decision that the Canadian Government has chosen not to appeal). See Halpern v. Toronto, 2003 WL 34950 (Ontario Ct. App.); Cohen, Dozens in Canada Follow Gay Couple's Lead, Washington Post, June 12, 2003, p. A25. At the end of its opinion—after having laid waste the foundations of our rational-basis jurisprudence—the Court says that the present case "does not involve whether the government must give formal recognition to any relationship that homosexual persons seek to enter." Do not believe it. More illuminating than this bald, unreasoned disclaimer is the progression of thought displayed by an earlier passage in the Court's opinion, which notes the constitutional protections afforded to "personal decisions relating to marriage, procreation, contraception, family relationships, child rearing, and education," and then declares that "[p]ersons in a homosexual relationship may seek autonomy for these purposes, just as heterosexual persons do." Today's opinion dismantles the structure of constitutional law that has permitted a distinction to be made between heterosexual and homosexual unions, insofar as formal recognition in marriage is concerned. If moral disapprobation of homosexual conduct is "no legitimate state interest" for purposes of proscribing that conduct and if, as the Court coos (casting aside all pretense of neutrality), "[w]hen sexuality finds overt expression in intimate conduct with another person, the conduct can be but one element in a personal bond that is more enduring"; what justification could there possibly be for denying the benefits of marriage to homosexual couples exercising "[t]he liberty protected by the Constitution." Surely not the encouragement of procreation, since the sterile and the elderly are allowed to marry. This case "does not involve" the issue of homosexual marriage only if one entertains the belief that principle and logic have nothing to do with the decisions of this Court. . . .

JUSTICE THOMAS, dissenting.

I join Justice Scalia's dissenting opinion. I write separately to note that the law before the Court today "is . . . uncommonly silly." Griswold v. Connecticut, 381 U.S. 479, 527 (1965) (Stewart, J., dissenting). If I were a member of the Texas Legislature, I would vote to repeal it. Punishing someone for expressing his sexual preference through noncommercial consensual conduct with another adult does not appear to be a worthy way to expend valuable law enforcement resources.

Notwithstanding this, I recognize that as a member of this Court I am not empowered to help petitioners and others similarly situated. My duty, rather, is to "decide cases 'agreeably to the Constitution and laws of the United States.'" And, just like Justice Stewart, I "can find [neither in the Bill of Rights nor any other part of the Constitution a] general right of privacy," or as the Court terms it today, the "liberty of the person both in its spatial and more transcendent dimensions."

Page 920. After section 3 of the Note, add the following:

4. *Crane.* An interesting substantive due process issue was resolved in Kansas v. Crane, 534 U.S. 407 (2002). The Kansas Sexually Violent Predator Act allows civil detention of certain sex offenders. Crane, a previously convicted sex offender, was found (by at least one of the state's psychiatric witnesses) to suffer from antisocial personality disorder and exhibitionism. A court ordered his confinement, but without finding that Crane was completely unable to control his conduct. The Supreme Court held that the due process clause did not require such a finding. At the same time, the Court required some kind of "lack-of-control determination." In the Court's view, "there must be proof of serious difficulty in controlling behavior." This difficulty might be shown by "such features of the case as the nature of the psychiatric diagnosis, and the severity of the mental abnormality itself." Without such a finding, the civil confinement would be unconstitutional. Justice Scalia, joined by Justice Thomas, disagreed, urging that it was sufficient to find that "the person previously convicted . . . is suffering from a mental abnormality or personality disorder" and that this condition "renders him likely to commit future acts of sexual violence."

5. *State Farm.* For a striking due process ruling, with strong substantive due process overtones, see State Farm Mutual Automobile Insurance Co. v. Campbell, 538 U.S. ___ (2003). At issue was a $145 million punitive damage award against an insurer for bad faith refusal to settle. The Court held that the award violated the due process clause. The Court said that in general, a state cannot punish a defendant for "unlawful acts committed outside of the State's jurisdiction"—and hence that a punitive damage award cannot be justified as a way of punishing a range of misconduct, some of which occurred outside the state. The Court also said that "courts must ensure that the measure of punishment is both reasonable and proportionate to the amount of harm to the plaintiff and to the general damages suffered"—an idea that would support "single digit multipliers" of the compensatory award as "more likely to comply with due process" than higher numbers. Thus the Court seemed to suggest that the due process clause would severely discipline punitive damage awards from juries, requiring a reasonable ratio, judicially policed, between those awards and compensatory awards.

State Farm is part of a series of cases in which the Court has confronted the question whether the Constitution imposes any substantive limit on the size of punitive damages awards. In Browning-Ferris Industries v. Kelco Disposal, Inc., 492 U.S.

257 (1989), the Court held that the Eighth Amendment's excessive fines clause did not apply to punitive damages awards in civil cases involving private parties. In Pacific Mutual Life Insurance Co. v. Haslip, 499 U.S. 1 (1991), the Court held that the due process clause imposes both a procedural and a substantive limit on the size of punitive damages awards. The procedural component requires that juries be properly instructed on the purposes of punitive damages and the factors to be taken into account in deciding whether and what amount of punitive damages to award. It also requires appellate review of jury awards to ensure reasonableness. The substantive component requires that the award in fact *be* reasonable, rather than "grossly excessive" or disproportionate. In ensuing cases, the Court reviewed awards of punitive damages, upholding some, see TXO Production Corporation v. Alliance Resources Corporation, 509 U.S. 443 (1993) (upholding a $10 million punitive damages award in a case where the plaintiff recovered $19,000 in compensatory damages), and striking down others, see B.M.W. of North America v. Gore, 517 U.S. 559 (1996) (rejecting a punitive damages award of $2 million in a case where the plaintiff recovered roughly $3000 in compensatory damages).

Why is the Court so willing to use substantive due process to control punitive damage awards if it is so reluctant to control other forms of arbitrariness?

H.   The Contracts and Takings Clauses

Page 992.   At the bottom of the page, add the following:

PALAZZOLO v. RHODE ISLAND
533 U.S. 606 (2001)

JUSTICE KENNEDY delivered the opinion of the Court.

Petitioner Anthony Palazzolo owns a waterfront parcel of land in the town of Westerly, Rhode Island. Almost all of the property is designated as coastal wetlands under Rhode Island law. After petitioner's development proposals were rejected by respondent Rhode Island Coastal Resources Management Council (Council), he sued in state court, asserting the Council's application of its wetlands regulations took the property without compensation in violation of the Takings Clause of the Fifth Amendment, binding upon the State through the Due Process Clause of the Fourteenth Amendment. . . .

I

The town of Westerly is on an edge of the Rhode Island coastline. The town's western border is the Pawcatuck River, which at that point is the boundary between

Rhode Island and Connecticut. . . . In later times Westerly's coastal location had a new significance: It became a popular vacation and seaside destination. . . . Westerly today has about 20,000 year-round residents, and thousands of summer visitors come to enjoy its beaches and coastal advantages.

One of the more popular attractions is Misquamicut State Beach, a lengthy expanse of coastline facing Block Island Sound and beyond to the Atlantic Ocean. The primary point of access to the beach is Atlantic Avenue, a well-traveled 3-mile stretch of road running along the coastline within the town's limits. At its western end, Atlantic Avenue is something of a commercial strip, with restaurants, hotels, arcades, and other typical seashore businesses. The pattern of development becomes more residential as the road winds eastward onto a narrow spine of land bordered to the south by the beach and the ocean, and to the north by Winnapaug Pond, an intertidal inlet often used by residents for boating, fishing, and shellfishing.

In 1959 petitioner, a lifelong Westerly resident, decided to invest in three undeveloped, adjoining parcels along this eastern stretch of Atlantic Avenue. To the north, the property faces, and borders upon, Winnapaug Pond; the south of the property faces Atlantic Avenue and the beachfront homes abutting it on the other side, and beyond that the dunes and the beach. To purchase and hold the property, petitioner and associates formed Shore Gardens, Inc. (SGI). After SGI purchased the property petitioner bought out his associates and became the sole shareholder. In the first decade of SGI's ownership of the property the corporation submitted a plat to the town subdividing the property into 80 lots; and it engaged in various transactions that left it with 74 lots, which together encompassed about 20 acres. During the same period SGI also made initial attempts to develop the property and submitted intermittent applications to state agencies to fill substantial portions of the parcel. Most of the property was then, as it is now, salt marsh subject to tidal flooding. The wet ground and permeable soil would require considerable fill—as much as six feet in some places—before significant structures could be built. SGI's proposal, submitted in 1962 to the Rhode Island Division of Harbors and Rivers (DHR), sought to dredge from Winnapaug Pond and fill the entire property. The application was denied for lack of essential information. A second, similar proposal followed a year later. A third application, submitted in 1966 while the second application was pending, proposed more limited filling of the land for use as a private beach club. These latter two applications were referred to the Rhode Island Department of Natural Resources, which indicated initial assent. The agency later withdrew approval, however, citing adverse environmental impacts. SGI did not contest the ruling.

No further attempts to develop the property were made for over a decade. Two intervening events, however, become important to the issues presented. First, in 1971, Rhode Island enacted legislation creating the Council, an agency charged with the duty of protecting the State's coastal properties. Regulations promulgated by the Council designated salt marshes like those on SGI's property as protected "coastal wetlands," on which development is limited to a great extent. Second, in 1978 SGI's corporate charter was revoked for failure to pay corporate income taxes; and title to the property passed, by operation of state law, to petitioner as the corporation's sole shareholder.

In 1983 petitioner, now the owner, renewed the efforts to develop the property. An application to the Council, resembling the 1962 submission, requested permission to construct a wooden bulkhead along the shore of Winnapaug Pond and to fill the entire marsh land area. The Council rejected the application, noting it was "vague and inadequate for a project of this size and nature." The agency also found that "the proposed activities will have significant impacts upon the waters and wetlands of Winnapaug Pond," and concluded that "the proposed alteration . . . will conflict with the Coastal Resources Management Plan presently in effect." Petitioner did not appeal the agency's determination.

Petitioner went back to the drawing board, this time hiring counsel and preparing a more specific and limited proposal for use of the property. The new application, submitted to the Council in 1985, echoed the 1966 request to build a private beach club. The details do not tend to inspire the reader with an idyllic coastal image, for the proposal was to fill 11 acres of the property with gravel to accommodate "50 cars with boat trailers, a dumpster, port-a-johns, picnic tables, barbecue pits of concrete, and other trash receptacles."

The application fared no better with the Council than previous ones. Under the agency's regulations, a landowner wishing to fill salt marsh on Winnapaug Pond needed a "special exception" from the Council. In a short opinion the Council said the beach club proposal conflicted with the regulatory standard for a special exception. To secure a special exception the proposed activity must serve "a compelling public purpose which provides benefits to the public as a whole as opposed to individual or private interests." . . .

Petitioner filed an inverse condemnation action in Rhode Island Superior Court, asserting that the State's wetlands regulations, as applied by the Council to his parcel, had taken the property without compensation in violation of the Fifth and Fourteenth Amendments.

[We] hold [that] the owner is not deprived of all economic use of his property because the value of upland portions is substantial. We remand for further consideration of the claim under the principles set forth in *Penn Central.*

II

[Since] *Mahon,* we have given some, but not too specific, guidance to courts confronted with deciding whether a particular government action goes too far and effects a regulatory taking. First, we have observed, with certain qualifications, that a regulation which "denies all economically beneficial or productive use of land" will require compensation under the Takings Clause. Where a regulation places limitations on land that fall short of eliminating all economically beneficial use, a taking nonetheless may have occurred, depending on a complex of factors including the regulation's economic effect on the landowner, the extent to which the regulation interferes with reasonable investment-backed expectations, and the character of the government action. *Penn Central.* . . .

[The Court held that the takings issue was ripe for review.] While a landowner must give a land-use authority an opportunity to exercise its discretion, once it becomes clear that the agency lacks the discretion to permit any development, or the permissible uses of the property are known to a reasonable degree of certainty, a takings claim is likely to have ripened. The case is quite unlike those upon which respondents place principal reliance, which arose when an owner challenged a land-use authority's denial of a substantial project, leaving doubt whether a more modest submission or an application for a variance would be accepted. . . . The rulings of the Council interpreting the regulations at issue, and the briefs, arguments, and candid statements by counsel for both sides, leave no doubt on this point: On the wetlands there can be no fill for any ordinary land use. There can be no fill for its own sake; no fill for a beach club, either rustic or upscale; no fill for a subdivision; no fill for any likely or foreseeable use. And with no fill there can be no structures and no development on the wetlands. Further permit applications were not necessary to establish this point.

We turn to the second asserted basis for declining to address petitioner's takings claim on the merits. When the Council promulgated its wetlands regulations, the disputed parcel was owned not by petitioner but by the corporation of which he was sole shareholder. . . . The theory underlying the argument that postenactment purchasers cannot challenge a regulation under the Takings Clause seems to run on these lines: Property rights are created by the State. See, e.g., Phillips v. Washington Legal Foundation, 524 U.S. 156, 163 (1998). So, the argument goes, by prospective legislation the State can shape and define property rights and reasonable investment-backed expectations, and subsequent owners cannot claim any injury from lost value. After all, they purchased or took title with notice of the limitation.

The State may not put so potent a Hobbesian stick into the Lockean bundle. The right to improve property, of course, is subject to the reasonable exercise of state authority, including the enforcement of valid zoning and land-use restrictions. The Takings Clause, however, in certain circumstances allows a landowner to assert that a particular exercise of the State's regulatory power is so unreasonable or onerous as to compel compensation. Just as a prospective enactment, such as a new zoning ordinance, can limit the value of land without effecting a taking because it can be understood as reasonable by all concerned, other enactments are unreasonable and do not become less so through passage of time or title. Were we to accept the State's rule, the postenactment transfer of title would absolve the State of its obligation to defend any action restricting land use, no matter how extreme or unreasonable. A

128

State would be allowed, in effect, to put an expiration date on the Takings Clause. This ought not to be the rule. Future generations, too, have a right to challenge unreasonable limitations on the use and value of land.

Nor does the justification of notice take into account the effect on owners at the time of enactment, who are prejudiced as well. Should an owner attempt to challenge a new regulation, but not survive the process of ripening his or her claim (which, as this case demonstrates, will often take years), under the proposed rule the right to compensation may not by asserted by an heir or successor, and so may not be asserted at all. The State's rule would work a critical alteration to the nature of property, as the newly regulated landowner is stripped of the ability to transfer the interest which was possessed prior to the regulation. The State may not by this means secure a windfall for itself. The proposed rule is, furthermore, capricious in effect. The young owner contrasted with the older owner, the owner with the resources to hold contrasted with the owner with the need to sell, would be in different positions. The Takings Clause is not so quixotic. A blanket rule that purchasers with notice have no compensation right when a claim becomes ripe is too blunt an instrument to accord with the duty to compensate for what is taken.

Direct condemnation, by invocation of the State's power of eminent domain, presents different considerations than cases alleging a taking based on a burdensome regulation. In a direct condemnation action, or when a State has physically invaded the property without filing suit, the fact and extent of the taking are known. In such an instance, it is a general rule of the law of eminent domain that any award goes to the owner at the time of the taking, and that the right to compensation is not passed to a subsequent purchaser. . . .

We have no occasion to consider the precise circumstances when a legislative enactment can be deemed a background principle of state law or whether those circumstances are present here. It suffices to say that a regulation that otherwise would be unconstitutional absent compensation is not transformed into a background principle of the State's law by mere virtue of the passage of title. This relative standard would be incompatible with our description of the concept in *Lucas,* which is explained in terms of those common, shared understandings of permissible limitations derived from a State's legal tradition, see [*Lucas*]. A regulation or common-law rule cannot be a background principle for some owners but not for others. The determination whether an existing, general law can limit all economic use of property must turn on objective factors, such as the nature of the land use proscribed. A law does not become a background principle for subsequent owners by enactment itself. For reasons we discuss next, the state court will not find it necessary to explore these matters on remand in connection with the claim that all economic use was deprived; it must address, however, the merits of petitioner's claim under *Penn Central.* That claim is not barred by the mere fact that title was acquired after the effective date of the state-imposed restriction.

III

[Petitioner] accepts the Council's contention and the state trial court's finding that his parcel retains $200,000 in development value under the State's wetlands regulations. He asserts, nonetheless, that he has suffered a total taking and contends the Council cannot sidestep the holding in *Lucas* "by the simple expedient of leaving a landowner a few crumbs of value."

Assuming a taking is otherwise established, a State may not evade the duty to compensate on the premise that the landowner is left with a token interest. This is not the situation of the landowner in this case, however. A regulation permitting a landowner to build a substantial residence on an 18-acre parcel does not leave the property "economically idle." *Lucas.*

In his brief submitted to us petitioner attempts to revive this part of his claim by reframing it. He argues, for the first time, that the upland parcel is distinct from the wetlands portions, so he should be permitted to assert a deprivation limited to the latter. This contention asks us to examine the difficult, persisting question of what is the proper denominator in the takings fraction. Some of our cases indicate that the extent of deprivation effected by a regulatory action is measured against the value of the parcel as a whole, see, e.g., Keystone Bituminous Coal Assn. v. DeBenedictis; but we have at times expressed discomfort with the logic of this rule, see *Lucas,* a sentiment echoed by some commentators, see, e.g., Epstein, Takings: Descent and Resurrection, 1987 Sup. Ct. Rev. 1, 16-17 (1987); Fee, Unearthing the Denominator in Regulatory Takings Claims, 61 U. Chi. L. Rev. 1535 (1994). Whatever the merits of these criticisms, we will not explore the point here. Petitioner did not press the argument in the state courts, and the issue was not presented in the petition for certiorari. The case comes to us on the premise that petitioner's entire parcel serves as the basis for his takings claim, and, so framed, the total deprivation argument fails. . . .

For the reasons we have discussed, the State Supreme Court erred in finding petitioner's claims were unripe and in ruling that acquisition of title after the effective date of the regulations barred the takings claims. The court did not err in finding that petitioner failed to establish a deprivation of all economic value, for it is undisputed that the parcel retains significant worth for construction of a residence. The claims under the *Penn Central* analysis were not examined, and for this purpose the case should be remanded.

The judgment of the Rhode Island Supreme Court is affirmed in part and reversed in part, and the case is remanded for further proceedings not inconsistent with this opinion.

It is so ordered.

JUSTICE O'CONNOR, concurring.

I join the opinion of the Court but with my understanding of how the issues discussed in Part II of the opinion must be considered on remand.

Part II of the Court's opinion addresses the circumstance, present in this case, where a takings claimant has acquired title to the regulated property after the enactment of the regulation at issue. As the Court holds, the Rhode Island Supreme Court erred in effectively adopting the sweeping rule that the preacquisition enactment of the use restriction ipso facto defeats any takings claim based on that use restriction. Accordingly, the Court holds that petitioner's claim under Penn Central Transp. Co. v. New York City "is not barred by the mere fact that title was acquired after the effective date of the state-imposed restriction."

The more difficult question is what role the temporal relationship between regulatory enactment and title acquisition plays in a proper *Penn Central* analysis. Today's holding does not mean that the timing of the regulation's enactment relative to the acquisition of title is immaterial to the *Penn Central* analysis. Indeed, it would be just as much error to expunge this consideration from the takings inquiry as it would be to accord it exclusive significance. Our polestar instead remains the principles set forth in *Penn Central* itself and our other cases that govern partial regulatory takings. Under these cases, interference with investment-backed expectations is one of a number of factors that a court must examine. Further, the regulatory regime in place at the time the claimant acquires the property at issue helps to shape the reasonableness of those expectations.

If investment-backed expectations are given exclusive significance in the *Penn Central* analysis and existing regulations dictate the reasonableness of those expectations in every instance, then the State wields far too much power to redefine property rights upon passage of title. On the other hand, if existing regulations do nothing to inform the analysis, then some property owners may reap windfalls and an important indicium of fairness is lost. As I understand it, our decision today does not remove the regulatory backdrop against which an owner takes title to property from the purview of the *Penn Central* inquiry. It simply restores balance to that inquiry. Courts properly consider the effect of existing regulations under the rubric of investment-backed expectations in determining whether a compensable taking has occurred. As before, the salience of these facts cannot be reduced to any "set formula." *Penn Central* (internal quotation marks omitted). The temptation to adopt what amount to per se rules in either direction must be resisted. The Takings Clause requires careful examination and weighing of all the relevant circumstances in this context. The court below therefore must consider on remand the array of relevant factors under *Penn Central* before deciding whether any compensation is due.

JUSTICE SCALIA, concurring.

I write separately to make clear that my understanding of how the issues discussed in Part II of the Court's opinion must be considered on remand is not Justice O'Connor's.

The principle that underlies her separate concurrence is that it may in some (unspecified) circumstances be "[un]fai[r]," and produce unacceptable "windfalls," to allow a subsequent purchaser to nullify an unconstitutional partial taking (though, inexplicably, not an unconstitutional total taking) by the government. The polar horrible, presumably, is the situation in which a sharp real estate developer, realizing (or indeed, simply gambling on) the unconstitutional excessiveness of a development restriction that a naïve landowner assumes to be valid, purchases property at what it would be worth subject to the restriction, and then develops it to its full value (or resells it at its full value) after getting the unconstitutional restriction invalidated.

This can, I suppose, be called a windfall—though it is not much different from the windfalls that occur every day at stock exchanges or antique auctions, where the knowledgeable (or the venturesome) profit at the expense of the ignorant (or the risk averse). There is something to be said (though in my view not much) for pursuing abstract "fairness" by requiring part or all of that windfall to be returned to the naïve original owner, who presumably is the "rightful" owner of it. But there is nothing to be said for giving it instead to the government—which not only did not lose something it owned, but is both the cause of the miscarriage of "fairness" and the only one of the three parties involved in the miscarriage (government, naïve original owner, and sharp real estate developer) which acted unlawfully—indeed unconstitutionally. Justice O'Connor would eliminate the windfall by giving the malefactor the benefit of its malefaction. It is rather like eliminating the windfall that accrued to a purchaser who bought property at a bargain rate from a thief clothed with the indicia of title, by making him turn over the "unjust" profit to the thief.

In my view, the fact that a restriction existed at the time the purchaser took title (other than a restriction forming part of the "background principles of the State's law of property and nuisance," Lucas v. South Carolina Coastal Council), should have no bearing upon the determination of whether the restriction is so substantial as to constitute a taking. The "investment-backed expectations" that the law will take into account do not include the assumed validity of a restriction that in fact deprives property of so much of its value as to be unconstitutional. Which is to say that a *Penn Central* taking, see Penn Central Transp. Co. v. New York City, no less than a total taking, is not absolved by the transfer of title.

[Justices Ginsburg and Breyer wrote separate opinions, dissenting on ripeness grounds.]

JUSTICE STEVENS, concurring in part and dissenting in part.

[I] have no doubt that [a property owner] has standing to challenge the restriction's validity whether she acquired title to the property before or after the regulation was adopted. For, as the Court correctly observes, even future generations "have a right to challenge unreasonable limitations on the use and value of land."

It by no means follows, however, that, as the Court assumes, a succeeding owner may obtain compensation for a taking of property from her predecessor in interest. A taking is a discrete event, a governmental acquisition of private property for which the state is required to provide just compensation. Like other transfers of property, it occurs at a particular time, that time being the moment when the relevant property interest is alienated from its owner. . . .

[To] the extent that the adoption of the regulations constitute the challenged taking, petitioner is simply the wrong party to be bringing this action. If the regulations imposed a compensable injury on anyone, it was on the owner of the property at the moment the regulations were adopted. Given the trial court's finding that petitioner did not own the property at that time, in my judgment it is pellucidly clear that he has no standing to claim that the promulgation of the regulations constituted a taking of any part of the property that he subsequently acquired.

[At] oral argument, petitioner contended that the taking in question occurred in 1986, when the Council denied his final application to fill the land. Though this theory, to the extent that it was embraced within petitioner's actual complaint, complicates the issue, it does not alter my conclusion that the prohibition on filling the wetlands does not take from Palazzolo any property right he ever possessed.

The title Palazzolo took by operation of law in 1978 was limited by the regulations then in place to the extent that such regulations represented a valid exercise of the police power. For the reasons expressed above, I think the regulations barred petitioner from filling the wetlands on his property. At the very least, however, they established a rule that such lands could not be filled unless the Council exercised its authority to make exceptions to that rule under certain circumstances.

[If] the existence of valid land-use regulations does not limit the title that the first postenactment purchaser of the property inherits, then there is no reason why such regulations should limit the rights of the second, the third, or the thirtieth purchaser. Perhaps my concern is unwarranted, but today's decision does raise the spectre of a tremendous—and tremendously capricious—one-time transfer of wealth from society at large to those individuals who happen to hold title to large tracts of land at the moment this legal question is permanently resolved.

In the final analysis, the property interest at stake in this litigation is the right to fill the wetlands on the tract that petitioner owns. Whether either he or his predecessors in title ever owned such an interest, and if so, when it was acquired by the State, are questions of state law. If it is clear—as I think it is and as I think the Court's disposition of the ripeness issue assumes—that any such taking occurred before he became the owner of the property, he has no standing to seek compensation for that taking. On the other hand, if the only viable takings claim has a different predicate that arose later, that claim is not ripe and the discussion in [the] Court's opinion is superfluous dictum. In either event, the judgment of the Rhode Island Supreme Court should be affirmed in its entirety.

Question: What, exactly, is the "Lockean" bundle involved in this case? How can we know what the property right is at the time of acquisition without knowing what the state's law says at that time?

Page 992.   After section 5 of the Note, add the following:

6. *Temporary takings*? Is the government permitted to impose a moratorium on economic development? What if the moratorium deprives the property owner of all valuable use of the property? In Tahoe-Sierra Preservation Council, Inc. v. Tahoe Regional Planning Agency, 535 U.S. 302 (2002), the Court held that a moratorium, imposed during a period for studying the impact of development on Lake Tahoe, would not be treated as a categorical taking, subject to a per se requirement of compensation. The Court stressed that the case did not involve a physical taking, and concluded that the rules for physical takings should not be used for "regulatory takings." Hence the *Penn Central* test, involving balancing, would be appropriate. The Court emphasized that *Lucas* involved a permanent taking, not a taking for a mere thirty-two months. The Court refused to accept the view "that we can effectively sever a 32-month segment from the remainder of each landowner's fee simple estate and then ask whether that segment has been taken in its entirety" by the moratorium. Hence the Court concluded that it was appropriate to rely on "the familiar *Penn Central* approach when deciding cases like this, rather than by attempting to craft a new categorical rule." Chief Justice Rehnquist dissented, in an opinion joined by Justices Scalia and Thomas.

7
FREEDOM OF EXPRESSION

A. Introduction

Page 997.   At the end of section 4 of the Note, add the following:

The framers themselves were unsure what a constitutional guarantee of "freedom of the speech or of the press" would mean. Benjamin Franklin observed, for example, that "Few of us, I believe, have distinct ideas of its nature and extent," and Alexander Hamilton asked "Who can give it any definition which would not leave the utmost latitude for evasion?" See Meyerson, The Neglected History of the Prior Restraint Doctrine, 34 Ind. L. Rev. 295, 320 (2001).

Page 998.   In section 6 of the Note, before the citation to R. Nye, add the following:

M. Curtis, Free Speech, "The People's Darling Privilege" (2000) (focusing on the Sedition Act of 1798, suppression of abolitionist speech and suppression of speech during the Civil War); D. Rabban, Free Speech in its Forgotten Years: 1870-1920 (1997);

After the citation to Rabban, add the following:

Stone, Abraham Lincoln's First Amendment, 78 N.Y.U. L. Rev. 1 (2003).

Page 1002. Before section 3 of the Note, add the following:

e. Post, Reconciling Theory and Doctrine in First Amendment Jurisprudence, in L. Bollinger & G. Stone, Eternal Vigilance: Free Speech in the Modern Era 153, 165-167 (2002):

[Under Meiklejohn's view, the] First Amendment is understood to protect the communicative processes necessary to disseminate the information and ideas required for citizens to vote in a fully informed and intelligent way. [Under this view,] the state is imagined as a moderator, [and] speech [that is] inconsistent with "responsible and regulated discussion" can and should be suppressed. . . .

The alternative account of democracy, which I shall call the "participatory" theory, does not locate self-governance in mechanisms of decisionmaking, but rather in the processes through which citizens come to identify a government as their own. [This] account postulates that it is a necessary precondition [that] a state be constitutionally prohibited from preventing its citizens from participating in the communicative processes relevant to the formation of democratic public opinion.

[This] approach views the function of the First Amendment to be the safeguarding of public discourse from regulations that are inconsistent with democratic legitimacy. State restrictions on public discourse can be inconsistent with democratic legitimacy in two distinct ways. To the extent that the state cuts off particular citizens from participation in public discourse, it *pro tanto* negates its claim to democratic legitimacy with respect to such citizens. To the extent that the state regulates public discourse so as to reflect the values and priorities of some vision of collective identity, it preempts the very democratic process by which collective identity is to be determined.

[The] Meiklejohnian and participatory perspectives [differ] in at least two fundamental respects. First, the Meiklejohnian approach interprets the First Amendment primarily as a shield against the "mutilation of the thinking process of the community," whereas the participatory approach understands the First Amendment [as] safeguarding the ability of individual citizens to participate in the formation of public opinion. The Meiklejohnian theory thus stresses the quality of public debate, whereas the participatory perspective emphasizes the autonomy of individual citizens.

Second, the Meiklejohnian perspective imagines the state [as] a neutral moderator, capable of saving public discourse from "mutilation" by distinguishing between relevant and irrelevant speech, abusive and nonabusive speech. . . . The participatory approach, in contrast, denies that there can be any possible neutral position within public discourse, because public discourse is precisely the site of political contention about the nature of collective identity, and it is only by reference to some vision of collective identity that speech can be categorized as relevant or irrelevant, abusive or nonabusive. . . .

Page 1003. At the end of section 4 of the Note, add the following:

c. *Free speech and character.* Consider Blasi, Free Speech and Good Character: From Milton to Brandeis to the Present, in L. Bollinger & G. Stone, Eternal Vigilance: Free Speech in the Modern Era 61, 62, 84-85 (2002):

[A] culture that prizes and protects expressive liberty nurtures in its members certain character traits such as inquisitiveness, distrust of authority, willingness to take initiative, and the courage to confront evil. Such character traits are valuable [for] their instrumental contribution to the collective well-being, social as well as political. . . .

The most important [consequence] of protecting free speech is the intellectual and moral pluralism, and thus disorder in a sense, thereby engendered. In matters of belief, conventional structures of authority are weakened, rebellion is facilitated, closure is impaired. Persons who live in a free-speech regime are forced to cope with persistent, and frequently intractable, differences of understanding. For most of us that is a painful challenge. . . . Being made to take account of such differences shapes our character.

Page 1004.   At the end of section 5 of the Note, add the following:

On the other hand, consider Post, Reconciling Theory and Doctrine in First Amendment Jurisprudence, in L. Bollinger & G. Stone, Eternal Vigilance: Free Speech in the Modern Era 153, 153 (2002): "Doctrine becomes confused when [it] is required to articulate the implications of inconsistent theories. First Amendment doctrine has unfortunately suffered from [this difficulty]."

6. *First Amendment decisionmaking.* Given what you have read about the history and philosophy underlying the first amendment, is it possible to decide in a principled manner whether the first amendment protects nude dancing in bars, or a $50,000 campaign contribution to a political candidate, or commercial advertising of toothpaste? Is first amendment decisionmaking realistically about anything "other than a particular set of social, political, and ideological moves that are available at a particular point in time?" Schauer, First Amendment Opportunism, in L. Bollinger & G. Stone, Eternal Vigilance: Free Speech in the Modern Era 175, 195 (2002).

Consider Strauss, Freedom of Speech and the Common-Law Constitution, in L. Bollinger & G. Stone, Eternal Vigilance: Free Speech in the Modern Era 33, 59 (2002):

[The] story of the development of the American system of freedom of expression is not a story about the text of the First Amendment. That text was part of the Constitution for a century and a half before the central principles of the American regime of free speech [became] established in the law. Nor is it a story about the wisdom of those who drafted the First Amendment. There is a habit of attributing to the framers [great] foresight about freedom of expression as well as other subjects. But the actual views of the drafters and ratifiers of the First Amendment are in many ways unclear; and to the extent we can determine their views, they did

137

not think they were establishing a system of free expression resembling what we have today. [In fact, the] central principles of the American system of freedom of expression were hammered out mostly over the course of the twentieth century, in fits and starts, in a series of judicial decisions and extrajudicial developments. The story of the emergence of the American constitutional law of free speech is a story of evolution and precedent, trial and error. . . .

[Our current free speech jurisprudence] emerged fitfully by a process in which principles were tried and sometimes abandoned, sometimes modified, in light of experience and of an explicit assessment of whether they were good principles as a matter of policy and political morality. The law of the First Amendment is one of the great creations of the law, and it is a creation of the common-law Constitution.

7. *Our Democratic Constitution.* Consider Justice Breyer's approach to constitutional interpretation. How would this approach shape the analysis of such issues as the constitutionality of campaign finance reform or the regulation of commercial advertising? Breyer, Our Democratic Constitution, 77 N.Y.U. L. Rev. 245, 247-249 (2002):

[T]he Constitution, considered as a whole, creates a framework for a certain kind of government. Its general objectives can be described abstractly as including: (1) democratic self-government; (2) dispersion of power (avoid concentration of too much power in too few hands); (3) individual dignity (through protection of individual liberties); (4) equality before the law (through equal protection of the law); and (5) the rule of law itself. [In interpreting specific provisions of the Constitution, the Court] must consider the document as a whole. . . .

[T]he real-world consequences of a particular interpretive decision, valued in terms of [these] basic constitutional purposes, [should] play an important role in constitutional decisionmaking. To that extent, my approach differs from that of judges who would place near exclusive interpretive weight upon language, history, tradition, and precedent. [The] more literal judges may hope to find, in language, history, tradition, and precedent, objective interpretive standards; they may seek to avoid an interpretive subjectivity that could confuse a judge's personal idea of what is good for that which the Constitution demands; and they may believe that these "original" sources more readily will yield rules that can guide other institutions, including lower courts. These objectives are desirable, but I do not think the literal approach will achieve them, and, in any event, the constitutional price is too high. [It] is important to place greater weight upon constitutionally valued consequences. . . .

B.   Content-Based Restrictions: Dangerous Ideas and Information

Page 1011.   At the end of section 1 of the Note, add the following:

For the arguments that Judge Hand correctly interpreted the Espionage Act of 1917 and that the bad tendency test distorted not only the Espionage Act but the common law understanding of "attempt," see Stone, Judge Learned Hand and the Espionage Act of 1917: A Mystery Unraveled, 70 U. Chi. L. Rev. 335 (2003); Stone, The Origins of the "Bad Tendency" Test: Free Speech in Wartime, 2002 Sup. Ct. Rev. 411.

Page 1013.   After the second paragraph of section 4 of the Note, add the following:

Should the government be required to prove *both* clear and present danger *and* that the speaker intended to create a clear and present danger? Consider Alexander, Incitement and Freedom of Speech, in D. Kretzmer & F. Hazan, Freedom of Speech and Incitement Against Democracy 101, 107-108 (2000):

> [N]either the value [nor] the danger of the speech [turns] on the speaker's purpose. [Suppose, for example,] the government interdicts a shipment of pamphlets written without any purpose to incite to violence but which are quite likely to do so. [The] question the government faces is not whether to prosecute but whether to destroy the pamphlets. Solely as a matter of freedom of speech, [it] is difficult to see why the answer to that question should turn on the authors' intention. . . .

Page 1028.   After the citation to Blasi in section 1 of the Note, add the following:

Consider Blasi, Free Speech and Good Character: From Milton to Brandeis to the Present, in L. Bollinger & G. Stone, Eternal Vigilance: Free Speech in the Modern Era 61, 83 (2002): "To Brandeis, the measure of courage in the civic realm is the capacity to experience change [without] losing perspective or confidence. [The] character conducive to the maintenance of that [capacity] is what he considered the principal benefit of a robust freedom of speech."

Page 1030. At the end of section 7 of the Note, add the following:

Although there were no major Supreme Court decisions concerning subversive advocacy during World War II, there were several prosecutions of individuals under both the Espionage Act of 1917 and the Smith Act of 1940. Most often, these were prosecutions of individuals who were leaders of fascist organizations in the United States. See R. Steele, Free Speech in the Good War (1999); M. St. George & L. Dennis, The Great Sedition Trial of 1944 (1946).

Page 1035. At the end of section 1 of the Note, add the following:

Who are the "real" targets of the prosecutions in cases like *Schenck, Abrams, Gitlow, Whitney* and *Dennis*? Consider M. St. George & L. Dennis, A Trial on Trial: The Great Sedition Trial of 1944 41-42 (1946):

> [True agitators] are never intimidated by sedition trials. The blood of martyrs is the seed of the Church. The people who are intimidated by sedition trials are the people who have not enough courage [ever] to say or do anything that would get them involved in a sedition trial. And it is mainly for the purpose of intimidating these more prudent citizens that sedition trials are held. The cautious, of course, would be the last persons in the world to see this.

Page 1036. At the end of section 2 of the Note, add the following:

Consider Posner, The Speech Market and the Legacy of *Schenck*, in L. Bollinger and G. Stone, Eternal Vigilance: Free Speech in the Modern Era 121, 125-126 (2002):

> If the benefits of challenged speech are given by B; the cost (a fire, desertion, riot, rebellion, and so on) if the speech is allowed by H (for harm) or O (for offensiveness); the probability that the cost will actually materialize if the speech is allowed by p; the rate at which future costs or benefits are discounted to the present by d (like p a number between 0 and 1); the number of years [or other unit of time] between when the speech occurs and the harm from the speech materializes or is likely to occur if the speech is allowed by n; then the speech should be allowed if but only if $B \geq pH/(1 + d)^n + O - A$ [the cost of administering the ban], which, in

words, is if but only if the benefits of the speech equal or exceed its costs discounted by their probability and by their futurity, and reduced by the costs of administering the ban.

But consider also Posner, Pragmatism versus Purposivism in First Amendment Analysis, 54 Stan. L. Rev. 737, 744 (2002):

[A] shortcoming of the pragmatic approach is that the costs of freedom of expression are often more salient than the benefits, and their salience may cause the balance to shift too far toward suppression. [Doubt] is the engine of progress, but because people hate being in a state of doubt they may prefer to silence the doubters rather than to alter their beliefs. [Because] the cost of heterodox speech is immediate and its benefit deferred, the benefit may be slighted. All this must be kept steadily in mind by judges called upon to uphold the suppression of expression. . . .

Page 1037. After section 4 of the Note, add the following:

5. *Understanding* Dennis. Consider Wiecek, The Legal Foundations of Domestic Anticommunism: The Background of *Dennis v. United States*, 2001 Sup. Ct. Rev. 375, 377-379, 417, 428-429:

In the 1927-47 period, and then again a decade later, the Court's speech decisions consistently expanded freedom to [communicate]. The 1950-56 decisions interrupted that trend. In those years, the Court regressed to the spirit of the 1919-1927 [era]. [The reason for this phenomenon] is found in the dominant outlook and anxieties of contemporary anticommunism. This outlook produced an image of Communists that depicted them as unscrupulous traitors controlled by Moscow, committed to subverting American freedom. [This] image of Communists was an artifact of the preceding eighty years of anticommunism. [The Justices] were not exempt from the fears and beliefs of other Americans. [Indeed, it] was natural for the Justices to employ the anticommunist image as a kind of general template to make sense of legal issues coming before them in cases implicating the liberties of Communists. . . .

[The] half-century that followed World War II was not merely a string of relatively low-level crises [*e.g.*, Berlin blockade, the fall of China, the Soviet atomic bomb, the Korean War, etc.], but a slow-motion hot war, conducted on the periphery of rival empires, sometimes by the principals themselves, sometimes by their proxies. It threatened to escalate to nuclear conflict at any time. Seeing the period of the Cold War [as] a nightmare from which we could not disengage

[that] threatened our annihilation at any moment [helps] us to understand the fears and reactions of another time. . . .

The [anticommunist] crusade after World War II [demonized] Communists, endowing them with extraordinary powers and malignity, making them both covert and ubiquitous. [Communists] became The Other. Popular culture, in movies like *On the Waterfront* [and] *Invasion of the Body Snatchers,* effectively delivered this image to a mass audience. [The] manufactured image of the domestic Communist, cultivated and propagated by J. Edgar Hoover, the Catholic Church, the American Legion, and political opportunists, made of Communists something less than full humans, full [citizens]. [To] resist the ideological and emotional pressures of the Cold War era would have required superhuman wisdom and equanimity. Whatever else might be said of the Justices of the *Dennis* Court, the majority of them did not have those qualities.

Does this seem right? Keep it in mind as you think in the present about the War on Terrorism.

Page 1044. At the end of section 4 of the Note, add the following:

d. Is the private solicitation of murder protected by *Brandenburg*? Consider Greenawalt, "Clear and Present Danger" and Criminal Speech, in L. Bollinger & G. Stone, Eternal Vigilance: Free Speech in the Modern Era 97, 116-119 (2002):

Such a solicitation differs importantly from public speech in which the speaker urges a specific crime for political reasons. [But this] distinction should not be grounded on the view that free speech is [only] about speech in public. . . . [Most] people discuss political, social, and moral issues [in private conversations, and it] would be paradoxical [to] say that the government may freely regulate what is said in these private settings. . . .

As Justice Brandeis emphasized, a crucial assumption about free speech concerns countervailing speech. If one person or group urges people to do one thing, others are free to urge the opposite. . . . Another aspect of public speech is that officials know what has been said; they may be able to take precautions to lessen the chance of a crime being successfully committed. However, when one person [privately] urges another to commit a crime, there is opportunity neither for directly countervailing speech nor for official precautions. [In] such circumstances, imminence and likelihood provide too much protection for dangerous speech. [This] sort of solicitation should receive First Amendment protection only if [the] speaker reasonably believes that the remark will not have a serious effect on the listener.

5. *From* Schenck *to* Brandenburg, *and beyond.* Consider the following views:

a. Stone, Dialogue, in L. Bollinger & G. Stone, Eternal Vigilance: Free Speech in the Modern Era 1, 4 (2002):

[In] its initial efforts to make sense of the First Amendment, the [Court] seemed rather innocently to believe that the government could effectively excise from public debate only those views that could be said to be "dangerous," without threatening free speech more generally. But over time the Court came increasingly to understand that although each generation's effort to suppress *its* idea of "dangerous speech" (antiwar speech during World War I; syndicalist expression during the 1920s; Communist advocacy during the 1950s) seemed warranted at the time, each seemed with the benefit of hindsight an exaggerated [response] to a particular political or social problem. The Court came to understand that there is a natural tendency of even well-meaning citizens, legislators, and judges to want to suppress ideas they find offensive or misguided, to inflate the potential dangers of such expression, and to undervalue the costs of its suppression.

b. Stone, Dialogue, in L. Bollinger & G. Stone, Eternal Vigilance: Free Speech in the Modern Era 1, 7-8 (2002):

Earlier, I offered a very rosy view of the evolution of First Amendment jurisprudence. . . . There is, however, a more cynical view of this process. [During] World War I the Court enunciated the seemingly speech-protective "clear and present danger" test, but then construed the test in such a way as to uphold the convictions of those who protested against the war. . . . In the 1920s, the Court looked back on the World War I cases with some dismay, and embraced a more speech-protective interpretation of the First Amendment [that] presumably would have reversed the convictions of the earlier era, but that enabled the Court to uphold the convictions of the syndicalists. In the 1950s, the Court strengthened its protection of free speech in such a way as to call into question both the World War I cases and the syndicalist decisions of the 1920s, while enabling it to uphold the convictions of the leaders of the Communist Party. [So], one might say that the Court learns just enough to correct the mistakes of the past, but never quite enough to avoid the mistakes of the present.

c. Posner, Pragmatism versus Purposivism in First Amendment Analysis, 54 Stan. L. Rev. 737, 741 (2002):

[W]hen the country feels very safe the Justices [can] without paying a large political cost plume themselves on their fearless devotion to freedom of speech and professors can deride the cowardice of the *Dennis* decision. But they are likely to

143

change their tune when next the country feels endangered. The word "feels" is important here. The country may have exaggerated the danger that Communism posed. But the fear of Communism was a brute fact that judges who wanted to preserve their power had to consider.

d. Bollinger, Epilogue, in L. Bollinger & G. Stone, Eternal Vigilance: Free Speech in the Modern Era 1, 312-313 (2002):

The question for the future [is] whether the scope of First Amendment rights articulated in the *Brandenburg* era reflects the distilled wisdom of historical experience, which makes it more likely to survive in future periods of social upheaval, or whether the *Brandenburg* era will turn out to be just one era among many, in which the freedom of speech varies widely and more or less according to the sense of security and tolerance prevailing in the nation at the time. The fact that the last thirty years since *Brandenburg* have been remarkably peaceful and prosperous means that the understandings we now have about the meaning of free speech have not really been tested. By the standards we now apply (that is, through the eyes of *Brandenburg*), just about every time the country has felt seriously threatened the First Amendment has retreated.

Page 1048.   At the end of section 6 of the Note, add the following:

After September 11, may the government refuse to employ as an airport screener any person who, in the past five years, has been a member of, or contributed to, any organization on the government's list of Islamic terrorist organizations?

Page 1055.   At the end of section 3 of the Note, add the following:

In the actual Nuremberg Files case, the web site was established after an unrelated individual had murdered three abortion providers after distributing similar posters naming them as "Wanted" persons. Is this relevant?

In Planned Parenthood v. American Coalition of Life Activists, 290 F.3d 1058 (9th Cir. 2002), the Court of Appeals, in a six-to-five *en banc* decision, held that the Nuremberg Files web site could be held liable in damages and enjoined because it constituted an unprotected threat:

If ACLA had merely endorsed or encouraged the violent actions of others, its speech would be protected. [Citing *Brandenburg*.] However, while advocating violence is protected, threatening a person with violence is not. [Although the] posters contain no language that is [literally] a threat, whether a particular statement may properly be considered to be a threat is governed by an objective standard—whether a reasonable person would foresee that the statement would be interpreted by those to whom the maker communicates the statement as a serious expression of intent to harm or assault. [It] is not necessary that the defendant intend to, or be able to carry out his threat; the only intent requirement for a true threat is that the defendant intentionally or knowingly communicate the [threat] *with the intent to intimidate.* [It] is making a threat to intimidate that makes ACLA's conduct unlawful. . . .

The true threats analysis [in this case] turns on the poster pattern. [The Website does not contain] any language that is overtly threatening. [It] is use of the "Wanted"-type format in the context of the poster pattern—poster followed by murder—that constitutes the threat. Because of the pattern, a "Wanted"-type poster naming a specific doctor who provides abortions was perceived by physicians, who are providers of reproductive health services, as a serious threat of death or bodily harm. [The] posters are a true threat because, [like] burning crosses, they connote something they do not literally say, yet both the actor and the recipient get the message. To the doctor who performs abortions, these posters meant "You'll be shot or killed."

[As] a direct result of having [a] poster out on them, physicians wore bulletproof vests and took other extraordinary security measures to protect themselves and their families. ACLA had every reason to foresee that its expression [would] elicit this reaction. Physicians' fear did not simply happen; ACLA intended to intimidate them from doing what they do. This [is] conduct that [lacks] any protection under the First Amendment. Violence is not a protected value. Nor is a true threat of violence with intent to intimidate.

The dissenting judges argued as follows:

[I]t is not illegal—and cannot be made so—merely to say things that would frighten or intimidate the listener. For example, when a doctor says, "You have cancer and will die within six months," it is not a threat, even though you almost certainly will be frightened. [By] contrast, "If you don't stop performing abortions, I'll kill you" is a true threat and surely illegal. The difference between a true threat and protected expression is this: A true threat warns of violence or other harm that the speaker controls. . . .

[As the majority argues,] because context matters, the statements [in this case] could reasonably be interpreted as an effort to intimidate plaintiffs into ceasing their abortion-related activities. If that were enough to strip the speech of First Amendment protection, there would be nothing left to decide. But the Supreme Court has told us that "[s]peech does not lose its protected character . . . simply because it may embarrass others *or coerce them into action."* [*Claiborne Hardware.*] In other words, some forms of intimidation enjoy constitutional protection.

The majority does not point to any statement by defendants that they intended to inflict bodily harm on plaintiffs, nor is there any evidence that defendants took any steps whatsoever to plan or carry out physical violence against anyone. Rather, the majority relies on the fact that "the poster format itself had acquired currency as a death threat for abortion providers." [But none of the doctors who were killed were killed by anyone connected with this web page.]

The majority tries to fill this gaping hole in the record by noting that defendants "kn[ew] the fear generated among those in the reproductive health services community who were singled out for identification on a 'wanted'-type poster." But a statement does not become a true threat because it instills fear in the listener; as noted above, many statements generate fear in the listener, yet are not true threats and therefore may not be punished or enjoined consistent with the First Amendment. In order for the statement to be a threat, it must send the message that the speakers themselves—or individuals acting in concert with them—will engage in physical violence. [Yet] the opinion points to no evidence that defendants [would] have been understood by a reasonable listener as saying that *they* will cause the harm.

From the point of view of the victims, it makes little difference whether the violence against them will come from the makers of the posters or from unrelated third parties; bullets kill their victims regardless of who pulls the trigger. But it makes a difference for the purpose of the First Amendment. Speech—especially political speech, as this clearly was—may not be punished or enjoined unless it falls into one of the narrow categories of unprotected speech recognized by the Supreme Court: true threat, incitement, fighting words, etc.

[The] posters can be viewed, at most, as a call to arms for *other* abortion protesters to harm plaintiffs. However, the Supreme Court made it clear that under *Brandenburg*, encouragement or even advocacy of violence is protected by the First Amendment [unless the harm is both likely and imminent]. . . .

The Nuremberg Files website is clearly an expression of a political point of view. The posters and the website are designed both to rally political support for the views espoused by defendants, and to intimidate plaintiffs and others like them into desisting abortion related activities. This political agenda may not be to the liking of many people—political dissidents are often unpopular—but the speech, including the intimidating message, does not constitute a direct threat because there is no evidence [that] the speakers intend to resort to physical violence if their threat is not heeded.

We have recognized that statements communicated directly to the target are much more likely to be true threats than those, as here, communicated as part of a public protest. [In] deciding whether the coercive speech is protected, it makes a big difference whether it is contained in a private communication—a face-to-face confrontation, a telephone call, a dead fish wrapped in newspaper—or is made during the course of public discourse. The reason for this distinction is obvious: Private speech is aimed only at its target. Public speech, by contrast, seeks to move public opinion and to encourage those of like mind. Coercive speech that is part of public discourse enjoys far greater protection than identical speech made in a purely private context.

In this case, defendants said nothing remotely threatening, yet they find themselves crucified financially. Who knows what other neutral statements a jury might imbue with a menacing meaning based on the activities of unrelated parties. . . .

See also Rothman, Freedom of Speech and True Threats, 25 Harv. J. L. & Pub. Pol. 283 (2001) (to prove a "true" threat, the prosecution must prove (a) that the speaker knowingly or recklessly made a statement that would frighten or intimidate the victim with the threat of harm; (b) that the speaker knowingly or recklessly suggested that the threat would be carried out by the speaker or his co-conspirators; and (c) that a reasonable person who heard the statement would conclude that it was meant to threaten the victim with harm). In what circumstances, if any, might the display of a swastika or a burning cross constitute a "true threat"?

Page 1056. At the end of the sentence immediately before *Cantwell*, add the following:

Consider Posner, The Speech Market and the Legacy of *Schenck*, in L. Bollinger & G. Stone, Eternal Vigilance: Free Speech in the Modern Era 121, 136 (2002):

There [is] a pragmatic argument against putting much weight on offensiveness as a ground for restricting freedom of speech. Offensiveness is often a by-product of challenging the values and beliefs that are important to people, and these challenges are an important part of the market in ideas and opinions. People get upset when their way of life is challenged, yet that upset may be the beginning of doubt and lead eventually to change. Think of all the currently conventional ideas and opinions that were deeply offensive when first voiced. Perhaps, therefore, a condition of being allowed to hear and utter ideas that may challenge other people's values and beliefs should be the willingness to extend that same right to others and thus agree that offensiveness will not be a permissible ground for punishing expression.

Page 1064.   At the end of section 1 of the Note, add the following:

On the problem of cross-burning as a "threat," see Virginia v. Black, 538 U.S. ___ (2003), section D6 infra, this Supplement.

Page 1086.   At the end of section 5 of the Note, add the following:

Suppose a newspaper gains information as a result of a third party's unlawful act, such as theft of a document or an illegal wiretap. Can the newspaper be enjoined, criminally punished, or held civilly liable for invasion of privacy for publishing the information? See Bartnicki v. Vopper, 532 U.S. 514 (2001), in which the Court held that federal and state antiwiretap statutes cannot constitutionally be applied to a radio station that broadcasts the tape of an unlawfully intercepted telephone call, where the subject of the call was a matter of public concern and the broadcaster did not participate directly in the unlawful wiretap, even though the broadcaster knew that the material had been obtained unlawfully.

Page 1090.   Before *Note: Dangerous Ideas and Information — Final Thoughts*, add the following:

Note: Terrorism and the First Amendment

1. *September 11.* To what extent do any of the events following September 11 raise significant first amendment concerns? Consider the following:

(a) Several days after the September 11 attack, New York City police arrested a man who was picketing at the site of the former World Trade Center carrying a placard with a large photograph of Osama bin Laden. The man was charged with attempting to incite a breach of the peace.

(b) In testimony before the Senate Judiciary Committee, Attorney General John Ashcroft accused critics of the administration's policies in the war on terrorism of being "fearmongers" who give "aid" to our enemies. Suppose he had described such critics as "traitors"? Suppose he said they should be "stifled"?

(c) The federal government seized the assets of a charitable organization that was sending funds to the Middle East. The government alleged that at least some of these funds were being used to support terrorism.

(d) The federal government refused to disclose to the press the names of hundreds of individuals of Middle Eastern descent who were arrested and detained for alleged immigration violations in the wake of September 11 and it insisted on closed legal proceedings against such individuals.

(e) The federal government refused to permit representatives of the press to observe combat missions or to inspect combat sites during the war in Afghanistan.

2. *Intelligence Activities.* Suppose in an investigation of alleged Communist infiltration of the NAACP, an FBI informant infiltrates the organization's leadership and reports regularly on its membership and activities. Or suppose a government official photographs all persons attending a public NOW rally. In what circumstances, if any, are these and similar forms of surveillance limited by the first amendment? The question is hardly hypothetical. Consider the 1976 findings of the Senate Select Committee to Study Governmental Operations with Respect to Intelligence Activities:

> The Government has often undertaken the secret surveillance of citizens on the basis of their political beliefs, even when those beliefs posed no threat of violence or illegal acts on behalf of a hostile foreign power. The Government, operating primarily through secret informants, [has] swept in vast amounts of information about the personal lives, views, and associations of American citizens. Investigations of groups deemed potentially dangerous—and even of groups suspected of associating with potentially dangerous organizations—have continued for decades, despite the fact that those groups did not engage in unlawful activity. [FBI] headquarters alone has developed over 500,000 domestic intelligence files. [The] targets of intelligence activity have included political adherents of the right and the left, ranging from activist to casual supporters.
>
> [Although] the FBI has admitted that the Socialist Workers Party has committed no criminal acts, [it] has investigated the [SWP] for more than three decades on the basis of its revolutionary rhetoric [and] its claimed international links. [As] part of their effort to collect information which "related even remotely" to people or groups "active" in communities which had "the potential" for civil disorder, Army intelligence agencies took such steps as: sending agents to a Halloween party for elementary school children [because] they suspected a local "dissident" might be present; monitoring protests of welfare mothers' organizations in Milwaukee; infiltrating a coalition of church youth groups in Colorado; and sending agents to a priests' conference in Washington, D.C., held to discuss birth control measures. [In] 1970 the FBI ordered investigations of every member of the Students for a Democratic Society and of "every Black Student Union and similar group regardless of their past or present involvement in disorders."

Senate Select Committee to Study Governmental Operations with Respect to Intelligence Activities, Final Report, Intelligence Activities and the Rights of Americans,

Book II, S. Doc. No. 13133-4, 94th Cong., 2d Sess. 5-9 (1976). See generally F. Donner, The Age of Surveillance (1980); A. Theoharis, Spying on Americans (1978); Symposium, National Securities and Civil Liberties, 69 Cornell L. Rev. 685 (1984). See also Laird v. Tatum, 408 U.S. 1 (1972) (plaintiffs have no standing to challenge army's "surveillance of lawful political activities" on ground that their first amendment rights are "chilled" where there is no evidence of "objective" harm).

In 1976, Attorney General Edward Levi promulgated a series of guidelines that sharply curtailed the FBI's authority to infiltrate or investigate political and religious organizations. In 1983, Attorney General William French Smith issued a new and less restrictive set of guidelines. The Smith Guidelines provided that "[a] domestic security/terrorism investigation may be initiated when facts or circumstances reasonably indicate that two or more persons are engaged in an enterprise for the purpose of furthering political or social goals wholly or in part through activities that involve force or violence and a violation of the criminal laws of the United States." Although the Levi guidelines had prohibited any investigation based on constitutionally protected expression, the Smith guidelines expressly authorize the FBI to open an investigation "when statements advocate criminal activity."

In May of 2002, Attorney General John Ashcroft granted the FBI broad new authority to monitor political rallies, religious services and Internet chat rooms for indications of terrorist activity, and to search commercial databases that maintain detailed information on consumers such as their magazine subscriptions, book purchases, charitable contributions, and travel itineraries. The only limit the new guidelines place on such monitoring is that it be "for the purpose of detecting or preventing terrorist activities." Attorney General Ashcroft tied the new powers to the FBI's efforts to transform itself from a law-enforcement organization into a domestic security agency dedicated to preventing future terrorist attacks. In what circumstances, if any, would the new guidelines violate the first amendment?

C. Overbreadth, Vagueness, and Prior Restraint

Page 1104. At the end of the section 1 of the Note, add the following:

Suppose a permit scheme provides that the official "may" deny a permit only in certain clearly specified circumstances. Does the word "may" render the scheme "standardless"? See Thomas v. Chicago Park District, 534 U.S. 316 (2002) (rejecting this argument because on this theory every law regulating expression "contains a constitutional flaw, since it merely permits, but does not require, prosecution").

Page 1106. After the citations to Blasi and Monaghan in section 5 of the Note, add the following:

See Thomas v. Chicago Park District, 534 U.S. 316 (2002) (a content-neutral licensing scheme regulating the time, place and manner of use of a public forum need not employ the procedural safeguards required by *Freedman* because such a scheme "does not authorize a licensor to pass judgment on the content of speech").

Page 1110. At the end of section 3 of the Note, add the following:

For a general analysis of the collateral bar rule, see Palmer, Collateral Bar and Contempt: Challenging a Court Order After Disobeying It, 88 Cornell L. Rev. 215 (2002).

Page 1112. After the citation to Scordato, add the following:

Meyerson, The Neglected History of the Prior Restraint Doctrine, 34 Ind. L. Rev. 295 (2001) (suggesting that the prior restraint doctrine can best be understood as an extension of concerns about the separation of powers).

D.   Content-Based Restrictions: "Low" Value Speech

Page 1120. At the end of section 4 of the Note, add the following:

e. BeVier, The Invisible Hand of the Marketplace of Ideas, in L. Bollinger & G. Stone, Eternally Vigilant: Free Speech in the Modern Era 233, 235 (2002):

[The] political information industry—the press—is the only major industry in the U.S. economy [that] is not routinely held accountable for the harms that defects in its products cause, either to the electorate as a whole or to particular victimized individuals. [The arguable explanation is] that the private market fails to produce [political information] in optimal amounts. [Because] property rights in [information] are so difficult to establish and maintain, those who gather information [encounter] systematic difficulty in appropriating the full social benefits of their efforts. Since the "investment they make in producing information will benefit others as well as themselves," they will tend [to] underproduce it relative to its social value. This general tendency of markets to underproduce information [is] regarded as an important source of "failure" in [the] market for political information, [and thus a reason to support *New York Times v. Sullivan* as a form of subsidy to offset this market failure].

Page 1128. Before section 1 of the Note, add the following:

1a. *False ideas*. Do you agree with Justice Powell that "under the First Amendment there is no such thing as a false idea"? Consider Stone, Dialogue, in L. Bollinger & G. Stone, Eternal Vigilance: Free Speech in the Modern Era 29-31 (2002):

[Perhaps] the Supreme Court's single most important [statement] on the freedom of speech [was] its declaration in *Gertz* that "under the First Amendment there is no such thing as a false idea." [In effect, the Court announced that] the First Amendment places out of bounds any law that attempts to freeze public opinion at a particular moment in time. A majority of the People, acting through their government, may decide an issue of policy for themselves, but they have no power irrevocably to decide that issue by preventing continuation of the debate.

[But why] should that be so? [The] explanation is that we [are] balancing two competing risks. On the one hand, there is the risk that, if permitted to consider all ideas, the People will not always act wisely and will sometimes embrace bad ideas. . . . On the other hand, there is the risk that, if given the power to censor "bad" ideas, the People will not always act wisely and will sometimes prohibit the consideration of "good" ideas.

In choosing between these risks, [we] must consider the nature of human nature. History teaches that people are prone to undue certitude, intolerance [and] even fanaticism. [We] have a deep need to believe that we are right, [to] silence others who disagree with us, and in the words of Justice Holmes to "sweep away all opposition." If we empower the People to act on this instinct, there is every danger that they will do so. It is not inherent in human nature to be skeptical, self-doubting, and tolerant of others. We are not naturally inclined to abide ideas "we loathe and believe to be fraught with death." The First Amendment, on this view, cuts against human nature. It demands of us that we be better than we would be. [For] the Supreme Court to declare that "under the First Amendment there is no such thing as a false idea" is, in effect, to insist on doubt.

Page 1139. At the end of section 3 of the Note, add the following:

Consider Gewirtz, Privacy and Speech, 2001 Sup. Ct. Rev. 139, 179, 185-189:

Publicizing a rape victim's name is a cruel invasion of privacy concerning a matter of great sensitivity to the victim. Furthermore, in most cases, why is the name of a rape victim a matter of legitimate public concern? The fact of the rape or even the name of the alleged perpetrator is one thing, but the victim's name is ordinarily not something the public profits from knowing. . . .

The flavor of the Court's [opinions] is that [it] will find any conceivable escape hatch for media liability. The Court gives only token recognition to the value of implementing legal protections of privacy. This extreme solicitude for [speech] and sharply limited solicitude for [privacy should] be reversed. . . .

Supreme courts and constitutional courts in most other democracies give greater weight to values of privacy [when] they conflict with free speech claims [citing cases from Great Britain, Germany, India and Canada]. Although the constitutional rules in these countries are somewhat different, the press is vibrant and robust. [To] other countries, our current free speech doctrines seem to have become quite extreme. . . .

4. *Information of public concern.* In Bartnicki v. Vopper, 532 U.S. 514 (2001), the Court held that federal and state anti-wiretap statutes cannot constitutionally be applied to a radio station that broadcasts the tape of an unlawfully intercepted telephone call, where the subject of the call was a matter of public concern (collective-bargaining negotiations between a union representing teachers at a public high school and the local school board) and where the broadcaster did not participate directly in the unlawful wiretap, even though the broadcaster knew that the material had been obtained unlawfully. Without deciding whether there might be some circumstances in which the privacy interest is "strong enough to justify the application" of the statute, such as when there is disclosure of "domestic gossip [of] purely private concern," the Court held that the enforcement of the statute in this case "implicates core purposes of the First Amendment because it imposes sanctions on the publication of truthful information of public concern." In such circumstances, "privacy concerns give way when balanced against the interest in publishing matters of public importance." Was the information disclosed in *Cox Broadcasting* and *Florida Star* "of public importance"? Suppose the newspaper in *Bartnicki* had intercepted the phone call. Should that lead to a different result?

Page 1157. Before the Note, add the following:

THOMPSON v. WESTERN STATES MEDICAL CENTER, 535 U.S. 357 (2002). Drug compounding is a process by which a pharmacist combines ingredients to create a medication tailored to the needs of an individual patient. Compounding is typically used to prepare medications that are not commercially available. It is a traditional component of the practice of pharmacy. The federal Food, Drug and Cosmetic Act of 1938 prohibits any person to manufacture or sell any "new drug" without prior FDA approval. Until the early 1990s, the FDA essentially left the regulation of drug compounding to the States. In the early 1990s, however, the FDA became increasingly concerned that the practice of drug compounding was occurring largely outside the scope of the FDCA's testing standards. Thus, in 1997 Congress enacted the Food and Drug Administration Modernization Act which, among other things, expressly exempted compounded drugs from the FDA's standard drug approval requirements, but only if the providers of those drugs do not advertise or otherwise promote the use of specific compounded drugs. The Court, in a five-to-four decision, held that this restriction of advertising violates the First Amendment.

Justice O'Connor delivered the opinion of the Court: "In *Virginia Pharmacy*, [we] recognized that a 'particular consumer's interest in the free flow of commercial information . . . may be as keen [as] his interest in the day's most urgent political debate.' [Although] several Members of the Court have expressed doubts about [whether our] *Central Hudson* analysis [is sufficient to protect that interest], *Central Hudson,* as applied in our more recent commercial speech cases, provides an adequate basis for decision [of this case].

"[T]he Government [notes] that the FDCA's [general] drug approval requirements are critical to the public health [because the safety] of a new drug needs to be established by rigorous, scientifically valid clinical studies, [rather than by the] impressions of individual doctors, who cannot themselves compile sufficient [data]. [But] 'because obtaining FDA approval for a new drug is a costly process, requiring [such] approval of all drug products compounded by pharmacies for the particular needs of an individual patient would, as a practical matter, eliminate the practice of compounding, and thereby eliminate availability of compounded drugs for those patients who have no alternative treatment.' [Thus], the Government needs to be able to draw a line between small-scale compounding and large-scale drug manufacturing. That line must distinguish compounded drugs produced on such a small scale that they could not [realistically] undergo [costly] safety and efficacy testing from drugs produced and sold on a large enough scale that they could undergo such testing and therefore must do so.

"The Government argues that the FDAMA's speech-related provisions provide just such a line [because they] use advertising as the trigger for requiring FDA approval—essentially, as long as pharmacists do not advertise particular compounded drugs, they may sell [them] without first [obtaining] FDA approval. If they advertise their compounded drugs, however, FDA approval is required. [The] Government argues [that] Congress' decision to limit the FDAMA's compounding exemption to pharmacies that do not engage in promotional activity was 'rationally calculated' to avoid creating "'a loophole that would allow unregulated drug manufacturing to occur under the guise of pharmacy compounding.'"

"Assuming [that] drugs cannot be marketed on a large scale without advertising, the FDAMA's prohibition on advertising compounded drugs might indeed 'directly

154

advanc[e]' the Government's interests. [But] the Government has failed to demonstrate that the speech restrictions are 'not more extensive than is necessary to serve [those] interest[s].' In previous cases [we] have made clear that if the Government could achieve its interests in a manner that does not restrict speech, or that restricts less speech, the Government must do so. [Citing *Rubin* and *44 Liquormart*.]

"Several non-speech related means of drawing a line between compounding and large-scale manufacturing might be possible here. [For] example, the Government could ban the use of 'commercial scale manufacturing [for] compounding drug products.' It could prohibit pharmacists from compounding more drugs in anticipation of receiving prescriptions than in response to prescriptions already received. It could prohibit pharmacists from '[o]ffering compounded drugs at wholesale to other state licensed [entities] for resale.' [It could cap] the amount of any particular compounded drug [that] a pharmacist may make or sell in a given period of time. [The] Government has not offered any reason why these possibilities, alone or in combination, would be insufficient to prevent compounding from occurring on such a scale as to undermine the new drug approval process. . . .

"The dissent describes another governmental interest—an interest in prohibiting the sale of compounded drugs to 'patients who may not clearly need them.' Nowhere in its briefs, however, does the Government argue that this interest motivated the advertising ban. [We] have generally sustained statutes on the basis of hypothesized justifications when reviewing [them] merely to determine whether they are rational. [The] *Central Hudson* test is significantly stricter than the rational basis test, however. . . .

"Even if the Government had argued that the FDAMA's speech-related restrictions were motivated by a fear that advertising compounded drugs would put people who do not need such drugs at risk by causing them to convince their doctors to prescribe the drugs anyway, that fear would fail to justify the restrictions. Aside from the fact that this concern rests on the questionable assumption that doctors would prescribe unnecessary medications, [this] concern amounts to a fear that people would make bad decisions if given truthful information about compounded drugs. We have previously rejected the notion that the Government has an interest in preventing the dissemination of truthful commercial information in order to prevent members of the public from making bad decisions with the information. [Citing *Virginia Pharmacy* and *44 Liquormart*.]

"If the Government's failure to justify its decision to regulate speech were not enough to convice us that the FDAMA's advertising provisions were unconstitutional, the amount of beneficial speech prohibited by the FDAMA would be. Forbidding the advertisement of compounded drugs would affect pharmacists other than those interested in producing drugs on a large scale. It would prevent pharmacists [who] serve clienteles with special medical needs from telling [doctors] about the alternative drugs available through compounding. For example, [this law] would prohibit a pharmacist from posting a notice informing customers that if their children refuse to take medications because of the taste, the pharmacist could change the flavor. The fact that the FDAMA would prohibit such seemingly useful speech even though doing so does not appear to directly further any asserted governmental objective confirms our belief that the prohibition is unconstitutional."

Justice Breyer, joined by Chief Justice Rehnquist and Justices Stevens and Ginsburg, dissented: "[The] exemption from testing requirements inherently creates risks simply by placing untested drugs in the hands of the consumer. Where an individual has a specific medical need for a specially tailored drug those risks are likely offset. But where an untested drug is a convenience, not a necessity, that offset is unlikely to be present. [The FDAMA reflects] the view that individualized consideration is more likely present, and convenience alone is more likely absent, when the demand for a compounding prescription originates with a doctor, not an advertisement. The restrictions try to assure that demand is generated doctor-to-patient-to-pharmacist, not pharmacist-to-patient-to-doctor. And they do so in order to diminish the likelihood that those who do not genuinely need untested compounded drugs will not receive them.

"[No one can] deny that [the] risks associated with the untested combination of ingredients [can] for some patients mean infection, serious side effects, or even death. [There] is considerable evidence that consumer oriented advertising will create strong consumer-driven demand for a particular drug, [and] there is strong evidence that doctors will often respond affirmatively to a patient's request for a specific drug that the patient has seen advertised. . . .

"Congress could [not] have achieved its safety objectives in significantly less restrictive ways. [The alternatives suggested by the Court do not] assure the kind of individualized doctor-patient need determination that the statute [was] designed to help achieve, [and they do not] successfully distinguish traditional compounding from unacceptable manufacturing.

"It is an oversimplication to say that the Government 'fear[s]' that doctors or patients 'would make bad decisions if given truthful information.' Rather, the Government fears the safety consequences of multiple compound-drug prescription decisions initiated not by doctors but by pharmacist-to-patient advertising. Those consequences flow from the adverse cumulative effects of multiple individual decisions each of which may seem perfectly reasonable considered on its own. The Government fears that, taken together, these apparently rational individual decisions will undermine the safety testing system, thereby producing overall a net balance of harm. . . .

"I do not deny that the statute restricts the circulation of some truthful information. [Nonetheless], this Court has not previously held that commercial advertising restrictions automatically violate the First Amendment. Rather, the Court has applied a more flexible test. [It] has done so because it has concluded that, from a constitutional perspective, commercial speech does not warrant application of the Court's strictest speech-protective tests. And it has reached this conclusion in part because restrictions on commercial speech do not often repress individual self-expression; they rarely interfere with the functioning of democratic political processes; and they often reflect a democratically determined governmental decision to regulate a commercial venture in order to protect, for example, the consumer.

"[The] Court, in my view, gives insufficient weight [in this case] to the Government's regulatory rationale, and too readily assumes the existence of practical alternatives. It thereby applies the commercial speech doctrine too strictly. [An] overly rigid 'commercial speech' doctrine will transform what ought to be a legislative or regulatory decision about the best way to protect the health and safety of the American public into a constitutional decision prohibiting the legislature from enacting necessary protections. As history in respect to the Due Process Clause shows, any such transformation would involve a tragic constitutional misunderstanding."

Page 1158.   At the end of section 1 of the Note, add the following:

LORILLARD TOBACCO CO. v. REILLY, 533 U.S. 525 (2001). In 1999, the Attorney General of Massachusetts promulgated comprehensive regulations governing the advertising and sale of cigarettes, smokeless tobacco products, and cigars. These regulations prohibited (a) outdoor advertising of such products within 1,000 feet of a public playground or elementary or secondary school; (b) point-of-sale advertising that is placed lower than five feet from the floor of any retail establishment located within 1,000 feet of a public playground or elementary or second school; and (c) placing such products within a retail establishment within reach of consumers. The purpose of these regulations was "to address the incidence" of tobacco use "by children." Petitioners—a group of cigarette, smokeless tobacco, and cigar manufacturers and retailers—challenged the constitutionality of these regulations.

The Court, in an opinion by Justice O'Connor, held that the outdoor advertising and point-of-sale advertising regulations were preempted by federal law with respect to cigarettes. The Court held that those regulations violated the first amendment with respect to advertising of both cigars and smokeless tobacco products. The Court found it unnecessary to discuss the continuing validity of *Central Hudson* because it found these regulations unconstitutional even under the *Central Hudson* standard.

"The final step of the *Central Hudson* analysis [requires] a reasonable fit between the means and ends of the regulatory scheme. The Attorney General's regulations [with respect to outdoor advertising and point-of-sale advertising] do not meet this standard. The broad sweep of the regulations indicate that the Attorney General did not 'carefully calculat[e] the costs and benefits associated with the burden on speech imposed' by the regulations.

"The outdoor advertising regulations [would] prevent advertising in 87% to 91% of Boston. [Indeed], in some geographical areas, these regulations would constitute nearly a complete ban on the communication of truthful information about smokeless tobacco and cigars to adult consumers. The breadth and scope of the regulations [do] not demonstrate a careful calculation of the speech interests involved. [The] effect of [these] regulations will vary based on whether a locale is rural, suburban, or urban. The uniformly broad sweep of the geographical limitation demonstrates a lack of tailoring.

"In addition, the range of communications restricted seems unduly broad. [A] ban on all signs of any size seems ill suited to target the problem of highly visible billboards, as opposed to smaller signs. To the extent that studies have identified particular advertising and promotion practices that appeal to youth, tailoring would involve targeting those practices while permitting others. . . .

"The State's interest in preventing underage tobacco use is substantial, and even compelling, but it is no less true that the sale and use of tobacco products by adults is a legal activity. [Tobacco] retailers and manufacturers have an interest in conveying truthful information about their products to adults, and adults have a corresponding interest in receiving truthful information about tobacco products. [The] Attorney General has failed to show that [these regulations] are not more extensive than necessary to advance the State's substantial interest in preventing underage tobacco use."

The Court similarly found the point-of-sale regulation invalid under *Central Hudson*: "[The] State's goal is to prevent minors from using tobacco products and to curb demand for that activity by limiting youth exposure to advertising. The 5 foot rule does not seem to advance that goal. Not all children are less than 5 feet tall, and those who are certainly have the ability to look up. [Massachusetts] may wish to target tobacco advertisements and displays that entice children, much like floor-level candy displays in a convenience store, but the blanket height restriction does not constitute a reasonable fit with that goal."

Finally, the Court upheld the regulations that barred the "use of self-service displays" and required "that tobacco products be placed out of the reach of all consumers in a location accessible only to salespersons." The Court explained that these regulations did not require the application of *Central Hudson* because they restricted conduct "for reasons unrelated to the communication of ideas." Thus, they were constitutional because "the State has demonstrated a substantial interest in preventing access to tobacco products by minors and has adopted an appropriately narrow means of advancing that interest." The Court reasoned that "unattended displays of tobacco products present an opportunity for access without the proper age verification provided by law," that the regulations "leave open ample channels of communication" and "do not significantly impede adult access to tobacco products," and that "retailers have other means of exercising any cognizable speech interest in the presentation of their products," such as by placing "empty tobacco packaging on open display."

In a concurring opinion, Justice Thomas argued that "there is no 'philosophical or historical basis for asserting that "commercial" speech is of "lower value" than "noncommercial" speech.'" Thus, the "asserted government interest in keeping people ignorant by suppressing expression 'is per se illegitimate and can no more justify regulation of "commercial" speech than it can justify regulation of "noncommercial" speech.'" Moreover, with respect to the specifics of these regulations, he added that "the theory that public debate should be limited in order to protect impressionable children has a long historical pedigree: Socrates was condemned for being 'a doer of evil, inasmuch as he corrupts the youth.' [Speech] 'cannot be suppressed solely to protect the young from ideas or images that a legislative body thinks unsuitable for them.'"

Justice Stevens, joined by Justices Ginsburg and Breyer, concurred in part and dissented in part. With respect to the outdoor advertising regulation, Justice Stevens argued that "when calculating whether a child-direction location restriction goes too far in regulating adult speech, one crucial question is whether the regulatory scheme leaves available sufficient 'alternative avenues of communication.'" Justice Stevens concluded that the record did not contain "sufficient information to enable us to answer that question." He therefore advocated a remand "for trial on that issue."

Justice Stevens agreed with the Court that the sales practice regulations prohibiting self-service sales of tobacco products were consistent with the first amendment: "[These restrictions] are best analyzed as regulating conduct, not speech. While the decision how to display one's products no doubt serves a marginal communicative function, the same can be said of virtually any human activity performed with the hope or intention of evoking the interest of others. This Court has long recognized the need to differentiate between legislation that targets expression and legislation that targets conduct for legitimate non-speech-related reasons but imposes an incidental burden on expression. [Citing United States v. O'Brien, page 1302 of the main text]. [Laws] requiring that stores maintain items behind counters and prohibiting self-service displays fall squarely on the conduct side of the line. [I] see nothing the least bit constitutionally problematic in requiring individuals to ask for the assistance of a salesclerk in order to examine or purchase a handgun, a bottle of penicillin, or a package of cigarettes." Justice Stevens reached the same conclusion with respect to the five-foot regulation.

Consider M. Redish, Money Talks, 57-60 (2001):

The arguments against First Amendment protection for tobacco advertising [underscore] every one of the theoretical flaws underlying the commercial speech distinction. No one could seriously dispute that smoking is a social and political issue of enormous intensity and import. [In] order to demonstrate that point, one need only inquire whether full First Amendment protection would extend to the commentary of anti-tobacco activists either asserting the scientific case for the link between smoking and illness or directly urging individuals not to smoke. [Even] the most ardent advocate of a narrow, politically based First Amendment would have to concede that such expression lies at the core of free speech protection. [But] if this is true for the expression of those advocating that individuals refrain from smoking, it [must] be equally true of speech on the other side of the issue. [To] uphold such a restriction would allow government to skew the democratic process in order to achieve an externally preordained result. It would, moreover, reflect government's paternalistic mistrust of its citizens' ability to make lawful choices on the basis of free and open debate. . . .

It could be argued [of course] that tobacco advertisements [do not make] a real contribution to the debate. [But] far from failing to contribute to a public debate, the advertisements [urge] individuals to risk the possibility of future health injury in order to obtain certain largely intangible social or personal benefits. [It] would be difficult to distinguish appeals made in tobacco advertisements from [other appeals that] promote lawful lifestyle choices available to the individual. [Regulation of tobacco advertising] takes on the ominous character of government orchestrated suppression, manipulation, and mind control—the epitome of the type of expressive regulation the First Amendment precludes.

Page 1158. Before section 2 of the Note, add the following:

1a. *Regulating truthful commercial adverstising.* Consider Post, The Constitutional Status of Commercial Speech, 48 UCLA L. Rev. 1, 2-4, 14, 49, 53-54 (2000):

[C]ommercial speech doctrine [is] a notoriously unstable and contentious domain of First Amendment jurisprudence. . . . Although the Court has persistently adjudged commercial speech to be "subordinate," it has never explained why this might be true. [In my view], core First Amendment protections extend to those forms of communication that are deemed necessary to ensure that a democratic state remains responsive to the views of its citizens. [Commercial] speech, by contrast, consists of communication about commercial matters that conveys information necessary for public decision making, but that does not itself form part of public discourse. Commercial speech differs from public discourse because it is constitutionally valued merely for the information it disseminates, rather than for being itself a valuable way of participating in democratic self-determination. . . .

This focus on information introduces an important point of difference from the First Amendment protections that apply to public discourse. It is a necessary condition for democratic legitimacy that citizens have free access to public discourse, because censoring a citizen's ability to contribute to public opinion renders the government, with respect to that citizen, "heteronomous and nondemocratic." From a constitutional point of view, the censorship of commercial speech does not endanger the process of democratic legitimation. [Instead] it merely jeopardizes the circulation of information relevant to "the voting of wise decisions.". . .

The reason why the First Amendment prohibits the state from suppressing public discourse on the grounds of its persuasiveness is that participation within democratic self-governance [assumes that] speakers seek to persuade others of their point of view and in this way to make the state responsive to their perspective; for the state deliberately to disrupt this communicative relationship is to negate the very constitutional raison d'etre of public discourse. This analysis, however, is not applicable to commercial speech, which is protected [only] to ensure "the free flow of information." [Thus, in] the particular environment of commercial speech, [the doctrine ought to focus not on whether the regulation is paternalistic, but on] whether the "informational function" of commercial speech has been unacceptably compromised. [A] workable rule of thumb might well be that government regulations entirely eliminating a category of truthful information are good candidates for heightened constitutional suspicion.

Page 1160.   After section 8 of the Note, add the following:

9. *Other forms of compelled commercial advertising.* In what circumstances may government compel commercial firms to pay assessments to support common advertising programs? Compare Glickman v. Wileman Brothers & Elliott, Inc., 512 U.S. 1145 (1997) (upholding an order of the Secretary of Agriculture requiring California agricultural producers to pay assessments to help defray the costs of generic advertising of California fruits, noting that the advertising at issue does not promote any "message other than encouraging consumers to buy California tree fruit," that the order does "not compel the producers to endorse or to finance any political or ideological views," and that "the mere fact that the objectors believe their money is not being well spent "does not mean [that] they have a First Amendment complaint'"), with United States v. United Foods, 533 U.S. 405 (2001) (invalidating a federal statute requiring producers of fresh mushrooms to fund a common advertising program promoting mushroom sales, and distinguishing *Glickman* on the ground that the compelled assessments in *Glickman* were ancillary to a comprehensive regulatory scheme of government-mandated collective action, whereas the compelled assessments in *United Foods* were not part of such a comprehensive scheme, other than a program "to generate the very speech to which some of the producers object"). For more on compelled speech, see pages 1159-1164 of the main text.

Page 1165. Before section 2 of the Note, add the following:

1b. *The freedom of imagination.* Consider Rubenfeld, The Freedom of Imagination: Copyright's Constitutionality, 112 Yale L. J. 1, 35-38 (2002):

Why does American law rebel at state aesthetic censors? [A] society with state control over art might never have known Pollock's great abstractions, Schoenberg's tone poems, or Carroll's captivating Jabberwocky. [It] is simply confusion to think that constitutional protection of [Britney Spears] depends on the quality of her singing or dancing, [or] on the fact that she actually spurs a great deal of conversation on "matters of public concern." [The] art/entertainment distinction has no place in First Amendment law. [It] would be better to dispense with the idea that the First Amendment protects works of high aesthetic, cultural, political, or individually-expressive value. We should say rather that the First Amendment protects—the freedom of imagination. . . .

This should be a First Amendment bedrock. . . . The freedom of imagination means the freedom to explore the world not present, creatively and communicatively. [It] means the freedom to explore, without state penalty, any thought, any image, any emotion, any melody, as far as the imagining mind may take it.

Page 1180. After section 4 of the Note, add the following:

4a. *Community standards on the Internet.* In Ashcroft v. American Civil Liberties Union, 535 U.S. 564 (2002), the Court held that a federal statute (the Child Online Protection Act) regulating obscene material on the Internet is not invalid on its face because it applies local community standards in determining whether particular material is obscene, even though an individual posting sexually explicit material on the Internet has no control over the geographic areas in which the material is accessible. The Court of Appeals had invalidated the use of local community standards because, in the special context of the Internet, such a test "would effectively force all speakers on the Web to abide by the 'most puritan' community's standards."

In a plurality opinion, Justice Thomas reasoned that the Internet is not sufficiently different from other media of communication, such as the mail, to "justify adopting a different approach than that set forth in *Hamling*." Moreover, "if a publisher chooses to send its material into a particular community, [it] is the publisher's responsibility to abide by that community's standards. If a publisher wishes for its material to be judged only by the standards of particular communities, then it need only take the simple step of utilizing a medium that enables it to target the release of its material into [only] those communities." Finally, Justice Thomas observed that the statute is not unconstitutionally overbroad because those challenging the statute had failed to demonstrate with "objective evidence" that local community standards differ *substantially* from one community to another.

Although concurring in the judgment that the statute was not unconstitutional on its face, Justice O'Connor observed that "given Internet speakers' inability to control the geographic location of their audience, expecting them to bear the burden of controlling the recipients of their speech [may] be entirely too much to ask, and would potentially suppress an inordinate amount of expression. For these reasons, adoption of a national standard is necessary [for] any reasonable regulation of Internet obscenity."

In another concurring opinion, Justice Breyer argued that "Congress intended the statutory word 'community' to refer to the Nation's adult community taken as a whole, not to geographically separate local areas." He added that "to read the statute as adopting the community standards of every locality in the United States would provide the most puritan of communities with a heckler's Internet veto affecting the rest of the Nation."

Justice Kennedy, joined by Justices Souter and Ginsburg, also filed a concurring opinion: "Unlike Justice Thomas, [I] would not assume that the Act is narrow enough to render the national variation in community standards unproblematic. [The] economics and technology of Internet communication differ in important ways from those of [other means of communication, and] it is no answer to say that the speaker should 'take the simple step of utilizing a [different] medium.' [The] nation variation in community standards constitutes a particular burden on Internet speech." Nonetheless, Justice Kennedy agreed with the plurality that the act was not unconstitutional on its face.

Justice Stevens dissented: "[In] light of [the] fundamental difference in technologies, the rules applicable to the mass mailing of an obscene montage [should] not be used to judge the legality of messages on the World Wide Web. [Because] communities differ widely in their attitudes toward sex, [the] Court of Appeals was correct to conclude that [applying] local community standards to the Internet will restrict a substantial amount of protected speech that would not be considered [obscene] in many communities. [It] is quite wrong to allow the standards of a minority consisting of the least tolerant communities to regulate access to relatively harmless messages in this burgeoning market."

Page 1181. After section 6 of the Note, add the following:

7. *Violence.* Suppose a city enacts an ordinance regulating the freedom of minors to play video games that "appeal predominantly to the morbid interest of minors in violence, are patently offensive to prevailing adult standards about what is suitable

for minors, lack serious literary, artistic, political or scientific value for minors, and contain graphic depictions of violence, such as decapitation, dismemberment, mutilation, maiming and bloodshed."

Consider American Amusement Machine Assn. v. Kendrick, 244 F.3d 572 (7th Cir.), *cert. denied,* 534 U.S. 994 (2001)), in which the court, in an opinion by Judge Richard Posner, invalidated such an ordinance:

> Violence and obscenity are distinct categories of objectionable depiction. [The] main worry about obscenity [is] that it is offensive. [But] offensiveness is not the basis on which [the challenged ordinance] seeks to regulate violent video games. [The] basis of the ordinance, rather, is a belief that violent video games cause temporal harm by engendering aggressive attitudes and behavior, which might lead to violence. [To restrict speech on this basis], a state would have to present a compelling basis for believing that [such] harms were actually caused [by the expression].
>
> No doubt the City would concede this point if the question were whether to forbid children to read [the] *Odyssey,* with its graphic descriptions of Odysseus's grinding out the eye of Polyphemus with a heated, sharpened stake, [or] the *Divine Comedy,* with its graphic descriptions of the tortures of the damned, [or] *War and Peace,* with its graphic descriptions [of] death from war wounds. [Violence] has always been and remains a central interest of humankind and a recurrent, even obsessive theme of culture both high and low. It engages the interest of children from an early age, as anyone familiar with the classic fairy tales [is] aware. To shield children right up to the age of 18 from exposure to violent descriptions and images would not only be quixotic, but deforming; it would leave them unequipped to cope with the world as we know it. . . .
>
> Most of the video games in the record of this case [are] stories. Take "The House of the Dead." The player is armed with a gun—most fortunately, because he is being assailed by a seemingly unending succession of hideous axe-wielding zombies, the living dead conjured back to life by voodoo. [Zombies] are supernatural beings, therefore difficult to kill. Repeated shots are necessary to stop them as they rush headlong toward the player. He must not only be alert to the appearance of zombies from any quarter, he must be assiduous about reloading his gun periodically, lest he be overwhelmed. . . .
>
> Self-defense, protection of others, dread of the "undead," fighting against overwhelming odds—these are all age-old themes of literature, and ones particularly appealing to the young. "The House of the Dead" is not distinguished literature. [We] are in the world of kids' popular culture. But it is not lightly to be suppressed.

7a. *Video games as "speech."* Are video games "speech" within the meaning of the first amendment? Are games such as bingo, blackjack, chess and baseball "speech" within the meaning of the first amendment? See Saunders, Regulating Youth Access to Violent Video Games: Three Responses to First Amendment Concerns, 2003 L. Rev. M.S.U.-D.C.L. 51, 99 ("Where there is no intent to or likelihood of passing information or communicating a message, even the principle that entertainment is protected [speech] does not apply.").

7b. *Internet filters for public libraries.* Can a public library use filters on its internet terminals designed to preclude patrons from accessing obscene web-sites? Suppose the filter is imprecise and inevitably will block access to non-obscene as well as obscene web-sites? See United States v. American Library Association, 539 U.S. ___ (2003), section E.2, *infra* this Supplement.

Page 1183.   At the end of the first full paragraph after the decision in *Ferber*, add the following:

Does it make sense under the first amendment to prohibit X from showing a movie because Y committed an unlawful act to create the movie? Consider Bartnicki v. Vopper, 532 U.S. 514 (2001), in which the Court held that federal and state anti-wiretap statutes cannot constitutionally be applied to a radio station that broadcasts the tape of an unlawfully intercepted telephone call, where the subject of the call was a matter of public concern and the broadcaster did not participate directly in the unlawful wiretap, even though the broadcaster knew that the material had been obtained unlawfully. The Court expressly distinguished *Ferber* on the ground that *Ferber* involved speech "considered of minimal value."

Page 1183.   At the end of the second full paragraph after the decision in *Ferber*, add the following:

Consider Adler, Inverting the First Amendment, 149 U. Pa. L. Rev. 921, 996 (2001):

> Congress significantly broadened the scope of child pornography laws in 1996 when it passed [the] Child Pornography Prevention Act ("CPPA"). [The] CPPA responded to a technological innovation, the development of wholly computer-generated or "virtual" child pornography, [by outlawing] materials that *appear* to be (but are not) depictions of children engaged in sexual conduct. According to Congress, such material [must] be prevented because [it] "inflames the desires of child molesters, pedophiles, and child pornographers" and it "encourages a societal perception of children as sexual objects." [The] CPPA is a total departure from *Ferber*, which was premised on preventing the abuse of children in the production

of the material. [CPPA] has, in effect, enacted Catherine MacKinnon's theory of speech into law.

Page 1184.   Before Section 5, add the following:

For the argument that, by unwittingly perpetuating and escalating the sexual representation of children, child pornography laws may perversely "reinforce the very problem they are designed to attack," see Adler, The Perverse Law of Child Pornography, 101 Colum. L. Rev. 209 (2001) ("sexual prohibitions invite their own violation by increasing the sexual allure of what they forbid" and child pornography laws may thus generate "a vast realm of discourse in which the image of the child as sexual is preserved and multiplied").

ASHCROFT v. THE FREE SPEECH COALITION, 535 U.S. 234 (2002). The Court invalidated the Child Pornography Prevention Act of 1996 (CPPA), which extended the prohibition against child pornography to sexually explicit images that *appear* to depict minors, but were in fact produced without using real children — either by computer imaging or by using adults who look like children. Justice Kennedy delivered the opinion of the Court:

"By prohibiting child pornography that does not depict an actual child, the statute goes beyond *Ferber*, which distinguished child pornography from other sexually explicit speech because of the State's interest in protecting the children exploited by the production process. [Although the statute] captures a range of depictions [that] do not [harm] any children in the production process[, Congress] decided the materials threaten children in other, less direct, ways. Pedophiles might use the materials to encourage children to participate in sexual activity [or they] might 'whet their own sexual appetites' with the pornographic images, 'thereby increasing the creation and distribution of child pornography and the sexual abuse and exploitation of actual children.' Under these rationales, harm flows from the content of the images, not from the means of their production. In addition, Congress [was concerned that the existence of] computer-generated images [can] can make it harder to prosecute pornographers who [use] real minors. As imaging technology improves, Congress found, it becomes more difficult to prove that a particular picture was produced using actual children. To ensure that defendants possessing child pornography using real minors cannot evade prosecution, Congress extended the ban to virtual child pornography. . . .

"The sexual abuse of a child is a most serious crime and an act repugnant to the moral instincts of a decent people. [Congress] may pass valid laws to protect children from abuse, and it has. The prospect of crime, however, by itself does not justify laws suppressing protected speech. See *Kingsley Pictures*. ('Among free men, the deterrents ordinarily to be applied to prevent crime are education and punishment for violations of the law, not abridgment of the rights of free speech'). . . .

"As a general principle, the First Amendment bars the government from dictating what we see or read or speak or hear. The freedom of speech has its limits; it does not embrace certain categories of speech, including defamation, incitement, obscenity, and pornography produced with real children. While these categories may be prohibited without violating the First Amendment, none of them includes the speech prohibited by the CPPA . . .

"[T]he CPPA [does not deal with] obscenity. Under *Miller*, the Government must prove that the work, taken as a whole, appeals to the prurient interest, is patently offensive in light of community standards, and lacks serious literary, artistic, political, or scientific value. The CPPA, however, [applies] without regard to the *Miller* requirements. . . .

"[The] statute proscribes the visual depiction of an idea—that of teenagers engaging in sexual activity—that is a fact of modern society and has been a theme in art and literature throughout the ages. [Citing, e.g., Romeo and Juliet; and the movies Traffic and American Beauty.] If [such works] contain a single graphic depiction of sexual activity within the statutory definition, the possessor [or distributor] would be subject to severe punishment without inquiry into the work's redeeming value. This is inconsistent with an essential First Amendment rule: The artistic merit of a work does not depend on the presence of a single explicit scene. Under *Miller*, the First Amendment requires that redeeming value be judged by considering the work as a whole. . . .

"The Government seeks to address this deficiency by arguing that speech prohibited by the CPPA is virtually indistinguishable from child pornography, which may be banned without regard to whether it depicts works of value. See *Ferber*. Where the images are themselves the product of child sexual abuse, *Ferber* recognized that the State had an interest in stamping it out without regard to any judgment about its content. The production of the work, not its content, was the target of the statute. The fact that a work contained serious literary, artistic, or other value did not excuse the harm it caused to its child participants. [*Ferber*] upheld a prohibition on the distribution and sale of child pornography, as well as its production, because these acts were 'intrinsically related' to the sexual abuse of children in two ways. First, as a permanent record of a child's abuse, the continued circulation itself would harm the child who had participated. Like a defamatory statement, each new publication of the speech would cause new injury to the child's reputation and emotional well-being. Second, because the traffic in child pornography was an economic motive for its production, the State had an interest in closing the distribution network. [Under] either rationale, the speech had what the Court in effect held was a proximate link to the crime from which it came. . . .

"In contrast to the speech in *Ferber*, [the] CPPA prohibits speech that records no crime and creates no victims by its production. Virtual child pornography is not 'intrinsically related' to the sexual abuse of children, as were the materials in *Ferber*. While the Government asserts that the images can lead to actual instances of child abuse, the causal link is contingent and indirect. The harm does not necessarily follow from the speech, but depends upon some unquantified potential for subsequent criminal acts.

"The Government says these indirect harms are sufficient because, as *Ferber* acknowledged, child pornography rarely can be valuable speech. This argument, however, suffers from two flaws. First, *Ferber*'s judgment about child pornography was based upon how it was made, not on what it communicated. [Second,] *Ferber* did not hold that child pornography is by definition without value. On the contrary, the Court recognized some works in this category might have significant value, but relied on virtual images—the very images prohibited by the CPPA—as an alternative and permissible means of expression. *Ferber,* then, not only referred to the distinction between actual and virtual child pornography, it relied on it as a reason supporting its holding. *Ferber* provides no support for a statute that eliminates the distinction and makes the alternative mode criminal as well.

"The CPPA [is thus] inconsistent with *Miller* and finds no support in *Ferber*. The Government seeks to justify its prohibitions in other ways. It argues that the CPPA is necessary because pedophiles may use virtual child pornography to seduce children. There are many things innocent in themselves, however, such as cartoons, video games, and candy, that might be used for immoral purposes, yet we would not expect those to be prohibited because they can be misused. The Government, of course, may punish adults who provide unsuitable materials to children, see *Ginsberg*, and it may enforce criminal penalties for unlawful solicitation. The precedents establish, however, that speech within the rights of adults to hear may not be silenced completely in an attempt to shield children from it. [Here, the] evil in question depends upon the actor's unlawful conduct, conduct defined as criminal quite apart from any link to the speech in question. This establishes that the speech ban is not narrowly drawn. The objective is to prohibit illegal conduct, but this restriction goes well beyond that interest by restricting the speech available to law-abiding adults.

"The Government submits further that virtual child pornography whets the appetites of pedophiles and encourages them to engage in illegal conduct. This rationale cannot sustain the provision in question. The mere tendency of speech to encourage unlawful acts is not a sufficient reason for banning it. [The] Court's First Amendment cases draw vital distinctions between words and deeds, between ideas and conduct. The government may not prohibit speech because it increases the chance an unlawful act will be committed 'at some indefinite future time.' [The] Government has shown no more than a remote connection between speech that might encourage thoughts or impulses and any resulting child abuse. Without a significantly stronger, more direct connection, the Government may not prohibit speech on the ground that it may encourage pedophiles to engage in illegal conduct. . . .

168

"Finally, the Government says that the possibility of producing images by using computer imaging makes it very difficult for it to prosecute those who produce pornography by using real children. Experts, we are told, may have difficulty in saying whether the pictures were made by using real children or by using computer imaging. The necessary solution, the argument runs, is to prohibit both kinds of images. The argument, in essence, is that protected speech may be banned as a means to ban unprotected speech. This analysis turns the First Amendment upside down. The Government may not suppress lawful speech as the means to suppress unlawful speech. Protected speech does not become unprotected merely because it resembles the latter."

Justice Thomas filed a concurring opinion in which he observed that "if technological advances" eventually reach a point where they actually (as opposed to speculatively) "thwart prosecution of 'unlawful speech,' the Government may well have a compelling interest [in] regulating some narrow category of 'lawful speech' in order to enforce effectively laws against pornography made through the abuse of real children."

Justice O'Connor, joined in part by Chief Justice Rehnquist and Justice Scalia, dissented in part. Justice O'Connor concluded that the CPPA was unconstitutional insofar as it restricts material created by using youthful-looking adults, but that it was constitutional insofar as it restricts virtual-child pornography. With respect to the latter, with which Chief Justice Rehnquist and Justice Scalia agreed, Justice O'Connor argued that if the CPPA is narrowly construed to limit only computer-generated images that are "virtually indistinguishable" from real child pornography, it would satisfy "strict scrutiny" because it would then be narrowly-tailed to serve the compelling governmental interest in eliminating real child pornography. She also noted that if any work falling within this category in fact has serious social, political, literary or scientific value, the possible "overbreadth" of the law in that regard could be considered in an "as applied" challenge. On the other hand, Justice O'Connor concurred with the Court in invalidating the law insofar as it restricts material created with youthful-looking adults because such material would not pose the same problem to the enforcement of the prohibition on actual child pornography as material created using computer images.

Chief Justice Rehnquist, with whom Justice Scalia joined, dissented. Chief Justice Rehnquist argued that the Court should interpret the CPPA narrowly, as extending the definition of child pornography only to computer-generated images that are "virtually indistinguishable" from real children engaged in sexually explicit conduct. So construed, he would uphold the statute for the reasons offered by Justice O'Connor.

Another provision of the CPPA, not at issue in this case, prohibits the use of computer morphing to alter the images of real children so they appear to be engaged in sexual activity. Is this different from the issues addressed in *Ashcroft*? The Court noted in passing that because such morphed images "implicate the interests of real children" they are closer to the issue considered in *Ferber*. Might this better be analyzed as a form of libel?

Suppose Congress re-enacted the CPPA verbatim, but recognized an affirmative defense to enable the defendant to prove that the image had been created without the abuse of a real child. Would that satisfy the first amendment?

What do you suppose is the "real" motivation underlying laws like the CPPA? Is it the concern that the existence of virtual child pornography will increase pedophilia? That it will make it more difficult to prosecute actual child pornography? That the images are themselves so offensive that they should not be tolerated? Of course, the answer must be some mix of the three. But to the extent the most candid answer is the third, the Court made clear its view of this in *Ashcroft*: "[S]peech may not be prohibited because it concerns subjects offending our sensibilities."

Page 1204. At the end of section 1 of the Note, add the following:

1a. *Solving the problems of the CDA.* After the Court's decision in *Reno*, Congress enacted the Child Online Protection Act, which was designed to address the problems the Court found with the CDA. COPA prohibits any person from knowingly making "any communication for commercial purposes" on the World Wide Web that is "available to any minor and that includes any material that is harmful to minors." Thus, unlike the CDA, COPA applies only to material displayed on the World Wide Web (and not to e-mail); only to material made for commercial purposes; and only to material that is "harmful to minors" (*i.e.,* "obscene for minors," as recognized in *Ginsberg*). COPA defines material that is "harmful to minors" as any communication that "the average person, applying contemporary community standards, would find, taking the material as a whole and with respect to minors, is designed to appeal [to] the prurient interest"; that depicts in "a manner patently offensive with respect to minors, an actual or simulated sexual act [or] lewd exhibition of the genitals"; and that "taken as a whole, lacks serious literary, artistic, political, or scientific value for minors." Like the CDA, COPA provides an affirmative defense if the defendant "in good faith has restricted access by minors to material that is harmful to minors by requiring the use of a credit card, debit account, adult access code, or adult personal identification number." Is COPA constitutional? Cf. Ashcroft v. American Civil Liberties Union, 535 U.S. 564 (2002) (holding that COPA is not unconstitutional on its face because it uses local community standards to determine whether material is "harmful to minors," but not otherwise addressing the constitutionality of COPA). Approximately 40% of all sexually explicit web sites are placed on the Internet by individuals not in the United States. Given the nature of the Internet, and the way search engines work, is there anything to be gained by a law like COPA, which cannot reach individuals not within the jurisdiction of the United States?

1b. *The moral faculties of children.* Consider Tubbs, Conflicting Images of Children in First Amendment Jurisprudence, 30 Pepperdine L. Rev. 1, 51 (2002): "Perhaps the most distressing thing about the majority opinion in *Playboy Entertainment* is [its] cavalier indifference toward the vulnerability of the young [and its assumption] that the moral faculties of children are indistinguishable from those of adults."

Page 1209. After *Renton*, add the following:

CITY OF LOS ANGELES v. ALAMEDA BOOKS, 535 U.S. 425 (2002). In 1977, the city of Los Angeles conducted a study that concluded that concentrations of adult entertainment establishments are associated with higher crimes rates. Accordingly, it enacted an ordinance prohibiting such establishments within 1,000 feet of each other or within 500 feet of a religious institution, school or public park. In 1983, to close a "loophole" in the original ordinance, the city amended the ordinance to prohibit "more than one adult entertainment business in the same building." Alameda Books, which operates a combined adult book store and adult video arcade in a single location, challenged the amendment on the ground that there was no evidence that combining these two activities in a single location causes higher crime rates. The lower court granted summary judgment to Alameda Books. The Supreme Court reversed.

Justice O'Connor, joined by Chief Justice Rehnquist and Justices Scalia and Thomas, delivered the plurality opinion: "[In *Renton*,] we stated that the ordinance would be upheld so long as the city [showed] that [it] was designed to serve a substantial government interest and that reasonable alternative avenues of communication remained available. [We agree with Justice Kennedy's observation in his concurring opinion in this case that a zoning] ordinance warrants intermediate scrutiny only if it is a time, place, and manner regulation and not a ban.

"[Although the 1977 study did not specifically consider the problem addressed by the 1983 amendment, it was] rational for the city to infer that reducing the concentration of adult operations in a neighborhood, whether within separate establishments or in one large establishment, will reduce crime rates. [We] conclude that the city, at this [very early] stage of the litigation, has [sufficiently] complied with the evidentiary requirement in *Renton* [to withstand a motion for summary judgment]."

Justice Kennedy concurred in the judgment: "If a city can decrease the crime and blight associated with certain speech by the traditional exercise of its zoning power, and at the same time leave the quantity and accessibility of the speech substantially undiminished, there is no First Amendment objection. This is so even if the measure identifies the problem outside by reference to the speech inside—that is, even if the measure is in that sense content-based. [But] the purpose and effect of [such] a zoning ordinance must be to reduce secondary effects and not to reduce speech.

"[In *Renton*,] the Court designated the restriction 'content neutral.' [This] was something of a fiction. [Whether] a statute is content-based or content neutral is something that can be determined on the face of it; if the statute describes speech by content then it is content based. [This ordinance is] content based and we should call [it] so. [Nevertheless], the central holding of *Renton* is sound: [zoning] regulations do not automatically raise the specter of impermissible content discrimination, even if they are content based, [because the] zoning context provides a built-in legitimate rationale, which rebuts the usual presumption that content-based restrictions are unconstitutional. [But] the necessary rationale for applying intermediate [rather than strict] scrutiny is the promise that zoning ordinances like this one may reduce the costs of secondary effects without substantially reducing speech. [It] is no trick to reduce secondary effects by reducing speech or its audience; but a city may not attack secondary effects [by] attacking speech.

"[If] two adult businesses are under the same roof, an ordinance requiring them to separate will have one of two results: One business will either move elsewhere or close. The city's premise cannot be the latter. [In] this case the proposition to be shown is supported by [the] 1977 study and common experience. [If respondent can prove otherwise] at trial, then the ordinance might not withstand intermediate scrutiny. [But it does] survive summary judgment."

Justice Souter, joined by Justices Stevens, Ginsburg and Breyer, dissented: "Because content-based regulation applies to expression by very reason of what is said, it carries a high risk that expressive limits are imposed for the sake of suppressing a message that is disagreeable to listeners or readers, or the government. [The regulation at issue here], though called content-neutral [in *Renton*, would better be] called content-correlated. [This] would not only describe it for what it is, but keep alert to a risk of content-based regulation that it poses. The risk lies in the fact that when a law applies selectively only to speech of particular content, the more precisely the content is identified, the greater is the opportunity for government censorship. [The] capacity of zoning regulations to address the [secondary effects] without eliminating the speech [is] the only possible excuse for [treating them] as akin to time, place and manner regulations.

"In this case, [the] government has not shown that bookstores containing viewing booths [increase] negative secondary effects, [and] we are thus left without substantial justification for viewing the [restriction as content neutral]. [If] we take the city's breakup policy at its face, enforcing it will mean that in every case two establishments will operate instead of [one]. Since the city presumably does not wish merely to multiply adult establishments, it makes sense to ask what offsetting gain the city may obtain from [its] breakup policy. The answer may lie in the fact that two establishments in place of one will entail two [overheads] in place of one. [Every] month business will be more expensive than it used to be. [That] sounds like a good strategy for driving out expressive adult businesses. In sounds, in other words, like a policy of content-based regulation."

Page 1218. After section g of the Note, add the following:

gg. R. Kennedy, Nigger 151, 154, 158-59 (2002):

[P]roponents of enhanced hate-speech regulation have typically failed to establish persuasively the asserted predicate for their campaign—that is, that verbal abuse [is] a "rising" [development] demanding countermeasures. Regulationists do cite racist incidents [but] too often the dramatic retelling of an anecdote is permitted to substitute for a more systematic, quantitative analysis. [An] examination of the substance of the regulationists' proposals turns up suggested reforms that are puzzlingly narrow, frighteningly broad, or disturbingly susceptible to discriminatory manipulation. . . .

The cumulative effect of [the Supreme Court's] speech-protective doctrines is a conspicuous toleration of speech [that] many people—in some instances the vast majority of people—find deeply, perhaps even viscerally, obnoxious, including flag burning, pornography, Nazis' taunting of Holocaust survivors, a jacket emblazoned with the phrase "Fuck the Draft," *The Satanic Verses, The Birth of a Nation, The Last Temptation of Christ.* And just as acute wariness [of] censorship has long furthered struggles for freedom of expression in all its many guises, so has resistance against censorship always been an important and positive feature of the great struggles against racist tyranny in the United States, from the fight against slavery to the fight against Jim Crow. For this reason, we may count ourselves fortunate that the anti-hate-speech campaign [has] fizzled and largely subsided. This [effort] was simply not worth the various costs that success would have exacted.

ggg. A. Tsesis, Destructive Messages 180, 192 (2002):

A general consensus among nations holds that hate propaganda [threatens] both outgroup participation in democracy and minority rights. Countries that have enacted laws penalizing the dissemination of hate speech include Austria, Belgium, Brazil, Canada, Cyprus, England, France, Germany, India, Israel, Italy, Netherlands, and Switzerland. [These] international examples demonstrate that the United States's pure speech jurisprudence is anomalous. A broad consensus holds that inciting others to hatred is detrimental to society. Democracies generally recognizes that preserving human rights supersedes a bigot's desire to spread venomous messages. [The] history of racism in the United States, from Native

American dislocations, to slavery, to Japanese internment, makes clear that here, as in other democracies, intolerance and persecution can exist in spite of socially held ideals of fairness and equality. Safeguards against the realistic effects of hate speech should be enacted to prevent the forces of bigotry from harnessing resources to strengthen socially regressive movements.

Page 1226. Before section 3 of the Note, add the following:

d. After *R.A.V.*, would the following law be constitutional: No person may incite "others to discriminate, persecute, oppress, or commit any similar acts against members of an identifiable group [where] it is substantially probable or reasonably foreseeable, based on the content and context of the message, that its dissemination will elicit such acts [and] where the speaker specifically intended the message to promote destructive behavior, [provided that no] one shall be convicted under this law [if] the statement was uttered as an expression of opinion on a neutral scientific, academic, or religious subject and/or the statement was made to eliminate the incidence of hatred toward an identifiable group." A. Tsesis, Destructive Messages 208-09 (2002).

Page 1228. Before the Note on *Pornography and the Victimization of Women*, add the following:

VIRGINIA v. BLACK
538 U.S. ___ (2003)

JUSTICE O'CONNOR announced the judgment of the Court and delivered the opinion of the Court with respect to Parts I, II, and III, and an opinion with respect to Parts IV and V, in which THE CHIEF JUSTICE, JUSTICE STEVENS, and JUSTICE BREYER join.

In this case we consider whether the Commonwealth of Virginia's statute banning cross burning with "an intent to intimidate a person or group of persons" violates the First Amendment. Va. Code Ann. §18.2-423 (1996). We conclude that while a State, consistent with the First Amendment, may ban cross burning carried out with the intent to intimidate, the provision in the Virginia statute treating any cross burning as prima facie evidence of intent to intimidate renders the statute unconstitutional. . . .

I

Respondents Barry Black, Richard Elliott, and Jonathan O'Mara were convicted separately of violating Virginia's cross-burning statute, §18.2-423. That statute provides:

> It shall be unlawful for any person or persons, with the intent of intimidating any person or group of persons, to burn, or cause to be burned, a cross on the property of another, a highway or other public place. . . . Any such burning of a cross shall be prima facie evidence of an intent to intimidate a person or group of persons.

On August 22, 1998, Barry Black led a Ku Klux Klan rally in Carroll County, Virginia. Twenty-five to thirty people attended this gathering, which occurred on private property with the permission of the owner, who was in attendance. The property was located on an open field. . . .

When the sheriff of Carroll County learned that a Klan rally was occurring in his county, he went to observe it from the side of the road. During the approximately one hour that the sheriff was present, about 40 to 50 cars passed the site, a "few" of which stopped to ask the sheriff what was happening on the property. [Rebecca] Sechrist, who was related to the owner of the property where the rally took place, "sat and watched to see wha[t] [was] going on" from the lawn of her in-laws' house. She looked on as the Klan prepared for the gathering and subsequently conducted the rally itself.

During the rally, Sechrist heard Klan members speak about "what they were" and "what they believed in." The speakers "talked real bad about the blacks and the Mexicans." One speaker told the assembled gathering that "he would love to take a .30/.30 and just random[ly] shoot the blacks." The speakers also talked about "President Clinton and Hillary Clinton," and about how their tax money "goes to . . . the black people." Sechrist testified that this language made her "very . . . scared."

At the conclusion of the rally, the crowd circled around a 25- to 30-foot cross. The cross was between 300 and 350 yards away from the road. According to the sheriff, the cross "then all of a sudden . . . went up in a flame." As the cross burned, the Klan played Amazing Grace over the loudspeakers. Sechrist stated that the cross burning made her feel "awful" and "terrible."

When the sheriff observed the cross burning, he informed his deputy that they needed to "find out who's responsible and explain to them that they cannot do this in the State of Virginia." The sheriff then went down the driveway, entered the rally, and asked "who was responsible for burning the cross." Black responded, "I guess I am because I'm the head of the rally." The sheriff then told Black, "[T]here's a law in the State of Virginia that you cannot burn a cross and I'll have to place you under arrest for this."

175

Black was charged with burning a cross with the intent of intimidating a person or group of persons, in violation of §18.2-423. At his trial, the jury was instructed that "intent to intimidate means the motivation to intentionally put a person or a group of persons in fear of bodily harm. Such fear must arise from the willful conduct of the accused rather than from some mere temperamental timidity of the victim." The trial court also instructed the jury that "the burning of a cross by itself is sufficient evidence from which you may infer the required intent." [The] jury found Black guilty, and fined him $2,500. The Court of Appeals of Virginia affirmed Black's conviction.

On May 2, 1998, respondents Richard Elliott and Jonathan O'Mara, as well as a third individual, attempted to burn a cross on the yard of James Jubilee. Jubilee, an African-American, was Elliott's next-door neighbor in Virginia Beach, Virginia. Four months prior to the incident, Jubilee and his family had moved from California to Virginia Beach. Before the cross burning, Jubilee spoke to Elliott's mother to inquire about shots being fired from behind the Elliott home. Elliott's mother explained to Jubilee that her son shot firearms as a hobby, and that he used the backyard as a firing range.

On the night of May 2, respondents drove a truck onto Jubilee's property, planted a cross, and set it on fire. Their apparent motive was to "get back" at Jubilee for complaining about the shooting in the backyard. Respondents were not affiliated with the Klan. The next morning, as Jubilee was pulling his car out of the driveway, he noticed the partially burned cross approximately 20 feet from his house. After seeing the cross, Jubilee was "very nervous" because he "didn't know what would be the next phase," and because "a cross burned in your yard . . . tells you that it's just the first round."

Elliott and O'Mara were charged with attempted cross burning and conspiracy to commit cross burning. O'Mara pleaded guilty to both counts, reserving the right to challenge the constitutionality of the cross-burning statute. The judge sentenced O'Mara to 90 days in jail and fined him $2,500. The judge also suspended 45 days of the sentence and $1,000 of the fine. At Elliott's trial, the judge [instructed] the jury that the Commonwealth must prove that "the defendant intended to commit cross burning," that "the defendant did a direct act toward the commission of the cross burning," and that "the defendant had the intent of intimidating any person or group of persons." The court did not instruct the jury on the meaning of the word "intimidate," nor on the prima facie evidence provision of §18.2-423. The jury found Elliott guilty of attempted cross burning and acquitted him of conspiracy to commit cross burning. It sentenced Elliott to 90 days in jail and a $2,500 fine. The Court of Appeals of Virginia affirmed the convictions of both Elliott and O'Mara. *O'Mara v. Commonwealth*, 33 Va. App. 525, 535 S.E. 2d 175 (2000).

Each respondent appealed to the Supreme Court of Virginia, arguing that §18.2-423 is facially unconstitutional. The Supreme Court of Virginia consolidated all three cases, and held that the statute is unconstitutional on its face. 262 Va. 764, 553

S.E. 2d 738 (2001). It held that the Virginia cross-burning statute "is analytically indistinguishable from the ordinance found unconstitutional in [R.A.V. v. St. Paul]. The Virginia statute, the court held, discriminates on the basis of content since it "selectively chooses only cross burning because of its distinctive message." The court also held that the prima facie evidence provision renders the statute overbroad because "[t]he enhanced probability of prosecution under the statute chills the expression of protected speech." . . .

II

Cross burning originated in the 14th century as a means for Scottish tribes to signal each other. [Cross] burning in this country, however, long ago became unmoored from its Scottish ancestry. Burning a cross in the United States is inextricably intertwined with the history of the Ku Klux Klan.

The first Ku Klux Klan began in Pulaski, Tennessee, in the spring of 1866. Although the Ku Klux Klan started as a social club, it soon changed into something far different. The Klan fought Reconstruction and the corresponding drive to allow freed blacks to participate in the political process. Soon the Klan imposed "a veritable reign of terror" throughout the South. The Klan employed tactics such as whipping, threatening to burn people at the stake, and murder. The Klan's victims included blacks, southern whites who disagreed with the Klan, and "carpetbagger" northern whites.

The activities of the Ku Klux Klan prompted legislative action at the national level. In 1871, [Congress] passed what is now known as the Ku Klux Klan Act (now codified at 42 U.S.C §§1983, 1985, and 1986). President Grant used these new powers to suppress the Klan [and by] the end of Reconstruction in 1877, the first Klan no longer existed.

The genesis of the second Klan began in 1905, with the publication of Thomas Dixon's The Clansmen: An Historical Romance of the Ku Klux Klan. Dixon's book was a sympathetic portrait of the first Klan, depicting the Klan as a group of heroes "saving" the South from blacks and the "horrors" of Reconstruction. Although the first Klan never actually practiced cross burning, Dixon's book depicted the Klan burning crosses to celebrate the execution of former slaves. Cross burning thereby became associated with the first Ku Klux Klan. When D.W. Griffith turned Dixon's book into the movie The Birth of a Nation in 1915, the association between cross burning and the Klan became indelible. [Soon] thereafter, in November 1915, the second Klan began.

From the inception of the second Klan, cross burnings have been used to communicate both threats of violence and messages of shared ideology. The first initiation ceremony occurred on Stone Mountain near Atlanta, Georgia. While a 40-foot cross burned on the mountain, the Klan members took their oaths of loyalty. [The] new

Klan's ideology did not differ much from that of the first Klan. As one Klan publication emphasized, "We avow the distinction between [the] races, . . . and we shall ever be true to the faithful maintenance of White Supremacy and will strenuously oppose any compromise thereof in any and all things." Violence was also an elemental part of this new Klan. . . .

Often, the Klan used cross burnings as a tool of intimidation and a threat of impending violence. For example, in 1939 and 1940, the Klan burned crosses in front of synagogues and churches. After one cross burning at a synagogue, a Klan member noted that if the cross burning did not "shut the Jews up, we'll cut a few throats and see what happens." In Miami in 1941, the Klan burned four crosses in front of a proposed housing project, declaring, "We are here to keep niggers out of your town . . . . When the law fails you, call on us." These cross burnings embodied threats to people whom the Klan deemed antithetical to its goals. And these threats had special force given the long history of Klan violence. [The] Klan continued to use cross burnings to intimidate after World War II. [These] incidents of cross burning, among others, helped prompt Virginia to enact its first version of the cross-burning statute in 1950.

The decision of this Court in *Brown v. Board of Education*, along with the civil rights movement of the 1950's and 1960's, sparked another outbreak of Klan violence. These acts of violence included bombings, beatings, shootings, stabbings, and mutilations. Members of the Klan burned crosses on the lawns of those associated with the civil rights movement, assaulted the Freedom Riders, bombed churches, and murdered blacks as well as whites whom the Klan viewed as sympathetic toward the civil rights movement.

Throughout the history of the Klan, cross burnings have also remained potent symbols of shared group identity and ideology. The burning cross became a symbol of the Klan itself and a central feature of Klan gatherings. [The] Klan has often published its newsletters and magazines under the name The Fiery Cross. [At] Klan gatherings across the country, cross burning became the climax of the rally or the initiation. [Throughout] the Klan's history, the Klan continued to use the burning cross in their ritual ceremonies. [For] its own members, the cross was a sign of celebration and ceremony. . . .

To this day, regardless of whether the message is a political one or whether the message is also meant to intimidate, the burning of a cross is a "symbol of hate." And while cross burning sometimes carries no intimidating message, at other times the intimidating message is the *only* message conveyed. For example, when a cross burning is directed at a particular person not affiliated with the Klan, the burning cross often serves as a message of intimidation, designed to inspire in the victim a fear of bodily harm. Moreover, the history of violence associated with the Klan shows that the possibility of injury or death is not just hypothetical. The person who burns a cross directed at a particular person often is making a serious threat, meant to coerce the victim to comply with the Klan's wishes unless the victim is willing to risk the wrath of the Klan. Indeed, as the cases of respondents Elliott and O'Mara indicate, individuals without Klan affiliation who wish to threaten or menace another person sometimes use cross burning because of this association between a burning cross and violence.

In sum, while a burning cross does not inevitably convey a message of intimidation, often the cross burner intends that the recipients of the message fear for their lives. And when a cross burning is used to intimidate, few if any messages are more powerful.

III

A

The protections afforded by the First Amendment [are] not absolute, and we have long recognized that the government may regulate certain categories of expression consistent with the Constitution. The First Amendment permits "restrictions upon the content of speech in a few limited areas, which are 'of such slight social value as a step to truth that any benefit that may be derived from them is clearly outweighed by the social interest in order and morality.'" [*R.A.V.*, quoting *Chaplinsky*]. . . .

Thus, for example, a State may punish [a] "true threat." [*Watts.*] "True threats" encompass those statements where the speaker means to communicate a serious expression of an intent to commit an act of unlawful violence to a particular individual or group of individuals. The speaker need not actually intend to carry out the threat. Rather, a prohibition on true threats "protect[s] individuals from the fear of violence" and "from the disruption that fear engenders," in addition to protecting people "from the possibility that the threatened violence will occur." Intimidation in the constitutionally proscribable sense of the word is a type of true threat, where a speaker directs a threat to a person or group of persons with the intent of placing the victim in fear of bodily harm or death. Respondents do not contest that some cross burnings fit within this meaning of intimidating speech, and rightly so. As noted in Part II, *supra*, the history of cross burning in this country shows that cross burning is often intimidating, intended to create a pervasive fear in victims that they are a target of violence.

B

The Supreme Court of Virginia ruled that in light of *R.A.V.*, even if it is constitutional to ban cross burning in a content-neutral manner, the Virginia cross-burning statute is unconstitutional because it discriminates on the basis of content and viewpoint. It is true [that] the burning of a cross is symbolic expression. The reason why the Klan burns a cross at its rallies, or individuals place a burning cross on someone else's lawn, is that the burning cross represents the message that the speaker wishes

179

to communicate. Individuals burn crosses as opposed to other means of communication because cross burning carries a message in an effective and dramatic manner.

The fact that cross burning is symbolic expression, however, does not resolve the constitutional question. [In] *R.A.V.*, we held that a local ordinance that banned certain symbolic conduct, including cross burning, when done with the knowledge that such conduct would "'arouse anger, alarm or resentment in others on the basis of race, color, creed, religion or gender'" was unconstitutional. We held that the ordinance did not pass constitutional muster because it discriminated on the basis of content by targeting only those individuals who "provoke violence" on a basis specified in the law. The ordinance did not cover "[t]hose who wish to use 'fighting words' in connection with other ideas—to express hostility, for example, on the basis of political affiliation, union membership, or homosexuality." This content-based discrimination was unconstitutional because it allowed the city "to impose special prohibitions on those speakers who express views on disfavored subjects."

We did not hold in *R.A.V.* that the First Amendment prohibits *all* forms of content-based discrimination within a proscribable area of speech. Rather, we specifically stated that some types of content discrimination did not violate the First Amendment:

> When the basis for the content discrimination consists entirely of the very reason the entire class of speech at issue is proscribable, no significant danger of idea or viewpoint discrimination exists. Such a reason, having been adjudged neutral enough to support exclusion of the entire class of speech from First Amendment protection, is also neutral enough to form the basis of distinction within the class.

Indeed, we noted that it would be constitutional to ban only a particular type of threat: "[T]he Federal Government can criminalize only those threats of violence that are directed against the President . . . since the reasons why threats of violence are outside the First Amendment . . . have special force when applied to the person of the President." And a State may "choose to prohibit only that obscenity which is the most patently offensive *in its prurience—i.e.,* that which involves the most lascivious displays of sexual activity." Consequently, while the holding of *R.A.V.* does not permit a State to ban only obscenity based on "offensive *political* messages," or "only those threats against the President that mention his policy on aid to inner cities," the First Amendment permits content discrimination "based on the very reasons why the particular class of speech at issue . . . is proscribable."

Similarly, Virginia's statute does not run afoul of the First Amendment insofar as it bans cross burning with intent to intimidate. Unlike the statute at issue in *R.A.V.*, the Virginia statute does not single out for opprobrium only that speech directed toward "one of the specified disfavored topics." It does not matter whether an individual burns a cross with intent to intimidate because of the victim's race, gender, or religion, or because of the victim's "political affiliation, union membership, or homosexuality." Moreover, as a factual matter it is not true that cross burners direct their intimidating conduct solely to racial or religious minorities. . . .

The First Amendment permits Virginia to outlaw cross burnings done with the intent to intimidate because burning a cross is a particularly virulent form of intimidation. Instead of prohibiting all intimidating messages, Virginia may choose to regulate this subset of intimidating messages in light of cross burning's long and pernicious history as a signal of impending violence. Thus, just as a State may regulate only that obscenity which is the most obscene due to its prurient content, so too may a State choose to prohibit only those forms of intimidation that are most likely to inspire fear of bodily harm. A ban on cross burning carried out with the intent to intimidate is fully consistent with our holding in *R.A.V.* and is proscribable under the First Amendment.

IV

The Supreme Court of Virginia ruled in the alternative that Virginia's cross-burning statute was unconstitutionally overbroad due to its provision stating that "[a]ny such burning of a cross shall be prima facie evidence of an intent to intimidate a person or group of persons." [The] Supreme Court of Virginia has . . . stated that "the act of burning a cross alone, with no evidence of intent to intimidate, [will] suffice for arrest and prosecution and will insulate the Commonwealth from a motion to strike the evidence at the end of its case-in-chief." . . .

The prima facie evidence provision . . . renders the statute unconstitutional. [The] prima facie provision strips away the very reason why a State may ban cross burning with the intent to intimidate. The prima facie evidence provision permits a jury to convict in every cross-burning case in which defendants exercise their constitutional right not to put on a defense. And even where a defendant [presents] a defense, the prima facie evidence provision makes it more likely that the jury will find an intent to intimidate regardless of the particular facts of the case. The provision permits the Commonwealth to arrest, prosecute, and convict a person based solely on the fact of cross burning itself.

It is apparent that the provision as so interpreted "'would create an unacceptable risk of the suppression of ideas.'" The act of burning a cross may mean that a person is engaging in constitutionally proscribable intimidation. But that same act may mean only that the person is engaged in core political speech. The prima facie evidence provision in this statute blurs the line between these two meanings of a burning cross. As interpreted by the jury instruction, the provision chills constitutionally protected political speech because of the possibility that a State will prosecute—and potentially convict—somebody engaging only in lawful political speech at the core of what the First Amendment is designed to protect.

As the history of cross burning indicates, a burning cross is not always intended to intimidate. Rather, sometimes the cross burning is a statement of ideology, a symbol of group solidarity. It is a ritual used at Klan gatherings, and it is used to represent the Klan itself. Thus, "[b]urning a cross at a political rally would almost certainly be protected expression." . . .

The prima facie provision makes no effort to distinguish among these different types of cross burnings. It does not distinguish between a cross burning done with the purpose of creating anger or resentment and a cross burning done with the purpose of threatening or intimidating a victim. It does not distinguish between a cross burning at a public rally or a cross burning on a neighbor's lawn. It does not treat the cross burning directed at an individual differently from the cross burning directed at a group of like-minded believers. It allows a jury to treat a cross burning on the property of another with the owner's acquiescence in the same manner as a cross burning on the property of another without the owner's permission. . . .

It may be true that a cross burning, even at a political rally, arouses a sense of anger or hatred among the vast majority of citizens who see a burning cross. But this sense of anger or hatred is not sufficient to ban all cross burnings. [The] prima facie evidence provision in this case ignores all of the contextual factors that are necessary to decide whether a particular cross burning is intended to intimidate. The First Amendment does not permit such a shortcut. . . .

JUSTICE STEVENS, concurring.

Cross burning with "an intent to intimidate" unquestionably qualifies as the kind of threat that is unprotected by the First Amendment. For the reasons stated in the separate opinions that Justice White and I wrote in *R.A.V.*, that simple proposition provides a sufficient basis for upholding the basic prohibition in the Virginia statute even though it does not cover other types of threatening expressive conduct. With this observation, I join Justice O'Connor's opinion.

JUSTICE THOMAS, dissenting.

In every culture, certain things acquire meaning well beyond what outsiders can comprehend. That goes for both the sacred, see *Texas v. Johnson* [section E3 *infra*] (describing the unique position of the American flag in our Nation's 200 years of history), and the profane. I believe that cross burning is the paradigmatic example of the latter.

Although I agree with the majority's conclusion that it is constitutionally permissible to "ban . . . cross burning carried out with intent to intimidate," I believe that the majority errs in imputing an expressive component to the activity in question. . . .

A

[The] majority's brief history of the Ku Klux Klan [reinforces the] understanding of the Klan as a terrorist organization, which, in its endeavor to intimidate, or even eliminate those its dislikes, uses the most brutal of methods. Such methods typically include cross burning—"a tool for the intimidation and harassment of racial minorities, Catholics, Jews, Communists, and any other groups hated by the Klan." For those not easily frightened, cross burning has been followed by more extreme measures, such as beatings and murder. [Indeed], the connection between cross burning and violence is well ingrained. . . . In our culture, cross burning has almost invariably meant lawlessness and understandably instills in its victims well-grounded fear of physical violence.

B

That in the early 1950s the people of Virginia viewed cross burning as creating an intolerable atmosphere of terror is not surprising. . . . [At] the time the statute was enacted, racial segregation was not only the prevailing practice, but also the law in Virginia. And, just two years after the enactment of this statute, Virginia's General Assembly embarked on a campaign of "massive resistance" in response to *Brown v. Board of Education.* [It] strains credulity to suggest that a state legislature that adopted a litany of segregationist laws self-contradictorily intended to squelch the segregationist message. [The] ban on cross burning with intent to intimidate demonstrates that even segregationists understood the difference between intimidating and terroristic conduct and racist expression. . . .

Accordingly, this statute prohibits only conduct, not expression. And, just as one cannot burn down someone's house to make a political point and then seek refuge in the First Amendment, those who hate cannot terrorize and intimidate to make their point. In light of my conclusion that the statute here addresses only conduct, there is no need to analyze it under any of our First Amendment tests.

II

Even assuming that the statute implicates the First Amendment, in my view, the fact that the statute permits a jury to draw an inference of intent to intimidate from the cross burning itself presents no constitutional problems. Therein lies my primary disagreement with the plurality. . . .

The plurality [is] troubled by the presumption because this is a First Amendment case. The plurality laments the fate of an innocent cross-burner who burns a cross, but does so without an intent to intimidate. The plurality fears the chill on expression because, according to the plurality, the inference permits "the Commonwealth to arrest, prosecute and convict a person based solely on the fact of cross burning itself." [But] the inference is rebuttable [and] Virginia law still requires the jury to find the existence of each element, including intent to intimidate, beyond a reasonable doubt. [The] plurality strikes down the statute because one day an individual might wish to burn a cross, but might do so without an intent to intimidate anyone. That

183

cross burning subjects its targets [to] extreme emotional distress, and is virtually never viewed merely as "unwanted communication," but rather, as a physical threat, is of no concern to the plurality. Henceforth, under the plurality's view, physical safety will be valued less than the right to be free from unwanted communications. . . .

Because I would uphold the validity of this statute, I respectfully dissent.

JUSTICE SCALIA, with whom JUSTICE THOMAS joins as to Parts I and II, concurring in part, concurring in the judgment in part, and dissenting in part.

I agree with the Court that, under our decision in *R.A.V.*, a State may, without infringing the First Amendment, prohibit cross burning carried out with the intent to intimidate. Accordingly, I join Parts I-III of the Court's opinion. I also agree that we should vacate and remand the judgment of the Virginia Supreme Court so that that Court can have an opportunity authoritatively to construe the prima-facie-evidence provision of Va. Code Ann. § 18.2-423 (1996). I write separately, however, to describe what I believe to be the correct interpretation of § 18.2-423, and to explain why I believe there is no justification for the plurality's apparent decision to invalidate that provision on its face.

I

Section 18.2-423 provides that the burning of a cross in public view "shall be prima facie evidence of an intent to intimidate." In order to determine whether this component of the statute violates the Constitution, it is necessary, first, to establish precisely what the presentation of prima facie evidence accomplishes.

Typically, "prima facie evidence" is defined as:

"Such evidence as, in the judgment of the law, is sufficient to establish a given fact . . . and which if not rebutted or contradicted, will remain sufficient. [Such evidence], if unexplained or uncontradicted, is sufficient to sustain a judgment in favor of the issue which it supports, but [it] may be contradicted by other evidence." Black's Law Dictionary 1190 (6th ed. 1990).

The Virginia Supreme Court has, in prior cases, embraced this canonical understanding of the pivotal statutory language. [That] is, presentation of evidence that a defendant burned a cross in public view is automatically sufficient, on its own, to support an inference that the defendant intended to intimidate *only until* the defendant comes forward with some evidence in rebuttal.

II

The question presented, then, is whether, given this understanding of the term "prima facie evidence," the cross-burning statute is constitutional. [We] have never held that the mere threat that individuals who engage in protected conduct will be subject to arrest and prosecution suffices to render a statute overbroad. Rather, our overbreadth jurisprudence has consistently focused on whether *the prohibitory terms* of a particular statute extend to protected conduct; that is, we have inquired whether individuals who engage in protected conduct can be *convicted* under a statute, not whether they might be subject to arrest and prosecution. [The plurality] notes that "[t]he prima facie evidence provision permits a jury *to convict* in every cross-burning case in which defendants exercise their constitutional right not to put on a defense." [And] this, according to the plurality, is constitutionally problematic because "a burning cross is not always intended to intimidate," and nonintimidating cross burning cannot be prohibited. [The] plurality is correct in all of this—and it means that some individuals who engage in protected speech may, because of the prima-facie-evidence provision, be subject to conviction. Such convictions, assuming they are unconstitutional, could be challenged on a case-by-case basis. The plurality, however, with little in the way of explanation, leaps to the conclusion that the *possibility* of such convictions justifies facial invalidation of the statute.

[W]e have noted that "[i]n a facial challenge to the overbreadth . . . of a law, a court's first task is to determine whether the enactment reaches a substantial amount of constitutionally protected conduct." [But here, as] the plurality concedes, the only persons who might impermissibly be convicted [because of the prima facie evidence provision] are those who adopt a particular trial strategy, to wit, abstaining from the presentation of a defense.

The plurality is thus left with a strikingly attenuated argument to support the claim that Virginia's cross-burning statute is facially invalid. The class of persons that the plurality contemplates could impermissibly be convicted under §18.2-423 includes only those individuals who (1) burn a cross in public view, (2) do not intend to intimidate, (3) are nonetheless charged and prosecuted, and (4) refuse to present a defense. [Conceding] (quite generously, in my view) that this class of persons exists, it cannot possibly give rise to a viable facial challenge, not even with the aid of our First Amendment overbreadth doctrine. For this Court has emphasized repeatedly that "where a statute regulates expressive conduct, the scope of the statute does not render it unconstitutional unless its overbreadth is not only real, but *substantial* as well, judged in relation to the statute's plainly legitimate sweep refused." . . .

JUSTICE SOUTER, with whom JUSTICE KENNEDY and JUSTICE GINSBURG join, concurring in the judgment in part and dissenting in part.

I agree with the majority that the Virginia statute makes a content-based distinction within the category of punishable intimidating or threatening expression, the very type of distinction we considered in *R.A.V.* I disagree that any exception should save Virginia's law from unconstitutionality under the holding in *R.A.V.* or any acceptable variation of it.

I

The ordinance struck down in *R.A.V.*, as it had been construed by the State's highest court, prohibited the use of symbols (including but not limited to a burning cross) as the equivalent of generally proscribable fighting words, but the ordinance applied only when the symbol was provocative "'on the basis of race, color, creed, religion or gender.'" Although the Virginia statute in issue here contains no such express "basis of" limitation on prohibited subject matter, the specific prohibition of cross burning with intent to intimidate selects a symbol with particular content from the field of all proscribable expression meant to intimidate. To be sure, that content often includes an essentially intimidating message, that the cross burner will harm the victim, most probably in a physical way, given the historical identification of burning crosses with arson, beating, and lynching. But even when the symbolic act is meant to terrify, a burning cross may carry a further, ideological message of white Protestant supremacy. The ideological message not only accompanies many threatening uses of the symbol, but is also expressed when a burning cross is not used to threaten but merely to symbolize the supremacist ideology and the solidarity of those who espouse it. . . .

The issue is whether the statutory prohibition restricted to this symbol falls within one of the exceptions to *R.A.V.*'s general condemnation of limited content-based proscription within a broader category of expression proscribable generally. Because of the burning cross's extraordinary force as a method of intimidation, the *R.A.V.* exception most likely to cover the statute is the first of the three mentioned there, which the *R.A.V.* opinion called an exception for content discrimination on a basis that "consists entirely of the very reason the entire class of speech at issue is proscribable." This is the exception the majority speaks of here as covering statutes prohibiting "particularly virulent" proscribable expression.

I do not think that the Virginia statute qualifies for this virulence exception as *R.A.V.* explained it. The statute fits poorly with the illustrative examples given in *R.A.V.*, none of which involves communication generally associated with a particular message, and in fact, the majority's discussion of a special virulence exception here moves that exception toward a more flexible conception than the version in *R.A.V.* . . . .

II

R.A.V. defines the special virulence exception to the rule barring content-based subclasses of categorically proscribable expression this way: prohibition by subcategory is nonetheless constitutional if it is made "entirely" on the "basis" of "the very reason" that "the entire class of speech at issue is proscribable" at all. The Court explained that when the subcategory is confined to the most obviously proscribable instances, "no significant danger of idea or viewpoint discrimination exists." . . .

The first example of permissible distinction is for a prohibition of obscenity unusually offensive "in its prurience." [Distinguishing] obscene publications on this basis does not suggest discrimination on the basis of the message conveyed. The opposite is true, however, when a general prohibition of intimidation is rejected in favor of a distinct proscription of intimidation by cross burning. The cross may have been selected because of its special power to threaten, but it may also have been singled out because of disapproval of its message of white supremacy, either because a legislature thought white supremacy was a pernicious doctrine or because it found that dramatic, public espousal of it was a civic embarrassment. Thus, there is no kinship between the cross-burning statute and the core prurience example.

Nor does this case present any analogy to the statute prohibiting threats against the President, the second of *R.A.V.*'s examples of the virulence exception and the one the majority relies upon. The content discrimination in that statute relates to the addressee of the threat and reflects the special risks and costs associated with threatening the President. Again, however, threats against the President are not generally identified by reference to the content of any message that may accompany the threat, let alone any viewpoint, and there is no obvious correlation in fact between victim and message. Millions of statements are made about the President every day on every subject and from every standpoint; threats of violence are not an integral feature of any one subject or viewpoint as distinct from others. Differential treatment of threats against the President, then, selects nothing but special risks, not special messages. A content-based proscription of cross burning, on the other hand, may be a subtle effort to ban not only the intensity of the intimidation cross burning causes when done to threaten, but also the particular message of white supremacy that is broadcast even by nonthreatening cross burning.

I thus read *R.A.V.*'s examples of the particular virulence exception as covering prohibitions that are not clearly associated with a particular viewpoint, and that are consequently different from the Virginia statute. On that understanding of things, I necessarily read the majority opinion as treating *R.A.V.*'s virulence exception in a more flexible, pragmatic manner than the original illustrations would suggest. Actually, another way of looking at today's decision would see it as a slight modification of *R.A.V.*'s third exception, which allows content-based discrimination within a proscribable category when its "nature" is such "that there is no realistic possibility that official suppression of ideas is afoot." The majority's approach could be taken as recognizing an exception to *R.A.V.* when circumstances show that the statute's ostensibly valid reason for punishing particularly serious proscribable expression probably is not a ruse for message suppression, even though the statute may have a greater (but not exclusive) impact on adherents of one ideology than on others.

III

[N]o content-based statute should survive . . . without a high probability that no "official suppression of ideas is afoot." I believe the prima facie evidence provision stands in the way of any finding of such a high probability here.

Virginia's statute provides that burning a cross on the property of another, a highway, or other public place is "prima facie evidence of an intent to intimidate a person or group of persons. [The primary effect of this provision] is to skew jury deliberations toward conviction in cases where the evidence of intent to intimidate is relatively weak and arguably consistent with a solely ideological reason for burning. [This] provision will encourage a factfinder to err on the side of a finding of intent to intimidate when the evidence of circumstances fails to point with any clarity either to the criminal intent or to the permissible one. . . . To the extent the prima facie evidence provision skews prosecutions, then, it skews the statute toward suppressing ideas. . . .

Page 1232.   Before section 3 of the Note, add the following:

i. Posner, The Speech Market and the Legacy of *Schenck*, in L. Bollinger & G. Stone, Eternal Vigilance: Free Speech in the Modern Era 121, 136-137 (2002):

In the case of both pornography and hate speech, [one] has the sense that the desire to crack down on these forms of speech has little to do with demonstrable harms [but] with an ideological project—[that] of denying or occluding the existence of deep-seated differences between groups (in particular men and women, and blacks and whites). Hate speakers are vociferous deniers of equality, and pornography caters primarily to a specifically male interest in women as sexual playthings for men. . . . Insofar as campaigns for the regulation of hate speech and pornography have the purpose and effect of correcting ideological or political "error," giving them the backing of the law interferes arbitrarily with the market in ideas and opinions.

E. Content-Neutral Restrictions: Limitations on the Means of Communication and the Problem of Content-Neutrality

Page 1240.   After *NAACP v. Alabama*, add the following:

BARTNICKI v. VOPPER, 532 U.S. 514 (2001). During contentious collective-bargaining negotiations between a union representing teachers at a public high school and the local school board, an unidentified person intercepted and recorded a cell phone conversation between the union negotiator and the union president. Vopper, a radio commentator, played a tape of the intercepted conversation on his public affairs talk show in connection with news reports about the settlement. The Court held that Vopper could not be held liable for damages under federal or state wiretap laws for broadcasting the unlawfully recorded phone call.

Justice Stevens delivered the opinion of the Court. The Court accepted that the information on the tapes had been obtained unlawfully by an unknown party, that Vopper had played no part in the illegal interception, that he knew or should have known that the phone call had been intercepted unlawfully, and that "the subject matter of the conversation was a matter of public concern."

The Court then explained that the relevant statutes, which prohibited the unauthorized disclosure of unlawfully intercepted communications, were "content-neutral" laws of general applicability. The Court then defined the issue as follows: "Where the punished publisher of information has obtained the information [in] a manner lawful in itself but from a source who has obtained it unlawfully, may the government punish the ensuing publication of that information?" The Court explained that, as a general proposition, "'if a newspaper unlawfully obtains truthful information about a matter of public significance then [government] officials may not constitutionally punish publication of the information, absent a need of the highest order'" [quoting Smith v. Daily Mail Publishing Co.].

The Court identified "two interests served by the statutes—first, the interest in removing an incentive for parties to intercept private conversations, and second, the interest in minimizing the harm to persons whose conversations have been illegally intercepted." With respect to the first of these interests, the Court reasoned that "the normal method of deterring unlawful conduct is to impose an appropriate punishment on the person who engages in it. If the sanctions that presently attach to [these unlawful acts] do not provide sufficient deterrence, perhaps those sanctions should be made more severe. But it would be quite remarkable to hold that speech by a law-abiding possessor of information can be suppressed in order to deter conduct by a non-law abiding third party."

The Court conceded that the second interest "is considerably stronger" because "privacy of communications is an important interest" and "the fear of public disclosure of private conversations might well have a chilling effect on private speech." Without deciding whether there might be some circumstances in which the privacy interest is "strong enough to justify the application" of the statutes, such as when there is disclosure of a trade secret or "domestic gossip [of] purely private concern," the Court held that the enforcement of the statutes in this case "implicates core purposes of the First Amendment because it imposes sanctions on the publication of truthful information of public concern." In such circumstances, "privacy concerns give way when balanced against the interest in publishing matters of public importance."

Justice Breyer, joined by Justice O'Connor, filed a concurring opinion: "I would ask whether the statutes strike a reasonable balance between their speech-restricting and speech-enhancing consequences. [What] this Court has called 'strict scrutiny' [is] normally out of place where, as here, important competing constitutional interests are implicated. [The] statutory restrictions before us directly enhance private speech. [The] assurance of privacy helps to overcome our natural reluctance to discuss private matters when we fear that our private conversations may become public. . . .

"But the statutes, as applied in these circumstances, do not reasonably reconcile the competing constitutional interests. Rather, they disproportionately interfere with media freedom. For one thing, the broadcasters here engaged in no unlawful activity other than the ultimate publication of the information. . . . For another thing, the speakers had little or no *legitimate* interest in maintaining the privacy of the particular conversation, [which] involved a suggestion [about] 'doing some work on some of these guys.' [Further], the speakers themselves [were] 'limited public figures,' for they voluntarily engaged in a public controversy. [Given these circumstances,] the speakers' legitimate privacy interests are unusually low and the public interest in defeating those expectations is unusually high."

Chief Justice Rehnquist, joined by Justices Scalia and Thomas, dissented: "[The] Court's decision diminishes, rather than enhances, the purposes of the First Amendment: chilling the speech of the millions of Americans who rely upon electronic technology to communicate each day. [These] are 'content-neutral laws of general applicability' which serve recognized interests of the highest order."

Chief Justice Rehnquist then argued that the *Smith v. Daily Mail* line of cases was irrelevant: "Each of the laws at issue in the *Daily Mail* cases regulated the content [of] speech. This fact alone was enough to trigger strict scrutiny. [These] laws are content-neutral; they only regulate information that was illegally obtained; they do not restrict republication of what is already in the public domain; they impose no special burdens upon the media; they have a scienter requirement to provide fair warning; and they promote the privacy and free speech of those using cellular telephones. [It] distorts our precedents to review these statutes under the often fatal standard of strict scrutiny. These laws should [be] upheld if they further a substantial governmental interest unrelated to the suppression of free speech, and they do." Consider Gewirtz, Privacy and Speech, 2001 Sup. Ct. Rev. 139, 149-151:

> Illegal conduct that yields stolen information can be every bit as wrongful and offensive as illegal conduct that yields stolen goods, and there is no reason why deterrence of the former should be disfavored any more than deterrence of the latter. [If] someone breaks into my home and steals my diary or personal letters, of course that person can be sanctioned for publishing the diary's or the letter's contents. This is usually a rule of government-created intellectual property law, and nothing in the First Amendment prohibits it. Similarly, nothing in the First Amendment should prohibit the government from creating an analogous rule of privacy law [in the wiretap statute].

Page 1242. At the end of section 2(e) of the Note, add the following:

Do you agree that there can be "no such thing as a free speech immunity based on the claim that someone wants to break an otherwise constitutional law for expressive purposes." Rubenfeld, The First Amendment's Purpose, 53 Stan. L. Rev. 767, 769 (2001) (arguing that "when a law is otherwise constitutional, and when an actor has not been singled out because of his expression, the actor has no free speech claim").

Page 1243. At the end of section 1 of the Note, add the following:

Consider Rubenfeld, The First Amendment's Purpose, 53 Stan. L. Rev. 767, 777 (2001):

> Whether a person is being punished for speaking [depends] on the kind [of] harm that the state seeks to prevent. Some harms arising out of our actions are independent of whatever we might be expressing through those actions. [But] other harms are communicative; the communicativeness of the action is a but-for cause of the harm. There are many kinds of harm [that] arise out of communication. The message communicated might be said to be immoral. Or the message might annoy or alarm its audience. Or the communication might be effective and lead others to take actions harmful either to themselves or others. The First Amendment is implicated when the government makes communicative harm the basis for liability.

[Indeed] this is why the distinction between "content-based" and "content-neutral" regulations is so important to First Amendment law.

Page 1244. At the end of Section 2 of the Note, add the following:

In City of Los Angeles v. Alameda Books, 535 U.S. 425 (2002), the Court revisited the issue of content-neutrality and secondary effects. Like *Renton*, *Alameda Books* concerned the constitutionality of a zoning ordinance that regulated the location of adult establishments. Although there was no majority opinion, four Justices expressly rejected the notion that such regulations should be characterized as "content-neutral." Justice Kennedy described as a "fiction" *Renton*'s designation of such ordinances as "content-neutral" and explained that "whether a statute is content neutral or content based is something that can be determined on the face of it; if the statute describes speech by content, then it is content based."

Justice Souter, joined by Justices Stevens and Ginsburg, observed that "this kind of regulation [occupies] a kind of limbo between full-blown, content-based restrictions and regulations that apply without any reference to the substance of what is said." He added that "it would in fact make sense to give this kind of zoning regulation a First Amendment label of its own, and if we called it content correlated, we would not only describe it for what it is, but keep alert to a risk of content-based regulation that it poses." Justice Souter explained that "when a law applies selectively only to speech of particular content, the more precisely the content is identified, the greater is the opportunity for government censorship."

Page 1248. Before *Schneider v. State*, add the following:

Consider C. Sunstein, republic.com 30-32 (2001):

[The public forum doctrine promotes three important goals. First, it ensures that speakers can have access to a wide array of people. [It allows speakers] to press their concerns that might otherwise be ignored by their fellow citizens. [Second, the doctrine] allows speakers [to have access] to specific people and specific institutions with whom they have a complaint. [The] public forum doctrine ensures that you can make your views heard by legislators, for example, by protesting in front of the state legislature. [Third, the doctrine] increases the likelihood that people generally will be exposed to a wide variety of people and views. [It] tends to ensure a range of experiences that are widely shared [and] a set of exposures to diverse views. [These] exposures can help promote understanding.

Page 1255. At the end of section 1 of the Note, add the following:

See also Thomas v. Chicago Park District, 534 U.S. 316 (2002) (a content-neutral licensing scheme regulating the time, place and manner of use of a public forum need not employ the *Freedman* safeguards because such a scheme "does not authorize a licensor to pass judgment on the content of speech").

If a city can use a "time, place and manner" based licensing scheme for individuals who want to parade on public streets, can it also use such a licensing scheme for speakers who want to go door-to-door to speak with homeowners and distribute literature? In Watchtower Bible & Tract Society v. Village of Stratton, 536 U.S. 150 (2002), the Court, in an eight-to-one decision, held such a scheme unconstitutional. Although acknowledging that the Village's interests in preventing fraud, preventing crime and protecting privacy are "important," the Court nonetheless held that the effect of the licensing scheme on the interests of speakers who want to maintain their anonymity, the administrative burden the scheme imposes on speakers, and the potential impact of the licensing requirement on "spontaneous speech" rendered the ordinance unconstitutional. The Court indicated that such a scheme limited to commercial activities and the solicitation of funds might not be invalid.

1a. *Overbreadth.* Suppose X is convicted of vandalizing a public park and is fined $100. The park district provides by regulation that anyone convicted of this offense is banned from the public park for three months from the date of conviction. A week after his conviction, X enters the public park in order to play basketball. He is arrested for trespass. Can X challenge the constitutionality of the park district regulation on the ground that it is overbroad—that is, on the ground that the regulation could not constitutionally be applied to a "banned" person who wants to enter the park for the purpose of speech? Should X lose because the regulation is not "substantially" overbroad? Suppose X enters the public park a week after his conviction in order to participate in a political rally. Is the regulation unconstitutional as applied? See Virginia v. Hicks, 539 U.S. ___ (2003), in which the Court rejected an overbreadth challenge to a regulation prohibiting any individual who had previously trespassed on the grounds of a public housing development from later entering the grounds of that development. The Court explained that the regulation was not "substantially" overboard and that "rarely, if ever, will an overbreadth challenge succeed against a law or regulation that is not specifically addressed to speech or conduct necessarily associated with speech (such as picketing or demonstrating)."

Page 1285.   After section 4 of the Note, add the following:

4a.   *Religious speech as viewpoint discrimination: another look.* In Good News Club v. Milford Central School, 533 U.S. 98 (2001), the school district authorized district residents to use school buildings after school hours for "instruction in education, learning, or the arts" and for "social, civic, recreational, and entertainment uses pertaining to the community welfare" but not for "religious purposes." The school district denied a request by the Good News Club, a private Christian organization for children ages six to twelve, to use school property to "sing songs, hear Bible lessons, memorize scripture and pray" on the ground that this constituted "religious purposes."

The Court, in a six-to-three decision, held that this was unconstitutional viewpoint discrimination in a limited public forum.   In his opinion for the Court, Justice Thomas explained that "the Club seeks to address a subject otherwise permitted under the rule, the teaching of morals and character, from a religious standpoint." He therefore concluded that this case was indistinguishable from *Lamb's Chapel* and *Rosenberger.*

In dissent, Justice Stevens argued that "speech for 'religious purposes' may reasonably be understood to encompass three different categories. First, there is religious speech that is simply speech about a particular topic from a religious point of view. [Second], there is religious speech that amounts to worship. [Third], there is [speech] that is aimed principally at proselytizing or inculcating a belief in a particular religious faith." In Justice Stevens's view, "the question is whether a school can [create] a limited public forum that admits the first type of religious speech without allowing the other two." He concluded that "just as a school may allow meetings to discuss current events from a political perspective without also allowing organized political recruitment, so too can a school allow discussion of topics such as moral development from a religious (or nonreligious) perspective without thereby opening its forum to religious proselytizing or worship."

In a separate dissenting opinion, Justice Souter, joined by Justice Ginsburg, argued that this case was distinguishable from *Lamb's Chapel* and *Rosenberger* because "Good News intends to use the public school premises not for the mere discussion of a subject from a particular, Christian point of view, but for an evangelical service of worship calling children to commit themselves in an act of Christian conversion." He maintained that the majority's position stands "for the remarkable proposition that any public school opened for civic meetings must be opened for use as a church, synagogue, or mosque."

In a concurring opinion, Justice Scalia responded to the dissenters: "The dissenters emphasize that the religious speech [of the Club is] 'aimed principally at proselytizing or inculcating belief in a particular religious faith.' [But this] does not distinguish the Club's activities from those of [political, social, and cultural organizations that also] may seek to inculcate children with their beliefs [and try to] 'recruit others to join their respective groups.'"

Page 1288. At the end of Forbes, add the following:

Consider Fiss, The Censorship of Television, in L. Bollinger & G. Stone, Eternally Vigilant: Free Speech in the Modern Era 257, 278 (2001):

[Justice Kennedy's argument that access must] be granted to overcome an exclusion based on disagreement with the candidate's views [does not seem] sensible. [Justice] Kennedy explained that such viewpoint discrimination would inevitably skew the electoral debate. [But] every exclusion [will] have this same effect. The only difference between a viewpoint-based exclusion and a viewpoint-neutral exclusion is the justification. [Suppose], for instance, that a station excludes a candidate not because it disagrees with the candidate's view, but because it believes the candidate is not popular, or is not likely to win, or does not have the economic resources needed to mount an effective campaign. [All] of these rationales strike me [as] insufficient to justify the skew that the exclusion will produce.

Page 1291. At the end of the material after *Pico*, add the following:

See also Nadel, The First Amendment's Limitations on the Use of Internet Filtering in Public and School Libraries, 78 Tex. L. Rev. 1117 (2000).

Most states permit individuals to purchase "vanity" license plates. May a state refuse to sell license plates that contain the following words or messages: "GODIZDED," "PRAY," "ARYAN," "FUK" and "DAGO"? See Jacobs, The Public Sensibilities Forum 95 Nw. U. L. Rev. 1357 (2001).

Page 1291. After the citation to *Loudoun*, add the following:

But see United States v. American Library Ass'n, 539 U.S. ___ (2003) (upholding the federal Children's Internet Protection Act, which required the use of filtering software by public libraries as a condition of the receipt of federal funding). On the issue of prior restraint, consider the fact that when a filter is used either some individual or some machine is screening material in advance, determining that it is "obscene," or whatever, and then denying it to the prospective user without any judicial determination.

In thinking about the use of filters, it may be useful to know that there are more than 2 billion Web pages on the Internet and that 10,000 new Web pages are added each hour. In this context, can filters possibly "work"? Consider R. Thornburgh & H. Lin (eds.), Youth, Pornography and the Internet (2002):

> In practice, the volume of material on the Internet is so large that it is impractical for human beings to evaluate every discrete piece of information for inappropriateness. Moreover, the content of some existing Web pages changes very quickly, and new Web pages appear at a rapid rate. Thus, identifying inappropriate material must rely either on an automated, machine-executable process for determining inappropriate content or on a presumption that everything that is not explicitly identified by a human being as appropriate is inappropriate. An approach based on machine-executable rules abstracted from human judgments inevitably misses nuances in those human judgments, which reduces the accuracy of this approach compared to that of humans, while the presumption-based approach necessarily identifies a large volume of appropriate material as inappropriate.

Is public education consistent with the First Amendment? Is there a danger that in structuring what individuals learn the government will engage in "thought control"? Are there circumstances in which the nature of public education may itself violate the First Amendment? Consider Redish & Finnerty, What Did You Learn in School Today? Free Speech, Values Inculcation, and the Democratic-Educational Paradox, 88 Corn. L. Rev. 62, 67-70 (2002):

> The problem [is] that by means of the public educational process, the state is able to engage is a dangerous form of political, social, or moral thought control that potentially interferes with a citizen's subsequent exercise of individual autonomy. [By] selectively instilling in students a predetermined set of normative values and empirical assumptions, the state effectively favors certain viewpoints over others. . . .
>
> [Although it] would be both practically and theoretically impossible to completely prevent the governmental values inculcation that occurs in the educational process, [it] is possible [for] the judiciary to reasonably police the educational process in order to restrict values inculcation to that essential minimum degree required for the educational process to function. [Under this view, the public school may] convey only those values that are both substantially related and incidental to the educational process. . . .

Page 1298. At the end of the Note, add the following:

LEGAL SERVICES CORP. v. VELAZQUEZ, 531 U.S. 533 (2001). In 1974, Congress established the Legal Services Corporation (LSC), whose mission is to distribute funds appropriated by Congress to eligible local grantee organizations "for the purpose of providing financial support for legal assistance in noncriminal proceedings . . . to persons financially unable to afford legal assistance." LSC grantees consist of hundreds of local organizations governed by local boards of directors. In many instances, the grantees are funded by a combination of LSC funds and other public or private sources. The grantee organizations hire and supervise lawyers to provide free legal assistance to indigent clients.

In a five-to-four decision, the Court distinguished *Rust* and held unconstitutional a congressionally imposed restriction prohibiting LSC-funded attorneys from challenging the legality or constitutionality of existing welfare laws. Justice Kennedy delivered the opinion of the Court: "The Court in *Rust* did not place explicit reliance on the rationale that the counseling activities of the doctors under Title X amounted to governmental speech; when interpreting the holding in later cases, however, we have explained *Rust* on this understanding. We have said that viewpoint-based funding decisions can be sustained in instances in which the government is itself the speaker, or instances, like *Rust*, in which the government 'used private speakers to transmit information pertaining to its own program.' As we said in *Rosenberger*, "[w]hen the government disburses public funds to private entities to convey a governmental message, it may take legitimate and appropriate steps to ensure that its message is neither garbled nor distorted by the grantee.' . . .

"[But] '[i]t does not follow . . . that viewpoint-based restrictions are proper when the [government] does not itself speak or subsidize transmittal of a message it favors but instead expends funds to encourage a diversity of views from private speakers. *Rosenberger*. Although the LSC program differs from the program at issue in *Rosenberger* in that its purpose is not to 'encourage a diversity of views,' the salient point is that, like the program in *Rosenberger*, the LSC program was designed to facilitate private speech, not to promote a governmental message. Congress funded LSC grantees to provide attorneys to represent the interests of indigent clients. [In] this vital respect this suit is distinguishable from *Rust*.

"The private nature of the speech involved here, and the extent of LSC's regulation of private expression, are indicated further by the circumstance that the Government seeks to use an existing medium of expression and to control it, in a class of cases, in ways which distort its usual functioning. Where the government uses or attempts to regulate a particular medium, we have been informed by its accepted usage in determining whether a particular restriction on speech is necessary for the program's purposes and limitations. [Citing FCC v. League of Women Voters; Arkansas Educational Television Commn. v. Forbes; and *Rosenberger*.]

"[Restricting] LSC attorneys in advising their clients and in presenting arguments and analyses to the courts distorts the legal system by altering the traditional role of the attorneys in much the same way broadcast systems or student publication networks were changed in the limited forum cases we have cited. Just as government in those cases could not elect to use a broadcasting network or a college publication structure in a regime which prohibits speech necessary to the proper functioning of those systems, it may not design a subsidy to effect this serious and fundamental restriction on advocacy of attorneys and the functioning of the judiciary. . . .

"Interpretation of the law and the Constitution is the primary mission of the judiciary when it acts within the sphere of its authority to resolve a case or controversy. Under [the challenged statute], however, cases would be presented by LSC attorneys who could not advise the courts of serious questions of statutory validity. The disability is inconsistent with the proposition that attorneys should present all the reasonable and well-grounded arguments necessary for proper resolution of the case. By seeking to prohibit the analysis of certain legal issues and to truncate presentation to the courts, the enactment under review prohibits speech and expression upon which courts must depend for the proper exercise of the judicial power. Congress cannot wrest the law from the Constitution which is its source. . . .

"It is no answer to say the restriction on speech is harmless because, under LSC's interpretation of the Act, its attorneys can withdraw. This misses the point. The statute is an attempt to draw lines around the LSC program to exclude from litigation those arguments and theories Congress finds unacceptable but which by their nature are within the province of the courts to consider.

"The restriction on speech is even more problematic because in cases where the attorney withdraws from a representation, the client is unlikely to find other counsel. [Thus], with respect to the litigation services Congress has funded, there is no alternative channel for expression of the advocacy Congress seeks to restrict. This is in stark contrast to *Rust*. There, a patient could receive the approved Title X family planning counseling funded by the Government and later could consult an affiliate or independent organization to receive abortion counseling. Unlike indigent clients who seek LSC representation, the patient in *Rust* was not required to forfeit the Government-funded advice when she also received abortion counseling through alternative channels. Because LSC attorneys must withdraw whenever a question of a welfare statute's validity arises, an individual could not obtain joint representation so that the constitutional challenge would be presented by a non-LSC attorney, and other, permitted, arguments advanced by LSC counsel.

"Finally, LSC and the Government maintain that [this restriction] is necessary to define the scope and contours of the federal program, a condition that ensures funds can be spent for those cases most immediate to congressional concern. [In the Government's] view, the restriction operates neither to maintain the current welfare system nor insulate it from attack; rather, it helps the current welfare system function in a more efficient and fair manner by removing from the program complex challenges to existing welfare laws.

"The effect of the restriction, however, is to prohibit advice or argumentation that existing welfare laws are unconstitutional or unlawful. Congress cannot recast a condition on funding as a mere definition of its program in every case, lest the First Amendment be reduced to a simple semantic exercise. Here, notwithstanding Congress' purpose to confine and limit its program, the restriction operates to insulate current welfare laws from constitutional scrutiny and certain other legal challenges, a condition implicating central First Amendment concerns. [There] can be little doubt that the LSC Act funds constitutionally protected expression; and in the context of this statute there is no programmatic message of the kind recognized in *Rust* and which sufficed there to allow the Government to specify the advice deemed necessary for its legitimate objectives. . . .

"Congress was not required to fund an LSC attorney to represent indigent clients; and when it did so, it was not required to fund the whole range of legal representations or relationships. The LSC and the United States, however, in effect ask us to permit Congress to define the scope of the litigation it funds to exclude certain vital theories and ideas. The attempted restriction is designed to insulate the Government's interpretation of the Constitution from judicial challenge. The Constitution does not permit the Government to confine litigants and their attorneys in this manner. We must be vigilant when Congress imposes rules and conditions which in effect insulate its own laws from legitimate judicial challenge."

Justice Scalia, joined by Chief Justice Rehnquist and Justices O'Connor and Thomas, dissented: "The LSC Act is a federal subsidy program, not a federal regulatory program, and '[t]here is a basic difference between [the two].' Regulations directly restrict speech; subsidies do not. [In *Rust*, the Court upheld] a statutory scheme that is in all relevant respects indistinguishable from [the provision challenged in this case]. The LSC Act, like the scheme in *Rust*, does not [discriminate] on the basis of viewpoint, since it funds neither challenges to nor defenses of existing welfare law. The provision simply declines to subsidize a certain class of litigation, and under *Rust* that decision 'does not infringe the right' to bring such litigation. . . . The Court's repeated claims that [the Act] 'restricts' and 'prohibits' speech, and 'insulates' laws from judicial review, are simply baseless. No litigant who, in the absence of LSC funding, would bring a suit challenging existing welfare law is deterred from doing so by [the Act]. *Rust* thus controls [this case] and compels the conclusion that [the Act] is constitutional.

"The Court contends that *Rust* is different because the program at issue subsidized government speech, while the LSC funds private speech. This is so unpersuasive it hardly needs response. If the private doctors' confidential advice to their patients at issue in *Rust* constituted 'government speech,' it is hard to imagine what subsidized speech would not be government speech. Moreover, the majority's contention that the subsidized speech in these cases is not government speech because the lawyers have a professional obligation to represent the interests of their clients founders on the reality that the doctors in *Rust* had a professional obligation to serve the interests of their patients. . . .

"The Court further asserts that these cases are different from *Rust* because the welfare funding restriction 'seeks to use an existing medium of expression and to control it . . . in ways which distort its usual functioning.' This is wrong on both the facts

199

and the law. It is wrong on the law because there is utterly no precedent for the novel and facially implausible proposition that the First Amendment has anything to do with government funding that—though it does not actually abridge anyone's speech —'distorts an existing medium of expression.' None of the three cases cited by the Court mentions such an odd principle. [The] Court's 'nondistortion' principle is also wrong on the facts, since there is no basis for believing that [the challenged provision], by causing 'cases [to] be presented by LSC attorneys who [can]not advise the courts of serious questions of statutory validity,' will distort the operation of the courts. It may well be that the bar of [the Act] will cause LSC-funded attorneys to decline or to withdraw from cases that involve statutory validity. But that means at most that fewer statutory challenges to welfare laws will be presented to the courts because of the unavailability of free legal services for that purpose. So what? The same result would ensue from excluding LSC-funded lawyers from welfare litigation entirely. . . .

"Finally, the Court is troubled 'because in cases where the attorney withdraws from a representation, the client is unlikely to find other counsel.' That is surely irrelevant, since it leaves the welfare recipient in no worse condition than he would have been in had the LSC program never been enacted. [*Rust*] rejected a similar argument. . . . There is no legitimate basis for declaring [this law] unconstitutional."

Page 1301.   At the end of *Finley*, add the following:

Consider Chemerinsky, Content Neutrality as a Central Problem of Freedom of Speech, 74 S. Cal. L. Rev. 49, 56, 59 (2000):

> The determination of whether a law is viewpoint based [is] crucial in determining its constitutionality. Two recent [decisions—*Forbes* and *Finley*]—are important because each [compromises] the protection against content-based regulation by adopting an unduly restrictive definition of viewpoint discrimination. [In] *Forbes*, the Court concluded that excluding a minor party candidate from a debate is viewpoint neutral. But the entire difference between minor party and major party candidates revolves around their views. In *Finley*, the Court said that a federal law that authorized the NEA to consider "decency and respect" for values was viewpoint neutral. Yet these terms are all about government examination of the viewpoint expressed. [The] Court has erred by adopting such an unduly restrictive definition of viewpoint discrimination in these cases.

Consider also Bezanson & Buss, The Many Faces of Government Speech, 86 Iowa L. Rev. 1377, 1382-1383, 1487 (2001):

> The imperative of government speaking, and the roles occupied by government when it speaks, are vastly multiplied in the modern state. [Government is] a crea-

tor [of] programs, a manager of economic and social relationships, a vast employer and purchaser, an educator, investor, curator, librarian, historian [and patron]. [It] taxes and spends, subsidizes and penalizes, encourages and discourages. None of these undertakings [could] be successfully pursued without speech by government. . . .

[In *Velazquez*], the Court drew upon the now established dichotomy between the *Rust* and *Rosenberger* paradigms: ". . . viewpoint-based funding decisions can be sustained [when] the government is itself the speaker [or uses] private speakers to transmit information pertaining to its own programs" [but not when the government] "expends funds to encourage a diversity of views from private speakers." [This distinction] rests on an incoherent theoretical premise [and] has left unanswered many important [questions]. For example, what [is] government "speech"? [Must] the message be specific [or] might [it] consist of nothing more than tacit government agreement with private messages that the government prefers? [Can the government speak] through private speakers whose messages [are] favored by subsidy or reward? [Can] it speak through exclusion of private speech as well as inclusion? [Is] government speaking when it acts as educator, [as] curator of a museum, as librarian, or as a patron of artistic [work]? Does it speak when it acts as a manager of [physical spaces]? . . .

We conclude that government speech should receive little or no immunity from the [ordinary requirement of viewpoint neutrality] when the government's speech creates a monopoly for a particular point of view, when it distorts the marketplace of ideas, and [when there is] government deception.

How would you apply "monopoly," "distortion" and "deception" to such cases as *Rosenberger, Mosley, Rust, Forbes, Finley, Pico* and *Velazquez*? Are these the right factors to consider in deciding these cases?

UNITED STATES v. AMERICAN LIBRARY ASSOCIATION, 539 U.S. ___ (2003). Two federal programs provide funds to public libraries to help them expand access to the Internet. The Children's Internet Protection Act (CIPA), however, forbids public libraries to receive federal under these programs unless they install software to block obscenity and child pornography and prevent minors from accessing material that is "harmful of minors." A group of libraries, library patrons and Web site publishers brought suit challenging CIPA's filtering provisions. A statutorily mandated three-judge district court held CIPA unconstitutional, but the Supreme Court reversed.

Chief Justice Rehnquist, joined by Justices O'Connor, Scalia and Thomas, authored a plurality opinion: "Even before Congress enacted CIPA, almost 17% of public libraries used such software on at least some of their Internet terminals, and 7% had filters on all of them. When a patron tries to view a site that falls within [a prohibited] category, a screen appears indicating that the site is blocked. [A] filter set to block pornography may sometimes block other sites that present neither obscene nor pornographic [material]. To minimize this problem, a library can [delete] specific sites from a blocking category, and [CIPA] permits [a library] library to 'disable' the filter 'to enable access for bona fide research or other lawful purposes. . . . '

"Congress has wide latitude to attach conditions to the receipt of federal assistance in order to further its policy objectives. But Congress may not 'induce' the recipient 'to engage in activities that would themselves be unconstitutional." To determine whether libraries would violate the First Amendment by employing the filtering software that CIPA requires, we must [examine] the role of libraries in our society. Public libraries pursue the worthy missions of facilitating learning and cultural enrichment. [To] fulfill [these] missions, public libraries must have broad discretion to decide what material to provide to their patrons. Although they seek to provide a wide array of information, their goal has never been to provide 'universal coverage.' Instead, public libraries seek to provide materials 'that would be of the greatest direct benefit or interest to the community.' To this end, libraries collect only those materials deemed to have 'requisite and appropriate quality.' . . .

"We have held in two analogous contexts that the government has broad discretion to make content-based judgments in deciding what private speech to make available to the public. [Citing *Forbes* and *Finley*.] Just as forum analysis and heightened judicial scrutiny are incompatible with the role of public television stations and the role of the NEA, they are also incompatible with the discretion that public libraries must have to fulfill their traditional missions. . . .

". . . Most libraries already exclude pornography from their print collections because they deem it inappropriate for inclusion. We do not subject these decisions to heightened scrutiny; it would make little sense to treat libraries' judgments to block online pornography any differently, when these judgments are made for just the same reason. . . .

"[The] dissents fault the tendency of filtering software to 'overblock' — that is, to erroneously block access to constitutionally protected speech that falls outside the categories that software users intend to block. [Assuming] that such erroneous blocking presents constitutional difficulties, any such concerns are dispelled by the ease with which patrons may have the filtering software disabled. When a patron encounters a blocked site, he need only ask a librarian to unblock it, [and CIPA] expressly authorizes library officials to 'disable' a filter altogether 'to enable access for bona fide research or other lawful purposes.' The Solicitor General confirmed that a [patron] would not 'have to explain . . . why he was asking a site to be unblocked or the filtering to be disabled.' The District Court viewed unblocking and disabling as inadequate because some patrons may be too embarrassed to request them. But the Constitution does not guarantee the right to acquire information at a public library without any risk of embarrassment.

"Appellees urge us to affirm the District Court's judgment on the alternative ground that CIPA imposes an unconstitutional condition on the receipt of federal assistance. Under this doctrine, 'the government may not deny a benefit to a person on a basis that infringes his constitutionally protected . . . freedom of speech even if he has no entitlement to that benefit.' Appellees argue that CIPA imposes an unconstitutional condition on libraries that receive [federal] subsidies by requiring them, as a condition on their receipt of federal funds, to surrender their First Amendment right to provide the public with access to constitutionally protected speech. The Government counters that this claim fails because Government entities do not have First Amendment rights. . . .

"We need not decide this question because, even assuming that appellees may assert an 'unconstitutional conditions' claim, this claim would fail on the merits. Within broad limits, 'when the Government appropriates public funds to establish a program it is entitled to define the limits of that program.' [Citing *Rust.*] The [Internet subsidy] programs were intended to help public libraries fulfill their traditional role of obtaining material of requisite and appropriate quality for educational and informational purposes. Congress may certainly insist that these 'public funds be spent for the purposes for which they were authorized.' Especially because public libraries have traditionally excluded pornographic material from their other collections, Congress could reasonably impose a parallel limitation on its Internet assistance programs. As the use of filtering software helps to carry out these programs, it is a permissible condition under *Rust.*

"Justice Stevens [asserts] that '[a] federal statute penalizing a library for failing to install filtering software on every one of its Internet-accessible computers would unquestionably violate [the First] Amendment.' But—assuming again that public libraries have First Amendment rights—CIPA does not 'penalize' libraries that choose not to install such software, or deny them the right to provide their patrons with unfiltered Internet access. Rather, CIPA simply reflects Congress' decision not to subsidize their doing so. To the extent that libraries wish to offer unfiltered access, they are free to do so without federal assistance. 'A refusal to fund protected activity, without more, cannot be equated with the imposition of a "penalty" on that activity.' *Rust.*

"Appellees mistakenly contend, in reliance on [*Velazquez*] that CIPA's filtering conditions '[d]istor[t] the [u]sual [f]unctioning of [p]ublic [l]ibraries.' In *Velazquez,* the Court concluded that [the] restriction on advocacy [in] welfare disputes would distort the usual functioning of the legal profession and the federal and state courts before which the lawyers appeared. Public libraries, by contrast, have no comparable role that pits them against the Government, and there is no comparable assumption that they must be free of any conditions that their benefactors might attach to the use of donated funds. . . .

"Relying on *Velazquez,* Justice Stevens argues mistakenly that *Rust* is inapposite because that case 'only involved and only applies to . . . situations in which the government seeks to communicate a specific message,' and unlike the Title X program in *Rust,* the [public library subsidy] programs 'are not designed to foster or transmit any particular governmental message.' But he misreads our cases discussing *Rust*

[and] misapprehends the purpose of providing Internet terminals in public libraries. *Velazquez* held only that viewpoint-based restrictions are improper 'when the [government] does not itself speak or subsidize transmittal of a message it favors *but instead expends funds to encourage a diversity of views from private speakers.*' [But] public libraries do not install Internet terminals to provide a forum for Web publishers to express themselves, but rather to provide patrons with online material of requisite and appropriate quality.

"Because public libraries' use of Internet filtering software does not violate their patrons' First Amendment rights, CIPA does not induce libraries to violate the Constitution, and is a valid exercise of Congress' spending power. Nor does CIPA impose an unconstitutional condition on public libraries."

Justice Kennedy concurred in the judgment: "If, on the request of an adult user, a librarian will unblock filtered material or disable the Internet software filter without significant delay, there is little to this case. The Government represents this is indeed the fact. [If] some libraries do not have the capacity to unblock specific Web sites or to disable the filter or if it is shown that an adult user's election to view constitutionally protected Internet material is burdened in some other substantial way, that would be the subject for an as-applied challenge, not the facial challenge made in this case. There are, of course, substantial Government interests at stake here. The interest in protecting young library users from material inappropriate for minors is legitimate, and even compelling, as all Members of the Court appear to agree. Given this interest, and the failure to show that the ability of adult library users to have access to the material is burdened in any significant degree, the statute is not unconstitutional on its face."

Justice Breyer also concurred in the judgment: "I would apply a form of heightened scrutiny, examining the statutory requirements in question with special care. The Act directly restricts the public's receipt of information. And it does so through limitations imposed by outside bodies (here Congress) upon two critically important sources of information—the Internet as accessed via public libraries. For that reason, we should not examine the statute's constitutionality as if it raised no special First Amendment concern—as if, like tax or economic regulation, the First Amendment demanded only a 'rational basis' for imposing a restriction. . . .

"At the same time, in my view, the First Amendment does not here demand application [of] 'strict scrutiny.' The statutory restriction in question is, in essence, a kind of 'selection' restriction (a kind of editing). It affects the kinds and amount of materials that the library can present to its patrons. And libraries often properly engage in the selection of materials, either as a matter of necessity (*i.e.,* due to the scarcity of resources) or by design (*i.e.,* in accordance with collection development policies). To apply 'strict scrutiny' to the 'selection' of a library's collection [would] unreasonably interfere with the discretion necessary to create, maintain, or select a library's 'collection' (broadly defined to include all the information the library makes available). . . .

204

"... I would examine [the] Act's restrictions here as the Court has examined speech-related restrictions in other contexts where circumstances call for heightened, but not 'strict,' scrutiny—where, for example, complex, competing constitutional interests are potentially at issue or speech-related harm is potentially justified by unusually strong governmental interests. Typically the key question in such instances is one of proper fit. [Citing *Denver Area*; *Red Lion, infra* section F.4; *Turner Broadcasting, infra* section F.4]. In such cases the Court has asked whether the harm to speech-related interests is disproportionate in light of both the justifications and the potential alternatives. It has considered the legitimacy of the statute's objective, the extent to which the statute will tend to achieve that objective, whether there are other, less restrictive ways of achieving that objective, and ultimately whether the statute works speech-related harm that, in relation to that objective, is out of proportion. . . .

"The Act's restrictions satisfy these constitutional demands. The Act seeks to restrict access to obscenity, child pornography, and, in respect to access by minors, material that is comparably harmful. These objectives are 'legitimate,' and indeed often 'compelling.' [Citing *Miller*; *Ferber*]. As the District Court found, software filters 'provide a relatively cheap and effective' means of furthering these goals. Due to present technological limitations, however, the software filters both 'overblock' [and] 'underblock.' [But] no one has presented any clearly superior or better fitting alternatives.

"At the same time, the Act contains an important exception that limits the speech-related harm that 'overblocking' might cause. As the plurality points out, the Act allows libraries to permit any adult patron access to an 'overblocked' Web site; the adult patron need only ask a librarian to unblock the specific Web site or, alternatively, ask the librarian, 'Please disable the entire filter.' The Act does impose upon the patron the burden of making this request. But it is difficult to see how that burden (or any delay associated with compliance) could prove more onerous than traditional library practices associated with segregating library materials in, say, closed stacks, or with interlibrary lending practices that require patrons to make requests that are not anonymous and to wait while the librarian obtains the desired materials from elsewhere. [Given] the comparatively small burden that the Act imposes upon the library patron seeking legitimate Internet materials, I cannot say that any speech-related harm that the Act may cause is disproportionate when considered in relation to the Act's legitimate objectives."

Justice Stevens dissented: "I agree with the plurality that it is neither inappropriate nor unconstitutional for a local library to experiment with filtering software as a means of curtailing children's access to Internet Web sites displaying sexually explicit images. I also agree with the plurality that the 7% of public libraries that decided to use such software on *all* of their Internet terminals in 2000 did not act unlawfully. Whether it is constitutional for the Congress of the United States to impose that requirement on the other 93%, however, raises a vastly different question. Rather than allowing local decisionmakers to tailor their responses to local problems,

[CIPA] operates as a blunt nationwide restraint on adult access to 'an enormous amount of valuable information' that individual librarians cannot possibly review. Most of that information is constitutionally protected speech. In my view, this restraint is unconstitutional.

". . . Because the software relies on key words or phrases to block undesirable sites, it does not have the capacity to exclude a precisely defined category of images. [Image] recognition technology is immature, ineffective, and unlikely to improve substantially in the near future. [Given] the quantity and ever-changing character of Web sites offering free sexually explicit material, it is inevitable that a substantial amount of such material will never be blocked. Because of this 'underblocking,' the statute will provide parents with a false sense of security without really solving the problem that motivated its enactment. Conversely, the software's reliance on words to identify undesirable sites necessarily results in the blocking of thousands of pages that 'contain content that is completely innocuous.' [A] statutory blunderbuss that mandates this vast amount of 'overblocking' abridges the freedom of speech. . . .

". . . Neither the interest in suppressing unlawful speech nor the interest in protecting children from access to harmful materials justifies this overly broad restriction on adult access to protected speech. 'The Government may not suppress lawful speech as the means to suppress unlawful speech.' [Quoting *Ashcroft v. Free Speech Coalition*].

"[T]he District Court expressly found that a variety of less restrictive alternatives are available at the local level: '[P]ublic libraries may enforce Internet use policies that make clear to patrons that the library's Internet terminals may not be used to access illegal speech. [They may require] parental consent [for] unfiltered access, or [restrict] minors' unfiltered access to terminals within view of library staff. [And] privacy screens, recessed monitors, and placement of unfiltered Internet terminals outside of sight-lines provide less restrictive alternatives for libraries to prevent patrons from being unwillingly exposed to sexually explicit content on the Internet.' [Such] local decisions tailored to local circumstances are more appropriate than a mandate from Congress.

"The plurality does not reject any of those findings. Instead, [it] relies on [the] assurance that the statute permits individual librarians to disable filtering mechanisms whenever a patron so requests. [This] does not cure the constitutional infirmity in the statute. Until a blocked site [is] unblocked, a patron is unlikely to know what is being hidden and therefore whether there is any point in asking for the filter to be removed. It is as though the statute required a significant part of every library's reading materials to be kept in unmarked, locked rooms or cabinets, which could be opened only in response to specific requests. Some curious readers would in time obtain access to the hidden materials, but many would not. [Unless] we assume that the statute is a mere symbolic gesture, we must conclude that it will create a significant prior restraint on adult access to protected speech. . . .

"The plurality incorrectly argues that the statute does not impose 'an unconstitutional condition on public libraries.' On the contrary, it impermissibly conditions the receipt of Government funding on the restriction of significant First Amendment rights. The plurality explains the 'worthy missions' of the public library in facilitating 'learning and cultural enrichment.' It then asserts that in order to fulfill these missions, 'libraries must have broad discretion to decide what material to provide to their patrons.' Thus the selection decision is the province of the librarians, a province into which we have hesitated to enter. [We] have always assumed that libraries have discretion when making decisions regarding what to include in, and exclude from, their collections. That discretion is comparable to the " 'business of a university . . . to determine for itself on academic grounds who may teach, what may be taught, how it shall be taught, and who may be admitted to study.' " Given our Nation's deep commitment 'to safeguarding academic freedom' and to the 'robust exchange of ideas,' a library's exercise of judgment with respect to its collection is entitled to First Amendment protection.

"A federal statute penalizing a library for failing to install filtering software on every one of its Internet-accessible computers would unquestionably violate [the First] Amendment. I think it equally clear that the First Amendment protects libraries from being denied funds for refusing to comply with an identical rule. An abridgment of speech by means of a threatened denial of benefits can be just as pernicious as an abridgment by means of a threatened penalty.

"The plurality argues that [*Rust*] requires rejection of [the] unconstitutional conditions claim. But, as subsequent cases have explained, *Rust* only involved and only applies to instances of governmental speech—that is, situations in which the government seeks to communicate a specific message. The [subsidies] involved in this case do not subsidize any message favored by the Government. As Congress made clear, these programs were designed '[t]o help public libraries provide their patrons with Internet access [to] a vast amount and wide variety of private speech. They are not designed to foster or transmit any particular governmental message. [This] Court should not permit federal funds to be used to enforce this kind of broad restriction of First Amendment rights. . . . "

Justice Souter, joined by Justice Ginsburg, also dissented: "I agree [with] Justice Stevens that the blocking requirements of [CIPA] impose an unconstitutional condition on the Government's subsidies to local libraries for providing access to the Internet. I also [conclude that] the blocking rule [is] invalid in the exercise of the spending power under Article I, §8 [because it] mandates action by recipient libraries that would violate the First Amendment's guarantee of free speech if the libraries took that action entirely on their own. . . .

". . . I have no doubt about the legitimacy of governmental efforts to put a barrier between child patrons of public libraries and the raw offerings on the Internet otherwise available to them there, and if the only First Amendment interests raised here were those of children, I would uphold application of the Act. [Nor] would I dissent if I agreed with the majority of my colleagues that an adult library patron could, consistently with the Act, obtain an unblocked terminal simply for the asking. I realize the Solicitor General represented this to be the Government's policy, and if that policy were communicated to every affected library as unequivocally as it was stated to us at argument, local librarians might be able to indulge the unblocking requests of adult patrons to the point of taking the curse off the statute. [But] the Federal Communications Commission, in its order implementing the Act, pointedly declined to set a federal policy on when unblocking by local libraries would be appropriate under the statute. [Moreover,] the District Court expressly found that 'unblocking may take days, and may be unavailable, especially in branch libraries, which are often less well staffed than main libraries.'

"In any event, we are here to review a statute, and the unblocking provisions simply cannot be construed [to] say that a library must unblock upon adult request, no conditions imposed and no questions asked. [We] have to take the statute on the understanding that adults will be denied access to a substantial amount of nonobscene material harmful to children but lawful for adult examination, and a substantial quantity of text and pictures harmful to no one. [This] is the inevitable consequence [of] current filtering mechanisms, which screen out material to an extent known only by the manufacturers of the blocking software.

"We likewise have to examine the statute on the understanding that the restrictions on adult Internet access have no justification in the object of protecting children. Children could be restricted to blocked terminals, and [screened] from casual glances. And of course the statute could simply have provided for unblocking at adult request, with no questions asked. The statute could, in other words, have protected children without blocking access for adults or subjecting adults to anything more than minimal inconvenience, just the way (the record shows) many librarians had been dealing with obscenity and indecency before imposition of the federal conditions. Instead, the Government's funding conditions engage in overkill. . . .

"The question for me, then, is whether a local library could itself constitutionally impose these restrictions on the content otherwise available to an adult patron through an Internet connection, at a library terminal provided for public use. The answer is no. A library that chose to block an adult's Internet access to material harmful to children (and whatever else the undiscriminating filter might interrupt) would be imposing a content-based restriction on communication of material in the library's control that an adult could otherwise lawfully see. This would simply be censorship. True, the censorship would not necessarily extend to every adult, for [an] Internet user might convince a librarian that he was a true researcher or had a 'lawful purpose' to obtain everything the library's terminal could provide. But as to those who did not qualify for discretionary unblocking, the censorship would be complete and, like all censorship by an agency of the Government, presumptively invalid owing to strict scrutiny in implementing [the] First Amendment. . . .

"The [plurality] does not treat blocking affecting adults as censorship, but chooses to describe a library's act in filtering content as simply an instance of the kind of selection from available material that every library [must] perform. But this position does not hold up. Public libraries are indeed selective in what they acquire to place in their stacks, as they must be. There is only so much money and so much shelf space, and the necessity to choose some material and reject the rest justifies the effort to be selective with an eye to demand, quality, and the object of maintaining the library as a place of civilized enquiry by widely different sorts of people. Selectivity is thus necessary and complex, and these two characteristics explain why review of a library's selection decisions must be limited: the decisions are made all the time, and only in extreme cases could one expect particular choices to reveal impermissible reasons (reasons even the plurality would consider to be illegitimate), like excluding books because their authors are Democrats or their critiques of organized Christianity are unsympathetic. [Citing *Pico*]. Review for rational basis is probably the most that any court could conduct, owing to the myriad particular selections that might be attacked by someone, and the difficulty of untangling the play of factors behind a particular decision.

"At every significant point, however, the Internet blocking here defies comparison to the process of acquisition. Whereas traditional scarcity of money and space require a library to make choices about what to acquire, and the choice to be made is whether or not to spend the money to acquire something, blocking is [a] choice made after the money for Internet access has been spent or committed. Since it makes no difference to the cost of Internet access whether an adult calls up material harmful for children or the Articles of Confederation, blocking (on facts like these) is not necessitated by scarcity of either money or space. [The] proper analogy therefore is not to passing up a book that might have been bought; it is either to buying a book and then keeping it from adults lacking an acceptable 'purpose,' or to buying an encyclopedia and then cutting out pages with anything thought to be unsuitable for all adults. . . .

"The plurality claims to find support for its conclusions in the 'traditional missio[n]' of the public library. The plurality thus argues, in effect, that the traditional responsibility of public libraries has called for denying adult access to certain books, or bowdlerizing the content of what the libraries let adults see. But, in fact, [the history of the public library in this nation over the past half-century offers] not a word about barring requesting adults from any materials in a library's collection, or about limiting an adult's access based on evaluation of his purposes in seeking materials. . . .

"There is no good reason [to] treat blocking of adult enquiry as anything different from the censorship [it] is. For this reason, I would hold in accordance with conventional strict scrutiny that a library's practice of blocking would violate an adult patron's [First] Amendment right to be free of Internet censorship, when unjustified (as here) by any legitimate interest in screening children from harmful material. On that ground, the Act's blocking requirement in its current breadth calls for unconstitutional action by a library recipient, and is itself unconstitutional."

Page 1310.   After the citation of Kagan in section 6 of the Note, add the following:

Rubenfeld, The First Amendment's Purpose, 53 Stan. L. Rev. 767, 769 (2001) ("there is no such thing as a free speech immunity based on the claim that someone wants to break an otherwise constitutional law for expressive purposes");

Page 1311.   At the end of section 6 of the Note, add the following:

For a more recent example, see Boy Scouts of America v. Dale, at page 1356 of the main text.

Page 1322.   At the end of *Pap's*, add the following:

Consider Leahy, The First Amendment Gone Awry, 150 U. Pa. L. Rev. 1021, 1059 (2002): "The *Pap's* decision is irreconcilable with [*Schad,* supra page 1210 of the main text, which held that a ban on all live entertainment in a town is unconstitutional]. Erie's nudity law in effect does exactly what [*Schad*] admonished could not be allowed, but the *Pap's* plurality was simply willing to ignore this. . . ." Is there a principled way to reconcile *Pap's* with *Schad*?

Page 1323.   After the Note on Political Boycotts, add the following:

Note: Computer Code

Another interesting, and increasingly important, example of symbolic speech involves the use of computer code. The Digital Millenium Copyright Act, 17 U.S.C. §1201 *et seq.*, provides that no person shall distribute any technology that is "primarily designed" to circumvent any technological measure that "effectively controls access to a work protected" by copyright. In Universal City Studios, Inc. v. Corley, 273 F.3d 429 (2d Cir. 2001), the Court of Appeals upheld an order enjoining the defendant, publisher of *The Hacker Quarterly*, from posting on his web site a decryption program known as DeCSS. DeCSS is an algorithm that enables users to circumvent the encryption scheme that protects movies on DVDs from limitless copying. DeCSS was developed by a Norwegian teenager who reverse-engineered the encryption system used by DVD producers.

Analogizing the code to a recipe or a music score, the Court of Appeals held that a computer code is "speech" for purposes of the first amendment. The court then noted that DeCSS combines "nonspeech and speech elements, *i.e.* functional and expressive elements." On the one hand, the code is like a recipe or a blueprint, which conveys information to a user. On the other hand, "unlike a blueprint or a recipe, which cannot yield any functional result without human comprehension of its content, human decision-making and human action, computer code can instantly cause a computer to accomplish tasks and instantly render the results of those tasks available throughout the world via the Internet."

Turning to the specific issue, the court noted that "the essential purpose of encryption code is to prevent unauthorized access. Owners of all property rights are entitled to prohibit access to their property by unauthorized persons." Here, the encryption code is "like a lock on a homeowner's door" or "a combination to a safe." Thus, "one might think that Congress has as much authority to regulate the distribution of a computer code to decrypt DVD movies as it has to regulate distribution of skeleton keys" or "combinations to safes." But "DeCSS differs from a skeleton key in one important respect: it not only is capable of performing the function of unlocking the encrypted DVD movie, it also is a form of communication, albeit written in a language not understood by the general public."

The court concluded that the prohibition on posting DeCSS on a web-site is a content-neutral restriction because it targets "the nonspeech" or "functional" capability of DeCSS to decrypt the DVD security code. In this sense, the court reasoned, DeCSS is merely a "skeleton key," and its regulation thus has only an "incidental effect" on speech. Applying *O'Brien*, the court then upheld the Act as applied.

Do you agree with this analysis? As the court observed, posting DeCSS has (at least) two effects. It is information that can be studied by people who are interested in understanding computer codes, and it is a device that can be downloaded to circumvent an encryption code. If the regulation is aimed at the second effect, is its "incidental impact" on the first effect permissible under *O'Brien*? Is a law aimed at the second effect analytically different under the First Amendment than a law restricting a book on how to make dynamite?

Page 1324. After the citation to *International Society for Krishna Consciousness v. Lee*, add the following:

See also Illinois ex rel. Madigan v. Telemarketing Associates, Inc., 538 U.S. ___ U.S. (2003), in which a non-profit organization retained Telemarketing Associates to solicit donations to aid Vietnam veterans. Under its contract with the non-profit organization, Telemarketing Associates was to keep 85% of the gross receipts. The state initiated an action for fraud on the ground that Telemarketing Associates had made false representations to donors about the percent of their contributions that would actually benefit Vietnam veterans. The Court distinguished *Schaumburg* and held that such an action is consistent with the First Amendment because under Illinois law the state must prove by clear and convincing evidence that the defendant knowingly made false representations of fact in order to mislead prospective donors and that the misrepresentations did mislead such donors.

Page 1333.   At the end of the first paragraph of section 1 of the Note, add the following:

Is this precept consistent with other aspects of first amendment jurisprudence? Consider Tushnet, Copyright as a Model for Free Speech Law, 42 B.C. L. Rev. 1, 2-3 (2000):

> When one speaker wishes to use another's words, [the] government may tell her that she cannot. [If] we believe standard First Amendment theory, then we should believe that copyright is unconstitutional because it is designed to suppress some speech to generate other speech, a result the Supreme Court condemned in [*Buckley*]. But that would be silly: copyright is constitutional, in large part because it does encourage speech by the people it protects. The problem is with the standard theory: Government is already involved in shaping available speech, and that's a good thing. Our objections to particular government regulations [must] be to their bias or ineffectiveness, not to the mere fact of government action.

Page 1343.   Before section 1 of the Note, add the following:

1a.   *Advocacy corporations.*   North Carolina Right to Life, a non-profit advocacy corporation that counsels pregnant women how to deal with unwanted pregnancies without resorting to abortion, challenged the constitutionality of 2 U.S.C. §441, which prohibits corporations from making political contributions directly to candidates for federal office, but permits them to establish, administer and solicit contributions to separately created PACs, which can themselves make such contributions. In Federal Election Commission v. Beaumont, 539 U.S. ___ (2003), the Court upheld §441, even as applied to non-profit advocacy corporations. In an opinion by Justice Souter, the Court noted that non-profit advocacy corporations, like for-profit corporations, benefit from state-created advantages and may thus be able to amass substantial political war chests. Moreover, §441 helps to prevent individuals and organizations from circumventing the contribution limits upheld in *Buckley*. Because restrictions on political contributions are "merely 'marginal' speech restrictions," and "lie closer to the edges than to the core of political expression," they are constitutional if they are "closely drawn" to serve a "sufficiently important interest," a test the Court held was satisfied in this case. Justice Thomas, joined by Justice Scalia, dissented.

Page 1344.   At the end of section 2 of the Note, add the following:

In order to prevent circumvention of the contribution limits, if an individual or organization makes campaign expenditures in *coordination* with a candidate, those expenditures ordinarily are treated not as independent expenditures but as contributions under both the Federal Election Campaign Act and the first amendment. But suppose a political party makes such coordinated expenditures on behalf of its electoral candidates? Should those expenditures also be treated as contributions, and thus be subjected to the limitations of the act? Would such an approach make sense, in light of the special nature and purpose of political parties?

In Federal Election Commission v. Colorado Republican Federal Campaign Committee, 533 U.S. 431 (2001) (*Colorado II*), the Court rejected the claim that a political party's *coordinated* expenditures on behalf of its electoral candidates should be treated as expenditures rather than contributions. The Court explained that "a party's right to make unlimited expenditures coordinated with a candidate would induce individual and other nonparty contributors to give to the party in order to finance coordinated spending for a favored candidate beyond the contribution limits, [and thus bypass the very limits] that *Buckley* upheld."

Page 1345.   After section 4 of the Note, add the following:

4a. *Regulating the speech of judicial candidates.* Minnesota elects its judges. It prohibits candidates for judicial office from announcing their views of any disputed legal issues that might come before them as judges. In Republican Party of Minnesota v. White, 536 U.S. 735 (2002), the Court, in a five-to-four decision, held that this prohibition (known as the "announce clause") violated the first amendment. (Minnesota has a separate provision, not challenged in this case, which prohibits candidates for judicial office from making "promises or pledges of conduct in office.")

Justice Scalia delivered the opinion of the Court. At the outset, Justice Scalia reasoned that because the "announce clause both prohibits speech on the basis of its content and burdens a category of speech that is 'at the very core of our First

Amendment freedoms' — speech about the qualifications for public office," the State must "prove that the announce clause is (1) narrowly tailored, to serve (2) a compelling state interest." Justice Scalia then observed that the State had asserted two interests: "preserving the impartiality of the state judiciary and preserving the appearance of the impartiality of the state judiciary." Defining the interest in "impartiality" as meaning that a judge should not have "a preconception in favor or against a particular legal view," Justice Scalia said that "it is virtually impossible to find a judge who does not have preconceptions about the law," and "pretending otherwise by attempting to preserve the 'appearance' of that type of impartiality can hardly be a compelling interest."

Justice Scalia also considered another version of impartiality: "openmindedness." This "sort of impartiality seeks to guarantee each litigant, not an *equal* chance to win the legal points in the case, but at least *some* chance of doing so." Justice Scalia conceded that impartiality and the appearance of impartiality in this sense "may well be . . . desirable in the judiciary" and that the announce clause serves these interests "because it relieves a judge from pressure to rule a certain way in order to maintain consistency with statements the judge has previously made. Justice Scalia nonetheless concluded, that "statements in election campaigns are such an infinitesimal portion of the public commitments to legal positions that judges (or judges to be) undertake, that this object of the prohibition is implausible." Justice Scalia offered as examples of such other statements rulings in earlier cases, statements made in classes judges teach, statements made in books, articles, speeches and so on.

Justice Scalia also rejected the argument that "statements made in an election campaign pose a special threat to openmindedness because the candidate, when elected judge, will have a *particular* reluctance to contradict them. Justice Scalia agreed that "that might be plausible [with] regard to campaign *promises*." But, he observed, Minnesota has "a separate prohibition on campaign 'pledges or promises' [by judicial candidates] which is not challenged here." Beyond that, Justice Scalia reasoned that "the proposition that judges feel significantly greater compulsion [to] maintain consistency with *nonpromissory* statements made during a judicial campaign than with such statements made before or after the campaign is not self-evidently true," and does not carry "the burden imposed by our strict-scrutiny test."

Responding to Justice Ginsburg's argument in dissent that "the announce clause must be constitutional because due process would be denied if an elected judge sat in a case involving an issue on which he had previously announced his view," Justice Scalia argued that elected judges "*always* face the pressure of an electorate who might disagree with their ruling and therefore vote them off the bench. Surely the judge who frees Timothy McVeigh places his job much more at risk than the judge who (horror of horrors!) reconsiders his previously announced view on a disputed legal view."

Finally, Justice Scalia concluded that the practice of restricting the speech of judicial candidates under the "announce clause," which for the most part developed since the 1920s and is not followed in four of the 31 states with elected judges, is not so "universal and long-established" that there should be any special "presumption" of constitutionality for that reason. Justices O'Connor and Kennedy filed concurring opinions.

Justice Stevens, joined by Justices Souter, Ginsburg and Breyer, dissented:

> By obscuring the fundamental distinction between campaigns for the judiciary and the political branches, [the] Court defies any sensible notion of the judicial office and the importance of impartiality in that context. [The] very purpose of most statements prohibited by the announce clause is to convey the message that the candidate's mind is not open on a particular issue.

Justice Ginsburg, joined by Justices Stevens, Souter and Breyer, also dissented:

> Legislative and executive officials act on behalf of the voters who placed them in office; 'judge[s] represen[t] the Law.' Unlike their counterparts in the political branches, judges are expected to refrain from catering to particular constituencies or committing themselves on controversial issues in advance of adversarial presentation. [I] would differentiate elections for political offices, in which the First Amendment holds full sway, from elections designed to select those who office it is to administer justice without respect to persons. Minnesota's choice to elect its judges [does] not preclude [it] from installing an election process geared to the judicial office. [The] rationale underlying unconstrained speech in elections for political office—that representative government depends on the public's ability to choose agents who will act at its behest—does not carry over to campaigns for the bench.
>
> All parties to this case agree that [the] State may constitutionally prohibit judicial candidates from pledging or promising certain results. [This is so because when] a judicial candidate promises to rule a certain way on an issue that may later reach the courts, the potential for due process violations is [grave]. If successful in her bid for office, [the judge] will be under pressure to resist the pleas of litigants who advance positions contrary to her pledges on the campaign trail. [A] judge in this position therefore may be thought to have a "direct, personal, substantial, [and] pecuniary interest" in ruling against certain litigants. [Given] this grave danger to litigants from judicial campaign promises, States are justified in barring expressing of such commitments. . . .
>
> The announce clause [is] equally vital to achieving these compelling ends, for without it, the pledges or promises provision would be feeble. [Uncoupled] from the announce clause, the ban on pledges or promises is easily circumvented. By prefacing a campaign commitment with the caveat, "although I cannot promise anything," [a] candidate could declare with impunity how she would

decide specific issues. Semantic sanitizing of the candidate's commitment would not, however, diminish its pernicious effects on actual and perceived judicial impartiality.

Page 1346. Before the Note on Regulating the Activities of Public Employees, add the following:

Note: The Bipartisan Campaign Finance Reform Act of 2002

1. *The key provisions of the Act.* Consider the following:

(a) "Soft money" consists of unregulated contributions to national political party committees (*e.g.*, the Democratic National Committee, the Republican National Committee, etc.). Prior to the Act, there were no limits on soft money contributions. Such contributions have been used for party-building activities, get-out-the-vote efforts, candidate recruitment, and candidate-specific campaign advertising. The Act prohibits soft money contributions and limits the amount that may be contributed to party committees.

(b) The Act prohibits corporations (including non-profit corporations), trade associations and labor organizations from financing "electioneering communications" within 60 days of a general election and 30 days of a primary election using "treasury money." An electioneering communication is a broadcast advertisement that refers to a clearly identified federal candidate and is targeted to the candidate's state or district. Corporations, trade associations and labor organizations may continue to finance such communications through their PACs.

2. *Soft money.* Is the ban on "soft money" contributions consistent with the reasoning of the Court upholding "contribution" limits? Consider Potter, New Law Follows Supreme Court Rulings, www.brook.edu:

> The soft money provisions of [the Act] were simply intended to prevent the circumvention of the existing contribution limits to candidates. *Buckley* did not distinguish between "hard" and "soft" money [because] "soft money" as a concept did not exist at the time of *Buckley*. The hard/soft money distinction evolved [because a loophole] made it possible for party committees to raise money not covered by the federal contribution limits to finance advertising that [promoted] their federal candidates. [This] created the explosion of "soft money" financing that has fundamentally undermined the effectiveness of the campaign finance laws.
>
> Large contributions to political parties and candidates — of individual as well as corporate and labor money — is a serious national problem, contributing to both

216

corruption and the appearance of corruption, and to diminished faith in government. The Court [has] consistently held that those concerns amply justify reasonable regulation.

3. *Electioneering communications.* Is the ban on electioneering communications constitutional under *Austin*? Consider the following argument, which is derived from a joint statement by such diverse groups as the ACLU, the NRA and the National Right to Life Coalition:

> We have heard a great deal about so-called "sham issue ads" and the need to regulate such advertising. [Congress] realizes that it would be unconstitutional to silence an individual who wants to take out broadcast advertising during [the period leading up to an election]; consequently, the Act does not silence wealthy individuals. But [it] does silence groups like ours that are collectively supported by millions of small contributors who band together to make their views known.
>
> Proponents of [the Act] argue that [it] does not silence our groups. They are wrong. [Its] net effect [is] to ban many of our national groups and their affiliates [from] funding TV or radio ads that even mention the name of a [candidate.] In effect, [our] groups are being cut out of the dialogue on major national issues.
>
> The Supreme Court has repeatedly held that only express advocacy [of a specific candidate's election] can be subject to campaign finance controls. [The Act] redefines express advocacy in a way that covers [issue-based ads if they even mention the name of a candidate]. If we dare applaud, criticize or even mention a candidate's name during this 30 day/60 day "blackout" period, we would have to create a PAC where donor names would have to be disclosed to the FEC. . . .
>
> We believe that no group that wants to express its views through broadcast ads should be forced to bear the significant and costly burden of establishing a PAC just to comment during this period. Separate accounting procedures, new legal compliance costs and separate administrative processes would be imposed on these groups—a high price to exercise their First Amendment rights to merely mention a candidate's name or comment on candidate records. . . .

4. *The Bipartisan Campaign Finance Reform Act of 2002 in the lower court.* In McConnell v. Federal Election Commission, ___ F. Supp. 2d ___ (D.D.C. 2003), a special three-judge panel divided sharply on the constitutionality of the 2002 Act. In more than 1,600 pages of opinions, the judges upheld the ban on party soft money for use in federal elections and the regulation of electioneering issue advocacy, but held that the soft-money ban could apply only to non-federal funds used to finance public communications that support or oppose federal candidates, not to other mixed activities such as voter registration and get-out-the-vote-drives. The judges also held that national parties can continue to raise non-federal funds as long as those funds are not used for "sham" issue ads. The Supreme Court has agreed to hear argument in the case in September, 2003.

5. *Voting with dollars.* Consider B. Ackerman & I. Ayres, Voting with Dollars 4-8, 156-157 (2002):

[The Bipartisan Campaign Reform Act of 2002 follows] the traditional reform repertoire [by attempting] to limit the amount of private money flowing into campaigns. [This effort] is positively misguided. If reformers ever succeeded in convincing the Court to change its mind [about limitations on campaign expenditures], they would not improve our democracy but degrade it further—making it even easier for incumbents to assure their endless reelection without serious challenge. [We] have something to fear from entrenched politicians as well as entrenched wealth; [reformers] should not be eager to exchange one master for another in the struggle for democracy. . . .

[Instead,] the American citizen should [be] given a more equal say in [campaign] funding decisions. Just as he receives a ballot on election day, he should also receive a special credit card to finance his favorite candidate. [Suppose] that Congress seeded every voter's account with fifty [dollars, which each voter could allocate among the candidates for federal office as he sees fit]. If the 100 million Americans who came to the polls in 2000 [each had fifty such dollars], their combined contributions would have amounted to $5 billion—overwhelming the $3 billion provided by private donors. [This approach] makes campaign finance into a new occasion for citizen sovereignty. . . .

[Additional private contributions should be permitted, but contributors should] be barred from giving money directly to candidates. They [should] instead pass their checks through a blind trust [so candidates] won't be able to identify who provided the funds. [There] are lots of reasons for contributing to campaigns, and this [approach] undercuts only one of them—the desire to obtain a quid pro quo from a victorious candidate. . . .

[This two-pronged approach] promises an effective increase in both political equality *and* political expression.

For a discussion of Ackerman and Ayres' proposal, see Karlan, Elections and Change Under "Voting with Dollars," 91 Cal. L. Rev. 706 (2003) (suggesting some contradictions between first amendment theory and the proposal's reliance on anonymous donation).

Page 1358.   At the end of section 4 of the Note, add the following:

Consider the following views of *Dale*:

a. Note, Freedom of Expressive Association—Antidiscrimination Laws, 114 Harv. L. Rev. 259, 263-265 (2000):

First Amendment jurisprudence draws a sharp distinction between direct and indirect burdens on speech. [This distinction] is practically and theoretically unavoidable, in part because its elimination would open the floodgates to First Amendment challenges to the incidental burdens that nearly all laws [impose] on speech. [To] avoid opening the floodgates, [the Court has taken a highly deferential approach to incidental restrictions except] when the effect on expression [is] substantial. . . .

The problem with the [Court's analysis in *Dale* was] its failure to recognize that "merely engag[ing] in expressive activity" cannot be a sound basis for invoking the right of association when the burdened message relates only tangentially to an organization's broader purposes. [BSA's] freedom of association claim [might] have failed as insubstantial had the Court looked to the centrality, rather than to the mere existence, of the organization's anti-homosexual views.

b. Epstein, The Constitutional Perils of Moderation: The Case of the Boy Scouts, 74 S. Cal. L. Rev. 119, 120, 139-140 (2000):

[The] majority reached the right decision [in *Dale*]. But its grounds for decision were too narrow. [The] right outcome in this case should not depend on a delicate balance of what kinds of organizations count as expressive organizations under the First Amendment. Rather, any proper decision must recognize that the state has no interest in counteracting discrimination by private associations that do not possess monopoly power. [All] private associations, regardless of their internal structure and stated purposes, should receive the same freedom afforded the Boy Scouts. . . .

If the reasoning underlying *Dale* is applied correctly, then Title VII is flatly unconstitutional. [The] core illustration of a nonexpressive organization has to be the profit-making corporation that ships goods [and] cares only for its bottom line. But it is sheer fantasy to assume that any successful organization fits this odd caricature of the firm, and is wholly indifferent to how it is perceived in the external world or by its own staff. [A] business firm that refuses to hire workers that have criminal records, or who lack certain religious affiliations, also makes a statement as to how it views itself. [If] the First Amendment applies [so] long as the organization "merely engage[s] in expressive activity that could be impaired," then it follows that every organization engages in expressive activity when it projects itself to its own members and to the rest of the world. [The] short, unhappy truth is that the phrase "expressive association" [cannot] bear the weight that is thrown onto its fragile shoulders.

c. Rubenfeld, The First Amendment's Purpose, 53 Stan. L. Rev. 767, 768-769 (2001):

> [The] Boy Scouts claim was a simple one. The Scouts wanted [to] discriminate for expressive reasons. If they could not exclude homosexuals, they would not be able effectively—or as effectively—to express their sincerely held anti-homo-sexual views. [But] people constantly want to violate laws for expressive reasons. Every person and every organization that wants to discriminate probably has good expressive reasons for doing so. Discrimination is profoundly expressive. It is by far the most effective way most people have of expressing their view of the superiority of their own group and the inferiority of others.
>
> Title VII has "significantly affected" the ability of countless employers to express their views about race or sex. Indeed, it has forced them to "send a message" of equality that many presumably oppose (or would oppose if permitted to do so), in the same way that New Jersey's law forced the Boy Scouts to do so. Should racist and sexist employers be able to come to court with First Amendment challenges to Title VII, demanding that judges accord them the same strict scrutiny that the Boy Scouts received? [Should] a person who can prove that he genuinely holds anti-government views, and that refusing to pay taxes is his most effective or only effective means of communicating these views, be exempt from the income tax?
>
> The answer to all these questions is no, and the reason is that there is no such thing as a free speech immunity based on the claim that someone wants to break an otherwise constitutional law for expressive purposes. [When] a law is otherwise constitutional, and when an actor has not been singled out *because of* his expression, the actor has no free speech claim. The Boy Scouts were not singled out in this way. As a result, the Scouts' claim should have been taken no more seriously than that of a tax protestor or that of a racist employer who demanded an exemption from Title VII on the theory that he wanted to discriminate for expressive, rather than merely commercial, reasons.

d. Sunder, Cultural Dissent, 54 Stan. L. Rev. 495, 498-501, 508, 557 (2001):

> [C]ultures now more than ever are characterized by cultural dissent: challenges by individuals within a community to modernize, or broaden, the traditional terms of cultural membership. [For example,] Gay Irish-Americans want to march in a St. Patrick's Day parade [and] Muslim feminists reinterpret the Koran and emphasize women's right [to] equality. [One response to] the rise of internal cultural debates [has] been to turn to law to protect against the dilution of cultural traditions. . . .
>
> In seeking to protect the Boy Scouts' expressive message against dilution, the Court [in *Dale*] ignored internal dissent in the Scouts over homosexuality and

treated Boy Scouts culture like a "thing" that is static, homogeneous, bounded, and distinct. [The decision therefore] ends up authorizing the exclusion of cultural dissenters because their speech conflicts with the speech of a cultural association's leaders. [A better approach would] recognize the plurality of meanings within a culture. [Where] law finds substantial disagreement over a culture's norms, law should be wary of uncritically granting [associational] leaders [the right] of private censorship.

   e.   Johnson, Expressive Association and Organizational Autonomy, 85 Minn. L. Rev. 1639, 1648-49 (2001):

   There is little doubt that different scouts disagree over whether to permit gay men to serve in leadership roles. The problem with accepting this argument, however, is that it would permit dissenting factions to circumvent an organization's established means of effecting internal change. [If] there is insufficient internal support for change, that suggests that those who dissent from the Scouts' official position are just that—dissenters—and courts should be wary of concluding that an organization's leadership does not speak for the organization as a whole. [One] aspect of associational freedom is the freedom to decide who decides. . . .

Page 1364.   In section 8 of the Note, after the citation to *Glickman,* add the following:

United States v. United Foods, 533 U.S. 405 (2001) (invalidating a federal statute requiring producers of fresh mushrooms to fund a common advertising program promoting mushroom sales, and distinguishing *Glickman* on the ground that the compelled assessments in *Glickman* were ancillary to a comprehensive regulatory scheme of government-mandated collective action, whereas the compelled assessments in *United Foods* were not part of such a comprehensive scheme, other than a program "to generate the very speech to which some of the producers object").

F.   Freedom of the Press

Page 1373.   After the first paragraph of section 5 of the Note, add the following:

   Is copyright protection consistent with the First Amendment? Consider Netanel, Locating Copyright Within the First Amendment, 54 Stan. L. Rev. 1, 39, 47-49, 81 (2001):

Copyright is often characterized as a property right. As such, to some, copyright "doesn't sound like censorship, just people enforcing their lawful property rights." To be certain, rights in real property do enjoy at least qualified First Amendment immunity. One cannot generally trespass on privately-owned land in order to speak. But that, in First Amendment terms, is because real property rights are general regulations that impose only isolated and incidental burdens on speech. [Property rights in information or expression, on the other hand,] are more properly characterized as speech regulations. [Moreover,] even if much slavish copying [is] properly viewed as the mere misappropriation of the economic value of copyrighted expression, [some] copyright regulation may have a chilling effect on speech that is protected under the First Amendment. . . .

[Some] commentators have suggested that copyright is content-based speech regulation [because] "[c]opyright liability turns on the content of what is published." But the fact that copyright law is content-sensitive does not mean that it is "content-based." [Copyright's] purpose is to provide an economic incentive for the creation and dissemination of original expression. Its target is not the viewpoint, subject matter, or even communicative impact [of the speech]. In enacting a copyright law, the government takes no position on the viewpoint or subject matter of restricted expression.

First Amendment challenges to copyright law [should] focus on whether the regulation leaves open "ample alternative channels" for communication of the burdened speech. [Consider], for example, Alan Cranston's translation, with critical commentary, of substantial portions of Hitler's *Mein Kampf*, which [a court in 1939] held to infringe the copyright in the original work. [Cranston] undertook his translation in order to counter the innocuous impression that the heavily edited official English translation had sought to impart. [Cranston] did not absolutely need to publish his own translation in order to covey his message. He might merely have drafted a critical review of the original *Mein Kampf*, [but] his publication of critical review [would have been] significantly less effective. . . .

Page 1373. Before the citation to Volokh and McDonnell in section 5 of the Note, add the following:

Rubenfeld, The Freedom of Imagination: Copyright's Constitutionality, 112 Yale L.J. 1 (2002); R. Tushnet, Copyright as a Model for Free Speech Law, 42 B.C. L. Rev. 1 (2000).

Page 1373. Before section 6 of the Note, add the following:

5a. *Copyright and the First Amendment.*   In Eldred v. Ashcroft, 537 U.S. ___ (2003), the Court upheld the 1998 Copyright Term Extension Act, which extended the duration of existing copyrights by an additional twenty years. The Court rejected the argument that the CTEA violated the first amendment because it limited the public's ability to use previously copyrighted material without serving a substantial government purpose:

> The Copyright Clause and First Amendment were adopted close in time. This proximity indicates that, in the Framers' view, copyright's limited monopolies are compatible with free speech principles. Indeed, copyright's purpose is to *promote* the creation and publication of free expression. As *Harper & Row* observed: "[T]he Framers intended copyright itself to be the engine of free expression. By establishing a marketable right to the use of one's expression, copyright supplies the economic incentive to create and disseminate ideas."
>
> In addition to spurring the creation and publication of new expression, copyright law contains built-in First Amendment accommodations. First, it distinguishes between ideas and expression and makes only the latter eligible for copyright protection. [As] we said in *Harper & Row*, this "idea/expression dichotomy strike[s] a definitional balance between the First Amendment and the Copyright Act by permitting free communication of facts while still protecting an author's expression." Due to this distinction, every idea, theory, and fact in a copyrighted work becomes instantly available for public exploitation at the moment of publication.
>
> Second, the "fair use" defense allows the public to use not only facts and ideas contained in a copyrighted work, but also expression itself in certain circumstances. [The] defense provides: "[T]he fair use of a copyrighted work, including such use by reproduction in copies . . . , for purposes such as criticism, comment, news reporting, teaching (including multiple copies for classroom use), scholarship, or research, is not an infringement of copyright." The fair use defense affords considerable "latitude for scholarship and comment," and even for parody.
>
> The CTEA itself supplements these traditional First Amendment safeguards. First, it allows libraries, archives, and similar institutions to "reproduce" and "distribute, display, or perform in facsimile or digital form" copies of certain published works "during the last 20 years of any term of copyright . . . for purposes of preservation, scholarship, or research" if the work is not already being exploited commercially and further copies are unavailable at a reasonable price. Second, Title II of the CTEA [exempts] small businesses, restaurants, and like entities from having to pay performance royalties on music played from licensed radio, television, and similar facilities. . . .
>
> . . . The CTEA [protects] authors' original expression from unrestricted exploitation. [The] First Amendment securely protects the freedom to make—or decline to make—one's own speech; it bears less heavily when speakers assert the right to make other people's speeches. To the extent such assertions raise First

Amendment concerns, copyright's built-in free speech safeguards are generally adequate to address them. . . .

As we read the Framers' instruction, the Copyright Clause empowers Congress to determine the intellectual property regimes that, overall, in that body's judgment, will serve the ends of the Clause. Beneath the facade of their inventive constitutional interpretation, petitioners forcefully urge that Congress pursued very bad policy in prescribing the CTEA's long terms. The wisdom of Congress' action, however, is not within our province to second guess. . . .

Page 1384.　At the very beginning of the Note, add the following:

1a.　*Detainees in deportation proceedings relating to the "War on Terrorism."* To what extent, if any, does the press have a right to information about individuals who are being detained by the Immigration and Naturalization Service and/or a right to attend deportation hearings? In New Jersey Media Group, Inc. v. Ashcroft, 205 F. Supp. 2d 288 (D.N.J. 2002), federal district judge John Bissell held unconstitutional an order issued by Chief Immigration Judge Michael Creppy on September 21, 2001, informing all immigration judges that "the Attorney General had implemented additional security procedures for certain cases in Immigration Court." Among these new "security procedures" that the immigration judges were to employ in proceedings involving "special interest" cases were that the hearings were to be closed to the public and the judges were to avoid "disclosing any information about the case to anyone outside the Immigration Court." The order explained further that the determination of which cases would be deemed "special interest" for the purposes of these new "security procedures" would be made by the Attorney General. The plaintiff, an association of New Jersey newspapers, filed this suit to enjoin the continued enforcement of this new policy. The government moved to dismiss the complaint for failure to state a claim. Judge Bissell rejected the government's argument that the judiciary has no jurisdiction over such procedural matters because the political branches have "plenary" authority over matters of immigration.

Judge Bissell then concluded that the principle recognized in *Richmond Newspapers* applied in this context because there has been a long "history of openness in deportation proceedings" and there "is no doubt that deportation hearings inherently involve a governmental process that affects a person's liberty interest and . . . must comport with constitutional guarantees of due process." Thus, Judge Bissell concluded that the government may "inhibit the disclosure of sensitive information in this context" only upon a showing "that denial is necessitated by a compelling governmental interest, and is narrowly tailored to serve that interest." The government asserted two interests in support of its policy of closing access to these proceedings: (1) avoidance of setbacks to the terrorism investigation caused by open hearings, and

(2) prevention of stigma or harm to detainees that might result if hearings were open. Judge Bissell held that these interests did not justify the sweeping nature of the closure order. With respect to the first interest, he determined that it could be dealt with by "a more narrow method of in camera disclosure of sensitive evidence" to enable a judicial determination of the necessity for closure. The second interest should be a matter of election for the individual detainee. Judge Bissell therefore held the policy unconstitutional. The United States Court of Appeals for the Third Circuit reversed, in a two-to-one decision. See Ashcroft v. New Jersey Media Group, 308 F. 3d 178 (3d Cir. 2002). See also Detroit Free Press v. Ashcroft, 195 F. Supp. 2d 937 (E.D. Mich. 2002) (reaching the same result as the District Court in *New Jersey Media Group*), aff'd, 303 F. 3d 68 (6th Cir. 2002).

Page 1407. After section 2c of the Note, add the following:

d. Kreimer, Technologies of Protest: Insurgent Social Movements and the First Amendment in the Era of the Internet, 150 U. Penn. L. Rev. 119, 122, 124, 143, 162, 168, 171 (2001):

> Given the structure of twentieth-century communications media, established or well-financed contenders in the public arena [had] a built-in advantage: the cost of disseminating arguments or information to a broad audience threatened effectively to exclude outsiders from public debate. [The Internet] has changed this dynamic, for [almost] any social movement can put up a website. [From] neo-Nazism and Christian Identity to gay liberation and disability rights, [the Internet] facilitates challenges to the status quo. . . .
> Does this mean the twenty-first century brings nothing but millennial prospects for insurgent social movements? Unfortunately, no. [As] sources of information proliferate, the constant stock of audience attention becomes the object of increased competition, [and] established groups are likely to hold a substantial advantage over insurgents in the production of expensive graphics, the purchase of online and offline advertising, and the paid placement of links on attractive websites. [Moreover, for] an insurgent social movement, transparency is not an unmixed blessing. Precisely the qualities of the Internet which enable insurgents to reach previously unaffiliated constituencies allow opponents to track [insurgent] activities. [A] First Amendment jurisprudence aimed at facilitating the potential of the Internet for "the poorly financed causes of little people" will [attend] both to the scarcity of attention and the vulnerabilities to surveillance which shadow the prospects of online activism.

e.   C. Sunstein, republic.com 8-9, 16, 54, 65, 71, 86 (2001):

[A] well-functioning system of free expression must meet two distinctive requirements. First, people should be exposed to materials that they would not have
chosen in advance. Unplanned [encounters] are central to democracy [and people
should] often come across views and topics that they have not specifically selected. Second, [citizens] should have a range of common experiences. Without
shared experiences, [people may] find it hard to understand one another. [There]
are serious dangers in a system in which individuals [restrict] themselves to opinions and topics of their own choosing. . . .

The specialization of Websites [and discussion groups] is obviously important
here. [For example], there are hundreds of Websites created [by] hate groups and
extremist organizations [which] provide links to one another. [Such Websites] are
being used [to] reinforce existing convictions. [They are] permitting people [to]
spread rumors, many of them paranoid and hateful. [This is an example of group
polarization, which] refers to something very simple: After deliberation, people
are likely to move toward a more extreme point in the direction to which the
group's members were originally inclined. . . .

With respect to the Internet, [the] implication is that groups of like-minded people, engaged in discussion with one another, will end up thinking the same thing
that they thought before—but in more extreme form. [Group] polarization is unquestionably occurring on the Internet, [which] is serving as a breeding ground
for extremism. [For] citizens of a heterogeneous democracy, a fragmented communications market creates considerable dangers.

Page 1408.   At the end of section 3 of the Note, add the following:

Should local community standards apply in deciding whether sexually explicit
material posted on the Internet is "obscene"? See Ashcroft v. American Civil Liberties Union, section D4 supra this Supplement.

8
THE CONSTITUTION AND RELIGION

A. Introduction

Page 1418. At the end of section 4 of the Note, add the following:

In Zelman v. Simmons-Harris, 536 U.S. 639 (2002), criticizing the Court's decision upholding a school voucher program that allowed vouchers to be used at religiously affiliated schools, Justice Souter discussed how, in his view, the risk that religion would be corrupted by government aid was "already being realized." He pointed to statutory provisions meaning that "the school may not give admission preferences to children who are members of the patron faith," suggesting that "a participating religious school may [be] forbidden to choose a member of its own clergy to serve as teacher or principal over a layperson of a different religion claiming equal qualification for the job," and suggesting that participating schools might not be allowed to "[teach] traditionally legitimate articles of faith as to the error, sinfulness, or ignorance of others, if they want government money for their schools." What basis is there for a constitutional rule that protects religious institutions from making decisions that judges believe to be contrary to the institutions' long-term interests?

Page 1421. After the quotation from Widmar v. Vincent, insert the following:

In Zelman v. Simmons-Harris, 536 U.S. 639 (2002), Justice Souter's dissenting opinion argued that "[religious] teaching at taxpayer expense simply cannot be cordoned from taxpayer politics, and every major religion currently espouses social positions that provoke intense opposition. Not all taxpaying Protestant citizens [will] be content to underwrite the teaching of the Roman Catholic Church condemning the death penalty. Nor will all of America's Muslims acquiesce in paying for the endorsement of the religious Zionism taught in many religious Jewish schools, which combines 'a nationalistic sentiment' in support of Israel with a 'deeply religious' element. Nor will every secular taxpayer be content to support Muslim views on differential treatment of the sexes, or, for that matter, to fund the espousal of a wife's obligation of obedience to her husband, presumably taught in any schools adopting the articles of faith of the Southern Baptist Convention. Views like these, and innumerable others, have been safe in the sectarian pulpits and classrooms of this Nation not only because the Free Exercise Clause protects them directly, but because the ban on supporting religious establishment has protected free exercise, by keeping it relatively private. With the arrival of vouchers in religious schools, that privacy will go, and along with it will go confidence that religious disagreement will stay moderate." Consider whether the combination of religious and political pluralism might combine to moderate disagreement, either through compromises that allow each religious institution to receive public assistance while maintaining its own views or through compromises that restrict all religious institutions. (Would the latter compromises violate the Free Exercise or Free Speech Clause?)

B.   The Establishment Clause

Page 1437.   At the end of section 3 of the Note, add the following:

Feldman, The Intellectual Origins of the Establishment Clause, 77 N.Y.U. L. Rev. 346, 351, 424 (2002), argues that "[liberty] of conscience [was] the central value invoked by the states that proposed constitutional amendments on the question of religion, and the purpose that underlay the Establishment Clause when it was enacted," and that "the Constitution never suggested that individual liberty of conscience should be protected from government actions that on their face have nothing to do with religion. [It] protects liberty of conscience [only] in the sphere of government action that relates *specifically to religion*." What does the establishment clause understood in this way add to the free exercise and free speech clauses?

Page 1437.   At the end of section 4 of the Note, add the following:

Does the distinction between permissible private speech and arguably impermissible government speech make sense in the contexts of *Lee* and *Santa Fe*? Consider the suggestion in Brady, The Push to Private Religious Expression: Are We Missing Something?, 70 Fordham L. Rev. 1147, 1199 (2002), that "the most promising approach is for students of all perspectives to 'opt in' to the educational process by voicing and defending differing views" in these contexts. Would school authorities have to develop guidelines setting out the limits beyond which student speech could not go in these contexts? If so, would those guidelines convert private into government speech? Would school authorities be barred from developing such guidelines by free speech principles?

Page 1446. At the end of section 2 of the Note, add the following:

Consider the argument in Feldman, From Liberty to Equality: The Transformation of the Establishment Clause, 90 Calif. L. Rev. 673, 677, 718 (2002), that the non-endorsement principle rests on a mistaken reduction of the establishment clause to a principle of equality: "Religious minorities are not uniquely vulnerable to political inequality, and religious discrimination in the United States has not been noticeably worse than discrimination on the basis of political ideology, immigrant status, or language. [The] political-equality approach [cannot] provide a compelling answer to the question 'what is special about religion?'" [The] harms associated with [exclusion] are no worse than the harms associated with other sorts of second-class citizenship and identity.

Page 1466. Before *Note: Purpose and Effect in Aid to Nonpublic Education—Benevolent Neutrality,* add the following:

ZELMAN v. SIMMONS-HARRIS, 536 U.S. 639 (2002). In an opinion by Chief Justice Rehnquist, the Court upheld a school voucher program with the following characteristics, as described in the syllabus to the Court's opinion. The program "gives educational choices to families in any Ohio school district that is under state control pursuant to a federal court order. The program provides tuition aid for certain students in the Cleveland City School District, the only covered district, to attend participating public or private schools of their parent's choosing and tutorial aid for students who choose to remain enrolled in public school. Both religious and nonreligious schools in the district may participate, as may public schools in adjacent school districts. Tuition aid is distributed to parents according to financial need, and where the aid is spent depends solely upon where parents choose to enroll their children. The number of tutorial assistance grants provided to students remaining in public school must equal the number of tuition aid scholarships. In the 1999-2000 school year, 82% of the participating private schools had a religious affiliation, none of the adjacent public schools participated, and 96% of the students participating in the scholarship program were enrolled in religiously affiliated schools. [Cleveland] schoolchildren also have the option of enrolling in community schools, which are funded under state law but run by their own school boards and receive twice the per-student funding as participating private schools, or magnet schools, which are public schools emphasizing a particular subject area, teaching method, or service, and for which the school district receives the same amount per student as it does for a student enrolled at a traditional public school."

Finding "no dispute that the program [was] enacted for the valid secular purpose of providing educational assistance to poor children in a demonstrably failing public school system, "the Court said that "[the] question presented is whether the Ohio program [has] the forbidden 'effect' of advancing or inhibiting religion." Relying on *Mueller, Witters,* and *Zobrest,* it concluded that it did not have such an effect. Those cases, the Court said, "make clear that where a government aid program is neutral with respect to religion, and provides assistance directly to a broad class of citizens who, in turn, direct government aid to religious schools wholly as a result of their own genuine and independent private choice, the program is not readily subject to challenge under the Establishment Clause. A program that shares these features permits government aid to reach religious institutions only by way of the deliberate choices of numerous individual recipients. The incidental advancement of a religious mission, or the perceived endorsement of a religious message, is reasonably attributable to the individual recipient, not to the government, whose role ends with the disbursement of benefits."

It continued, "[the] Ohio program is neutral in all respects toward religion. It is part of a general and multifaceted undertaking by the State of Ohio to provide educational opportunities to the children of a failed school district. It confers educational assistance directly to a broad class of individuals defined without reference to religion, *i.e.,* any parent of a school-age child who resides in the Cleveland City School District. The program permits the participation of *all* schools within the district, religious or nonreligious. Adjacent public schools also may participate and have a financial incentive to do so. Program benefits are available to participating families on neutral terms, with no reference to religion. The only preference stated anywhere in the program is a preference for low-income families, who receive greater assistance and are given priority for admission at participating schools.

"There are no 'financial incentives' that 'skew' the program toward religious schools. [*Witters*]. Such incentives '[are] not present . . . where the aid is allocated on the basis of neutral, secular criteria that neither favor nor disfavor religion, and is made available to both religious and secular beneficiaries on a nondiscriminatory basis.' [*Agostini*]. The program here in fact creates financial *dis*incentives for religious schools, with private schools receiving only half the government assistance given to community schools and one-third the assistance given to magnet schools. Adjacent public schools, should any choose to accept program students, are also eligible to receive two to three times the state funding of a private religious school. Families too have a financial disincentive to choose a private religious school over other schools. Parents that choose to participate in the scholarship program and then to enroll their children in a private school (religious or nonreligious) must copay a portion of the school's tuition. Families that choose a community school, magnet school, or traditional public school pay nothing. Although such features of the program are not necessary to its constitutionality, they clearly dispel the claim that the program 'creates . . . financial incentives for parents to choose a sectarian school.' [*Zobrest*]."

On whether the program gave "genuine opportunities for Cleveland parents to select secular educational options for their school-age children," the Court argued that "Cleveland schoolchildren enjoy a range of educational choices: They may remain in public school as before, remain in public school with publicly funded tutoring aid, obtain a scholarship and choose a religious school, obtain a scholarship and choose a nonreligious private school, enroll in a community school, or enroll in a magnet school. That 46 of the 56 private schools now participating in the program are religious schools does not condemn it as a violation of the Establishment Clause. The Establishment Clause question is whether Ohio is coercing parents into sending their children to religious schools, and that question must be answered by evaluating *all* options Ohio provides Cleveland schoolchildren, only one of which is to obtain a program scholarship and then choose a religious school."

Relying on *Mueller*, the Court rejected the argument that "we should attach constitutional significance to the fact that 96% of scholarship recipients have enrolled in religious schools. They claim that this alone proves parents lack genuine choice, even if no parent has ever said so. We need not consider this argument in detail, since it was flatly rejected in *Mueller*, where we found it irrelevant that 96% of parents taking deductions for tuition expenses paid tuition at religious schools." Explaining why it rejected the argument, the Court pointed out that "[the] 96% figure [discounts] entirely (1) the more than 1,900 Cleveland children enrolled in alternative community schools, (2) the more than 13,000 children enrolled in alternative magnet schools, and (3) the more than 1,400 children enrolled in traditional public schools with tutorial assistance. Including some or all of these children in the denominator of children enrolled in nontraditional schools during the 1999-2000 school year drops the percentage enrolled in religious schools from 96% to under 20%. The 96% figure also represents but a snapshot of one particular school year. In the 1997-1998 school year, by contrast, only 78% of scholarship recipients attended religious schools."

Justices O'Connor and Thomas wrote concurring opinions. Justices Stevens, Souter, Ginsburg, and Breyer dissented. Justice Souter's dissent asserted that "the espoused criteria of neutrality in offering aid, and private choice in directing it, [are] nothing but examples of verbal formalism." To apply the neutrality test, he argued, "it makes sense to focus on a category of aid that may be directed to religious as well as secular schools, and ask whether the scheme favors a religious direction. Here, one would ask whether the voucher provisions [were] written in a way that skewed the scheme toward benefiting religious schools. [The] majority looks not to the provisions for tuition vouchers, but to every provision for educational [opportunity]. The majority then finds confirmation that 'participation of *all* schools' satisfies neutrality by noting that the better part of total state educational expenditure goes to public schools, thus showing there is no favor of religion. The illogic is patent. If regular, public schools (which can get no voucher payments) 'participate' in a voucher scheme with schools that can, and public expenditure is still predominantly on public schools, then the majority's reasoning would find neutrality in a scheme of vouchers available for private tuition in districts with no secular private schools at all. 'Neutrality' as the majority employs the term is, literally, verbal and nothing more." Justice Souter also criticized the Court for what he described as its abandonment of the previously enforced limitation on provision of "substantial" aid to religious institutions.

Page 1466. Replace section 1 of the Note with the following:

1. *Vouchers.* What, if any, limits does the Establishment Clause place on voucher programs? What are the criteria for determining whether a program allows participants to exercise "genuine choice" among secular and religious options? Justice O'Connor's concurring opinion in *Zelman* argued that choice should be determined by "consider[ing] all reasonable educational alternatives to religious schools that are available to parents," and pointed out that "[when] one considers the option to attend community schools, the percentage of students enrolled in religious schools falls to 62.1 percent. If magnet schools are included, [this] percentage falls to 16.5 percent."

Justice Souter's dissent criticized this focus as "confused" because it "ignores the reason for having a private choice criterion in the first place. [It] is a criterion for deciding whether indirect aid to a religious school is legitimate because it passes through private hands that can spend or use the aid in a secular school. The question is whether the private hand is genuinely free to send the money in either a secular direction or a religious one. The majority now has transformed this question [into] a question about selecting from examples of state spending (on education) including direct spending on magnet and community public schools that goes through no private hands and could never reach a religious school under any circumstance. When the choice test is transformed from where to spend the money to where to go to school, it is cut loose from its very purpose." He concluded, "If 'choice' is present whenever there is any educational alternative to the religious school to which vouchers can be endorsed, then there will always be a choice and the voucher can always be constitutional, even in a system in which there is not a single private secular school as an alternative to the religious school."

For an analysis of the fiscal and political limits on voucher programs, see Ryan & Heise, The Political Economy of School Choice, 111 Yale L.J. 2043 (2002).

Page 1468.   After section 6 of the Note, add the following:

7. *Neutrality, steering, and "real choice."*   What considerations are relevant in determining whether a neutral program offers participants a real choice or steers them towards religious institutions? Lupu & Tuttle, Sites of Redemption: A Wide Angle Look at Government Vouchers and Sectarian Service Providers, 18 J. L. & Politics 537, 561, 565 (2002), suggest the following considerations: the extent to which participants are constrained in choosing the religious provider rather than not participating in the program at all; the extent to which there are nonreligious institutions providing the services and able to accept the vouchers; the ease with which new providers can start up, making the market more or less dynamic in response to demand; and the degree to which the government's purpose is connected to a character change itself tied to religious transformation. How might these factors bear on voucher programs for the provision of child care services? For the provision of drug treatment programs offered as alternatives to incarceration?

Page 1469.   Before Section C, add the following:

Lupu, Government Messages and Government Money: *Santa Fe, Mitchell v. Helms*, and the Arc of the Establishment Clause, 42 Wm. & Mary L. Rev. 771, 801 (2001), argues that

> [i]ssues involving government resources in support of religion quite frequently [are] truly about "church." [When] the state provides resources to such entities, it typically does so on the theory that churches may effectively assist in the state's secular work. [Government] message cases [are] very different in their character: [They] involve officials of the state doing the work of faith institutions—that is, preaching, proselytizing, [and] generally spreading the Word or respect for the Word. [Government] message cases are not about institutional connection between agencies of government and agencies of faith. [They are] about the political misappropriation of religious themes.

Does the distinction between money and message cases account for differences in the outcomes of the cases you have studied?

Page 1484.   At the end of section 2(a) of the Note, add the following:

Consider Brownstein, Protecting Religious Liberty: The False Messiahs of Free Speech Doctrine and Formal Neutrality, 18 J. L. & Politics 119, 191-92 (2002): Under the individualized determination exception, "religion is granted something like most favored nation status. If any secular interest can justify an exemption from a law, then the state must recognize that religious interests also deserve to be exempt from the law. [But an] extraordinary range of laws contain exemptions to their application, including most civil rights laws [and] even homicide statutes. [This] militates against such an understanding." See also Duncan, Free Exercise is Dead, Long Live Free Exercise: *Smith, Lukumi*, and the General Applicability Requirement, 3 U. Pa. J. Const. L. 850, 868 (2001): "[A] law burdening religious conduct is underinclusive, with respect to any particular government interest, if the law fails to pursue that interest uniformly against other conduct that causes similar damage to that government interest." Does this meet Brownstein's concerns?

Page 1485.   At the end of section 2(b) of the Note, add the following:

Consider Brownstein, Protecting Religious Liberty: The False Messiahs of Free Speech Doctrine and Formal Neutrality, 18 J. L. & Politics 119, 191-92 (2002): "A hybrid rights situation involves a neutral law of general applicability that substantially burdens the exercise of religion and sufficiently burdens some other constitutionally protected interested to invoke the application of the requisite standard of review [short] of strict scrutiny." Brownstein argues that this idea is coherent but inconsistent with "basic constitutional intuitions." He uses the example of an informed-consent requirement for abortion: If the requirement is "applied to a woman seeking an abortion for secular reasons, the regulation is reviewed under the undue burden standard and is upheld. If the woman is seeking an abortion for religious reasons, this application of the law will be reviewed under strict scrutiny and invalidated." Brownstein says that this is an "odd conclusion" because "it justifies treating people differently with regard to their exercise of fundamental rights. Hybrid rights analysis suggests that religious people should be treated preferentially with regard to the exercise of fundamental rights when their religious beliefs influence the way they exercise their rights. [That] cannot be right. There is an equality dimension to liberty rights. [Religious] people do not get special treatment with respect to these basic freedoms. No one does."

D.   Permissible Accommodation

Page 1497.   At the conclusion of the first paragraph of section 1 of the Note, add the following:

The Court followed *Lamb's Chapel* in Good News Club v. Milford Central School, 533 U.S. 98 (2001), which involved a club that would conduct prayer meetings and Bible lessons after school hours in a room at a school attended by children from kindergarten through the twelfth grade. Again finding that excluding the club would amount to viewpoint discrimination, the Court concluded that parents, who had to give permission for their children to attend the club's meetings, would not be coerced into participating or "confused about whether the school was endorsing religion." Nor did the evidence support the claim that students not attending the club's meetings would perceive endorsement. Indeed, "we cannot say the danger that children would misperceive the endorsement of religion is any greater than the danger that they would perceive a hostility toward religious viewpoint if the Club were excluded from the public forum. [We] decline to employ Establishment Clause jurisprudence using a modified heckler's veto, in which a group's religious activity can be proscribed on the basis of what the youngest members of the audience might misperceive."

Page 1500.   After the first paragraph of the Note, add the following:

Sullivan, The New Religion and the Constitution, 116 Harv. L. Rev. 1397 (2003), develops a taxonomy of ways of understanding the relation between religious associations and government. "(1) Religion as Quasi-Government: Here religious associations are seen "as unique in their power to interpret the world and express shared understandings," and "exert a quasi-sovereign authority over their members." Sullivan argues that this view "favors weak judicial enforcement of the Free Exercise Clause and strong judicial enforcement of the Establishment Clause. If religion poses the danger of quasi-sovereign competition with government, then judges [should] not afford religious groups special exemptions from general laws [nor] should they permit public subsidies to flow to religious activities." (2) "Religion as Private Expressive Association": Here religious associations are "on a continuum with other forms of private expressive association," but "with the twist that government is uniquely disabled [from] speaking in a religious voice." This view calls for "strong enforcement" of both religion clauses. "[Courts] would review strictly both government refusals to exempt religious associations from general laws that inhibit their collective expressive practices, and government inclusion of religious organizations within the scope of public subsidies." (3) "Religion as Discrete and Insular Minority": Here religion associations "are entitled not only to protection from unequal treatment, but also to preferential treatment in order to offset historical and structural disadvantages. [The] judicial prescription that follows [consists] of strong enforcement of the Free Exercise Clause but weak enforcement of the Establishment Clause." (4) "Religion as Ordinary Interest Group": Here religious associations "are best conceived as ordinary interest groups that may participate freely in politics but should expect no particular judicial solicitude from courts interpreting either of the Religion Clauses." Descriptively, which position do today's justices take? Prescriptively, on what basis should a judge choose among these approaches?

9

THE CONSTITUTION, BASELINES, AND THE PROBLEM OF PRIVATE POWER

C. Constitutionally Impermissible Departures from Neutrality: State Subsidization, Approval, and Encouragement

Page 1544. **Before Section D, add the following:**

BRENTWOOD ACADEMY v. TENNESSEE SECONDARY SCHOOL ATHLETIC ASSOCIATION

531 U.S. 288 (2001)

JUSTICE SOUTER delivered the opinion of the Court.

The issue is whether a statewide association incorporated to regulate interscholastic athletic competition among public and private secondary schools may be regarded as engaging in state action when it enforces a rule against a member school. The association in question here includes most public schools located within the State, acts through their representatives, draws its officers from them, is largely funded by their dues and income received in their stead, and has historically been seen to regulate in lieu of the State Board of Education's exercise of its own authority. We hold that the association's regulatory activity may and should be treated as state action owing to the pervasive entwinement of state school officials in the structure of the association, there being no offsetting reason to see the association's acts in any other way.

pervasive entwinement

I

Respondent Tennessee Secondary School Athletic Association (Association) is a not-for-profit membership corporation organized to regulate interscholastic sport among the public and private high schools in Tennessee that belong to it. No school is forced to join, but without any other authority actually regulating interscholastic athletics, it enjoys the memberships of almost all the State's public high schools (some 290 of them or 84% of the Association's voting membership), far outnumbering the 55 private schools that belong. A member school's team may play or scrimmage only against the team of another member, absent a dispensation.

The Association's rulemaking arm is its legislative council, while its board of control tends to administration. The voting membership of each of these nine-person committees is limited under the Association's bylaws to high school principals, assistant principals, and superintendents elected by the member schools, and the public school administrators who so serve typically attend meetings during regular school hours. Although the Association's staff members are not paid by the State, they are eligible to join the State's public retirement system for its employees. Member schools pay dues to the Association, though the bulk of its revenue is gate receipts at member teams' football and basketball tournaments, many of them held in public arenas rented by the Association.

The constitution, bylaws, and rules of the Association set standards of school membership and the eligibility of students to play in interscholastic games. Each school, for example, is regulated in awarding financial aid, most coaches must have a Tennessee state teaching license, and players must meet minimum academic standards and hew to limits on student employment. Under the bylaws, "in all matters pertaining to the athletic relations of his school," the principal is responsible to the Association, which has the power "to suspend, to fine, or otherwise penalize any member school for the violation of any of the rules of the Association or for other just cause."

Ever since the Association was incorporated in 1925, Tennessee's State Board of Education (State Board) has (to use its own words) acknowledged the corporation's functions "in providing standards, rules and regulations for interscholastic competition in the public schools of Tennessee." More recently, the State Board cited its statutory authority, Tenn. Code Ann. §49-1-302 (App. 220), when it adopted language expressing the relationship between the Association and the Board. Specifically, in 1972, it went so far as to adopt a rule expressly "designat[ing]" the Association as "the organization to supervise and regulate the athletic activities" in which the public junior and senior high schools in Tennessee participate on an interscholastic basis." [That] same year, the State Board specifically approved the Association's rules and regulations, while reserving the right to review future changes. Thus, on several occasions over the next 20 years, the State Board reviewed, approved, or reaffirmed its approval of the recruiting Rule at issue in this case. In 1996,

238

however, the State Board dropped the original Rule expressly designating the Association as regulator; it substituted a statement "recogniz[ing] the value of participation in interscholastic athletics and the role of [the Association] in coordinating interscholastic athletic competition," while "authoriz[ing] the public schools of the state to voluntarily maintain membership in [the Association]."

The action before us responds to a 1997 regulatory enforcement proceeding brought against petitioner, Brentwood Academy, a private parochial high school member of the Association. The Association's board of control found that Brentwood violated a rule prohibiting "undue influence" in recruiting athletes, when it wrote to incoming students and their parents about spring football practice. The Association accordingly placed Brentwood's athletic program on probation for four years, declared its football and boys' basketball teams ineligible to compete in playoffs for two years, and imposed a $3,000 fine. When these penalties were imposed, all the voting members of the board of control and legislative council were public school administrators.

Brentwood sued the Association and its executive director in federal court under Rev. Stat. §1979, 42 U.S.C. §1983 claiming that enforcement of the Rule was state action and a violation of the First and Fourteenth Amendments. . . .

II

A

Our cases try to plot a line between state action subject to Fourteenth Amendment scrutiny and private conduct (however exceptionable) that is not. [*Tarkanian; Jackson.*] The judicial obligation is not only to " 'preserv[e] an area of individual freedom by limiting the reach of federal law' and avoi[d] the imposition of responsibility on a State for conduct it could not control" [*Tarkanian* (quoting *Lugar*)], but also to assure that constitutional standards are invoked "when it can be said that the State is responsible for the specific conduct of which the plaintiff complains" [*Blum*]. If the Fourteenth Amendment is not to be displaced, therefore, its ambit cannot be a simple line between States and people operating outside formally governmental organizations, and the deed of an ostensibly private organization or individual is to be treated sometimes as if a State had caused it to be performed. Thus, we say that state action may be found if, though only if, there is such a "close nexus between the State and the challenged action" that seemingly private behavior "may be fairly treated as that of the State itself."

What is fairly attributable is a matter of normative judgment, and the criteria lack rigid simplicity. From the range of circumstances that could point toward the State behind an individual face, no one fact can function as a necessary condition across the board for finding state action; nor is any set of circumstances absolutely sufficient, for there may be some countervailing reason against attributing activity to the government.

Our cases have identified a host of facts that can bear on the fairness of such an attribution. We have, for example, held that a challenged activity may be state action when it results from the State's exercise of "coercive power" [*Blum*], when the State provides "significant encouragement, either overt or covert," ibid., or when a private actor operates as a "willful participant in joint activity with the State or its agents" [*Lugar* (internal quotation marks omitted)]. We have treated a nominally private entity as a state actor when it is controlled by an "agency of the State," Pennsylvania v. Board of Directors of City Trusts of Philadelphia, 353 U.S. 230, 231 (1957) (per curiam), when it has been delegated a public function by the State, cf., e.g., [West v. Atkins]; Edmonson v. Leesville Concrete Co., 500 U.S. 614, 627-628 (1991), when it is "entwined with governmental policies" or when government is "entwined in [its] management or control," Evans v. Newton, 382 U.S. 296, 299, 301 (1966).

Amidst such variety, examples may be the best teachers, and examples from our cases are unequivocal in showing that the character of a legal entity is determined neither by its expressly private characterization in statutory law, nor by the failure of the law to acknowledge the entity's inseparability from recognized government officials or agencies. Lebron v. National Railroad Passenger Corporation, 513 U.S. 374 (1995), held that Amtrak was the Government for constitutional purposes, regardless of its congressional designation as private; it was organized under federal law to attain governmental objectives and was directed and controlled by federal appointees. Pennsylvania v. Board of Directors of City Trusts of Philadelphia held the privately endowed Gerard College to be a state actor and enforcement of its private founder's limitation of admission to whites attributable to the State, because, consistent with the terms of the settlor's gift, the college's board of directors was a state agency established by state law. Ostensibly the converse situation occurred in Evans v. Newton, which held that private trustees to whom a city had transferred a park were nonetheless state actors barred from enforcing racial segregation, since the park served the public purpose of providing community recreation, and "the municipality remain[ed] entwined in [its] management [and] control."

These examples of public entwinement in the management and control of ostensibly separate trusts or corporations foreshadow this case, as this Court itself anticipated in *Tarkanian*. *Tarkanian* arose when an undoubtedly state actor, the University of Nevada, suspended its basketball coach, Tarkanian, in order to comply with rules and recommendations of the National Collegiate Athletic Association (NCAA). The coach charged the NCAA with state action, arguing that the state university had delegated its own functions to the NCAA, clothing the latter with authority to make and apply the university's rules, the result being joint action making the NCAA a state actor.

To be sure, it is not the strict holding in *Tarkanian* that points to our view of this case, for we found no state action on the part of the NCAA. We could see, on the one hand, that the university had some part in setting the NCAA's rules, and the Supreme Court of Nevada had gone so far as to hold that the NCAA had been delegated the university's traditionally exclusive public authority over personnel. But on the other side, the NCAA's policies were shaped not by the University of Nevada alone, but by several hundred member institutions, most of them having no connection with Nevada, and exhibiting no color of Nevada law. Since it was difficult to see the NCAA, not as a collective membership, but as surrogate for the one State, we held the organization's connection with Nevada too insubstantial to ground a state action claim.

But dictum in *Tarkanian* pointed to a contrary result on facts like ours, with an organization whose member public schools are all within a single State. "The situation would, of course, be different if the [Association's] membership consisted entirely of institutions located within the same State, many of them public institutions created by the same sovereign." To support our surmise, we approvingly cited two cases: Clark v. Arizona Interscholastic Assn., 695 F.2d 1126 (CA9 1982), cert. denied, 464 U.S. 818 (1983), a challenge to a state high school athletic association that kept boys from playing on girls' interscholastic volleyball teams in Arizona; and Louisiana High School Athletic Assn. v. St. Augustine High School, 396 F.2d 224 (CA5 1968), a parochial school's attack on the racially segregated system of interscholastic high school athletics maintained by the athletic association. In each instance, the Court of Appeals treated the athletic association as a state actor.

B

Just as we foresaw in *Tarkanian*, the "necessarily fact-bound inquiry" [*Lugar*], leads to the conclusion of state action here. The nominally private character of the Association is overborne by the pervasive entwinement of public institutions and public officials in its composition and workings, and there is no substantial reason to claim unfairness in applying constitutional standards to it.

The Association is not an organization of natural persons acting on their own, but of schools, and of public schools to the extent of 84% of the total. Under the Association's bylaws, each member school is represented by its principal or a faculty member, who has a vote in selecting members of the governing legislative council and board of control from eligible principals, assistant principals and superintendents.

Although the findings and prior opinions in this case include no express conclusion of law that public school officials act within the scope of their duties when they represent their institutions, no other view would be rational, the official nature of their involvement being shown in any number of ways. Interscholastic athletics obviously play an integral part in the public education of Tennessee, where nearly every public high school spends money on competitions among schools. Since a pickup system of interscholastic games would not do, these public teams need some mechanism to produce rules and regulate competition. The mechanism is an organization overwhelmingly composed of public school officials who select representatives (all of them public officials at the time in question here), who in turn adopt and

241

enforce the rules that make the system work. Thus, by giving these jobs to the Association, the 290 public schools of Tennessee belonging to it can sensibly be seen as exercising their own authority to meet their own responsibilities. Unsurprisingly, then, the record indicates that half the council or board meetings documented here were held during official school hours, and that public schools have largely provided for the Association's financial support. A small portion of the Association's revenue comes from membership dues paid by the schools, and the principal part from gate receipts at tournaments among the member schools. Unlike mere public buyers of contract services, whose payments for services rendered do not convert the service providers into public actors, see [Rendell-Baker], the schools here obtain membership in the service organization and give up sources of their own income to their collective association. The Association thus exercises the authority of the predominantly public schools to charge for admission to their games; the Association does not receive this money from the schools, but enjoys the schools' moneymaking capacity as its own.

In sum, to the extent of 84% of its membership, the Association is an organization of public schools represented by their officials acting in their official capacity to provide an integral element of secondary public schooling. There would be no recognizable Association, legal or tangible, without the public school officials, who do not merely control but overwhelmingly perform all but the purely ministerial acts by which the Association exists and functions in practical terms. Only the 16% minority of private school memberships prevents this entwinement of the Association and the public school system from being total and their identities totally indistinguishable.

To complement the entwinement of public school officials with the Association from the bottom up, the State of Tennessee has provided for entwinement from top down. State Board members are assigned ex officio to serve as members of the board of control and legislative council, and the Association's ministerial employees are treated as state employees to the extent of being eligible for membership in the state retirement system.

It is, of course, true that the time is long past when the close relationship between the surrogate association and its public members and public officials acting as such was attested frankly. [But] the removal of the designation language from Rule 0520-1-2-.08 affected nothing but words. Today the State Board's member-designees continue to sit on the Association's committees as nonvoting members, and the State continues to welcome Association employees in its retirement scheme. The close relationship is confirmed by the Association's enforcement of the same preamendment rules and regulations reviewed and approved by the State Board (including the recruiting Rule challenged by Brentwood), and by the State Board's continued willingness to allow students to satisfy its physical education requirement by taking part in interscholastic athletics sponsored by the Association. The most one can say on the evidence is that the State Board once freely acknowledged the Association's official character but now does it by winks and nods.

[The] entwinement down from the State Board is therefore unmistakable, just as the entwinement up from the member public schools is overwhelming. Entwinement will support a conclusion that an ostensibly private organization ought to be charged with a public character and judged by constitutional standards; entwinement to the degree shown here requires it.

C

Entwinement is also the answer to the Association's several arguments offered to persuade us that the facts would not support a finding of state action under various criteria applied in other cases. These arguments are beside the point, simply because the facts justify a conclusion of state action under the criterion of entwinement, a conclusion in no sense unsettled merely because other criteria of state action may not be satisfied by the same facts.

The Association places great stress, for example, on the application of a public function test, as exemplified in Rendell-Baker v. Kohn. There, an apparently private school provided education for students whose special needs made it difficult for them to finish high school. The record, however, failed to show any tradition of providing public special education to students unable to cope with a regular school, who had historically been cared for (or ignored) according to private choice. It was true that various public school districts had adopted the practice of referring students to the school and paying their tuition, and no one disputed that providing the instruction aimed at a proper public objective and conferred a public benefit. But we held that the performance of such a public function did not permit a finding of state action on the part of the school unless the function performed was exclusively and traditionally public, as it was not in that case. The Association argues that application of the public function criterion would produce the same result here, and we will assume, arguendo, that it would. But this case does not turn on a public function test, any more than *Rendell-Baker* had anything to do with entwinement of public officials in the special school.

For the same reason, it avails the Association nothing to stress that the State neither coerced nor encouraged the actions complained of. "Coercion" and "encouragement" are like "entwinement" in referring to kinds of facts that can justify characterizing an ostensibly private action as public instead. Facts that address any of these criteria are significant, but no one criterion must necessarily be applied. When, therefore, the relevant facts show pervasive entwinement to the point of largely overlapping identity, the implication of state action is not affected by pointing out that the facts might not loom large under a different test.

D

This is not to say that all of the Association's arguments are rendered beside the point by the public officials' involvement in the Association, for after application of the entwinement criterion, or any other, there is a further potential issue, and the Association raises it. Even facts that suffice to show public action (or, standing alone, would require such a finding) may be outweighed in the name of some value at odds with finding public accountability in the circumstances. In [Polk County v. Dodson, 454 U.S. 312 (1981)], a defense lawyer's actions were deemed private even though she was employed by the county and was acting within the scope of her duty as a public defender. Full-time public employment would be conclusive of state action for some purposes, see West v. Atkins, accord, *Lugar,* but not when the employee is doing a defense lawyer's primary job; then, the public defender does "not ac[t] on behalf of the State; he is the State's adversary." *Polk County.* The state-action doctrine does not convert opponents into virtual agents.

The assertion of such a countervailing value is the nub of each of the Association's two remaining arguments, neither of which, however, persuades us. The Association suggests, first, that reversing the judgment here will somehow trigger an epidemic of unprecedented federal litigation. Even if that might be counted as a good reason for a *Polk County* decision to call the Association's action private, the record raises no reason for alarm here. Save for the Sixth Circuit, every Court of Appeals to consider a statewide athletic association like the one here has found it a state actor. [No] one, however, has pointed to any explosion of §1983 cases against interscholastic athletic associations in the affected jurisdictions. [If] Brentwood's claim were pushing at the edge of the class of possible defendant state actors, an argument about the social utility of expanding that class would at least be on point, but because we are nowhere near the margin in this case, the Association is really asking for nothing less than a dispensation for itself. Its position boils down to saying that the Association should not be dressed in state clothes because other, concededly public actors are; that Brentwood should be kept out of court because a different plaintiff raising a different claim in a different case may find the courthouse open. Pleas for special treatment are hard to sell, although saying that does not, of course, imply anything about the merits of Brentwood's complaint; the issue here is merely whether Brentwood properly names the Association as a §1983 defendant, not whether it should win on its claim.

The judgment of the Court of Appeals for the Sixth Circuit is reversed, and the case is remanded for further proceedings consistent with this opinion.

It is so ordered.

JUSTICE THOMAS, with whom THE CHIEF JUSTICE, JUSTICE SCALIA, and JUSTICE KENNEDY join, dissenting.

We have never found state action based upon mere "entwinement." Until today, we have found a private organization's acts to constitute state action only when the organization performed a public function; was created, coerced, or encouraged by the government; or acted in a symbiotic relationship with the government. The majority's holding—that the Tennessee Secondary School Athletic Association's (TSSAA) enforcement of its recruiting rule is state action—not only extends state-action doctrine beyond its permissible limits but also encroaches upon the realm of individual freedom that the doctrine was meant to protect. I respectfully dissent.

I

Like the state-action requirement of the Fourteenth Amendment, the state-action element of 42 U.S.C. §1983 excludes from its coverage "merely private conduct, however discriminatory or wrongful." American Mfrs. Mut. Ins. Co. v. Sullivan, 526 U.S. 40, 50 (1999) (internal quotation marks omitted). "Careful adherence to the 'state action' requirement" thus "preserves an area of individual freedom by limiting the reach of federal law and federal judicial power." [*Lugar.*] The state-action doctrine also promotes important values of federalism, "avoid[ing] the imposition of responsibility on a State for conduct it could not control." [*Tarkanian.*] Although we have used many different tests to identify state action, they all have a common purpose. Our goal in every case is to determine whether an action "can fairly be attributed to the State." [*Blum.*] *American Mfrs., supra,* at 52.

A

Regardless of these various tests for state action, common sense dictates that the TSSAA's actions cannot fairly be attributed to the State, and thus cannot constitute state action. The TSSAA was formed in 1925 as a private corporation to organize interscholastic athletics and to sponsor tournaments among its member schools. Any private or public secondary school may join the TSSAA by signing a contract agreeing to comply with its rules and decisions. Although public schools currently compose 84% of the TSSAA's membership, the TSSAA does not require that public schools constitute a set percentage of its membership, and, indeed, no public school need join the TSSAA. The TSSAA's rules are enforced not by a state agency but by its own board of control, which comprises high school principals, assistant principals, and superintendents, none of whom must work at a public school. Of course, at the time the recruiting rule was enforced in this case, all of the board members happened to be public school officials. However, each board member acts in a representative capacity on behalf of all the private and public schools in his region of Tennessee, and not simply his individual school.

The State of Tennessee did not create the TSSAA. The State does not fund the TSSAA and does not pay its employees. In fact, only 4% of the TSSAA's revenue comes from the dues paid by member schools; the bulk of its operating budget is derived from gate receipts at tournaments it sponsors. The State does not permit the TSSAA to use state-owned facilities for a discounted fee, and it does not exempt the TSSAA from state taxation. No Tennessee law authorizes the State to coordinate interscholastic athletics or empowers another entity to organize interscholastic athletics on behalf of the State. The only state pronouncement acknowledging the

245

TSSAA's existence is a rule providing that the State Board of Education permits public schools to maintain membership in the TSSAA if they so choose.

Moreover, the State of Tennessee has never had any involvement in the particular action taken by the TSSAA in this case: the enforcement of the TSSAA's recruiting rule prohibiting members from using "undue influence" on students or their parents or guardians "to secure or to retain a student for athletic purposes." There is no indication that the State has ever had any interest in how schools choose to regulate recruiting. In fact, the TSSAA's authority to enforce its recruiting rule arises solely from the voluntary membership contract that each member school signs, agreeing to conduct its athletics in accordance with the rules and decisions of the TSSAA.

B

Even approaching the issue in terms of any of the Court's specific state-action tests, the conclusion is the same: The TSSAA's enforcement of its recruiting rule against Brentwood Academy is not state action.

[The] TSSAA has not performed a function that has been "traditionally exclusively reserved to the State." [*Jackson.*] The organization of interscholastic sports is neither a traditional nor an exclusive public function of the States. [Certainly,] in Tennessee, the State did not even show an interest in interscholastic athletics until 47 years after the TSSAA had been in existence and had been orchestrating athletic contests throughout the State. Even then, the State Board of Education merely acquiesced in the TSSAA's actions and did not assume the role of regulating interscholastic athletics. Cf. *Blum* ("Mere approval of or acquiescence in the initiatives of a private party is not sufficient to justify holding the State responsible for those initiatives . . ."); see also [*Flagg Brothers*]. The TSSAA no doubt serves the public, particularly the public schools, but the mere provision of a service to the public does not render such provision a traditional and exclusive public function. See [*Rendell-Baker*].

It is also obvious that the TSSAA is not an entity created and controlled by the government for the purpose of fulfilling a government objective, as was Amtrak in Lebron v. National Railroad Passenger Corporation. See also Pennsylvania v. Board of Directors of City Trusts of Philadelphia (per curiam) (holding that a state agency created under state law was a state actor). Indeed, no one claims that the State of Tennessee played any role in the creation of the TSSAA as a private corporation in 1925.

[In] addition, the State of Tennessee has not "exercised coercive power or . . . provided such significant encouragement [to the TSSAA], either overt or covert" [*Blum*] that the TSSAA's regulatory activities must in law be deemed to be those of the State. The State has not promulgated any regulations of interscholastic sports, and nothing in the record suggests that the State has encouraged or coerced the TSSAA in enforcing its recruiting rule. To be sure, public schools do provide a small portion of the TSSAA's funding through their membership dues, but no one argues

246

that these dues are somehow conditioned on the TSSAA's enactment and enforcement of recruiting rules. Likewise, even if the TSSAA were dependent on state funding to the extent of 90%, as was the case in *Blum*, instead of less than 4%, mere financial dependence on the State does not convert the TSSAA's actions into acts of the State.

Finally, there is no "symbiotic relationship" between the State and the TSSAA. [The] TSSAA provides a service—the organization of athletic tournaments—in exchange for membership dues and gate fees, just as a vendor could contract with public schools to sell refreshments at school events. Certainly the public school could sell its own refreshments, yet the existence of that option does not transform the service performed by the contractor into a state action. Also, there is no suggestion in this case that, as was the case in *Burton,* the State profits from the TSSAA's decision to enforce its recruiting rule.

Because I do not believe that the TSSAA's action of enforcing its recruiting rule is fairly attributable to the State of Tennessee, I would affirm.

II

Although the TSSAA's enforcement activities cannot be considered state action as a matter of common sense or under any of this Court's existing theories of state action, the majority presents a new theory. Under this theory, the majority holds that the combination of factors it identifies evidences "entwinement" of the State with the TSSAA, and that such entwinement converts private action into state action. The majority does not define "entwinement," and the meaning of the term is not altogether clear. But whatever this new "entwinement" theory may entail, it lacks any support in our state-action jurisprudence.

[Because] the majority never defines "entwinement," the scope of its holding is unclear. If we are fortunate, the majority's fact-specific analysis will have little bearing beyond this case. But if the majority's new entwinement test develops in future years, it could affect many organizations that foster activities, enforce rules, and sponsor extracurricular competition among high schools—not just in athletics, but in such diverse areas as agriculture, mathematics, music, marching bands, forensics, and cheerleading. Indeed, this entwinement test may extend to other organizations that are composed of, or controlled by, public officials or public entities, such as firefighters, policemen, teachers, cities, or counties. I am not prepared to say that any private organization that permits public entities and public officials to participate acts as the State in anything or everything it does, and our state-action jurisprudence has never reached that far. The state-action doctrine was developed to reach only those actions that are truly attributable to the State, not to subject private citizens to the control of federal courts hearing §1983 actions.

I respectfully dissent.